Schools of Linguistics

Schools of Linguistics

Geoffrey Sampson

Stanford University Press
Stanford, California

Stanford University Press
Stanford, California

© Geoffrey Sampson 1980

Originating publisher: Hutchinson & Co. (Publishers) Ltd
First published in the United States by
Stanford University Press in 1980
Printed in the United States of America

Cloth ISBN 0-8047-1084-8
Paper ISBN 0-8047-1125-9

Last figure below indicates year of this printing:
90

For Vera
who told me to get back to linguistics

Contents

Preface

The study of linguistics has grown up in many widely separated parts of the Western world. Often one individual or a small group of original minds has founded a tradition which has continued to mould approaches to language in the university or the nation in which that tradition began; between adherents of different traditions there has usually been relatively limited contact. Hence this book. It cannot fail to be an advantage to any student of linguistics (whether he is a 'student' in the formal or the amateur sense) to learn something of the ideas that have been current in traditions other than the one with which he is most familiar. This is not only because some of the ideas he has been taught as received truth are likely to be wrong (although I do believe that there are fundamental errors in the thinking of the most fashionable contemporary linguistic school, and I hope this book may encourage questioning of those points). In many cases one school has directed its attention to issues which simply have not been considered by another school, so that one can gain by studying other orthodoxies without necessarily rejecting any elements of one's own. Furthermore, it is impossible fully to appreciate a scholar's ideas without some understanding of the intellectual atmosphere within which, and in reaction to which, those ideas were evolved; so that one needs to learn something about past theories if only, in some cases, to see why they were wrong.

In a book of this size it is not possible to do more than sketch broad, general tendencies of thought shared, more or less, by sizable groups of linguistic scholars. Happily, scholars do not come in well-defined categories. Some individuals mentioned here conform more clearly than others to the tendencies I ascribe to their 'schools'; even those who seem easiest to categorize will often be found to have made remarks at some point in their careers which, taken in isolation, might appear to place them in a different camp altogether.

I cannot claim that the book is wholly comprehensive. I know less about developments outside the English-speaking world than within it; in particular, I suspect that I should have found the French 'linguistic geography' movement and Italian 'neolinguistics' worthy of extended discussion, if I had known more about them. No doubt there are other developments about which I do not even know that I am ignorant. And on the other hand there is only one group represented here (the 'stratificationalist' followers of Sydney Lamb) about whom I can claim to be unusually knowledgeable. However, I have had the fortune, during my time as a student and a teacher at ten British and American universities and university colleges, to be exposed perhaps more than most colleagues to a variety of linguistic orthodoxies in their respective native habitats. In case partisans of one school or another should feel tempted to refer to the proverb about Jack of all trades, let me say that to my mind by far the greatest danger in scholarship (and perhaps especially in linguistics) is not that the individual may fail to master the thought of a school but that a school may succeed in mastering the thought of the individual.

I have intentionally limited the book to 'core' linguistics, excluding various peripheral branches of the field. Subjects such as sociology, psychology and anthropology are discussed when they are particularly relevant (as they often are) to the linguistic theories of given schools. But there also exist brands of 'hyphenated linguistics' (socio-linguistics, psycho-linguistics, and the like) which involve investigating the relationships between, for example, sociology and a current linguistic theory irrespective of whether that particular version of linguistics forces one to think in sociological terms. Such studies can be quite legitimate, but I ignore them here.

Still less do I discuss so-called 'applied linguistics', which in practice means the study of language-teaching methods. This is because I do not believe that linguistics has any contribution to make to the teaching of English or the standard European languages. The many people who claim that it has seem to me to deceive themselves and others. (This would not matter, were it not for the extent to which the 'applied linguistics' industry, like so many other dubious modern enterprises, is financed not by those who see it as having some value but by taxpayers helpless in the grip of a voracious and tyrannical state.) Linguistics has an honourable role to play in the teaching of 'exotic' languages lacking a pedagogical tradition, which is presumably likely always to be a small-scale activity; but what is relevant there is not a special applied version of linguistics, but straightforward descriptive linguistics as discussed in this book.

I have not hesitated to allow my own views about the various issues treated in the book to become apparent, although I hope I have avoided the danger of confusing my views with those of the various writers I discuss. A book of this kind does its readers more service by offering reasoned judgements with which they may agree or disagree, than by treating each figure and each school at their own self-evaluation and thus leaving the reader no wiser than if he had been given a bibliography and left to read the sources for himself. Furthermore I have not striven, as scholars often do, to eradicate all expression of the personal tastes, foibles, and unscientific prejudices which may have affected my judgement of the issues discussed. As an admirer of the philosophy of Imre Lakatos, I regard such a procedure as positively undesirable, serving only to lend to the writer's work the appearance of an impartial authority which no product of a human mind possesses in reality. It goes without saying that the reader should feel free to disagree frequently and strongly with my opinions. All my friends do.

I owe a special debt of gratitude in connexion with this book to Dick Hudson, who first asked me, six years ago, to give the course of lectures out of which the book has finally grown. He has furthermore been kind enough to comment on drafts of the manuscript, as have Richard Hogg and Nigel Vincent on part of it. The book owes a great deal also to Charles Hockett, from whom I have learned much without ever meeting him. Over and over again I have discovered the source of some idea which I had fondly imagined to be original on re-reading *The State of the Art* or another of his publications. None of these people, of course, are to be blamed for the shortcomings of my work.

It is a pleasure to thank the library staffs of Lancaster University and the British Museum for their very considerable help, always given with willing enthusiasm; and I must thank

Lancaster University also for permitting me the leisure to write. I thank the American Association for the Advancement of Science, and the Linguistic Society of America, for permission to quote passages by Edward Sapir on pages 82–3.

To Vera, my debt is inexpressible.

Ingleton, Yorks.
September 1977

1 Prelude: the nineteenth century

This book deals primarily with linguistics as it has developed in the twentieth century. The scientific study of language did not, of course, begin in this century; but the years around 1900 happen to have marked an important turning-point in the history of modern linguistics. At very roughly that time, independently in Europe and America, linguistics shifted its orientation in such a way that much nineteenth-century work in the subject has become relatively remote from the concerns of the linguist of recent years. Not that twentieth-century linguistics is a wholly new enterprise quite lacking connections with the past; far from it. Noam Chomsky, in some ways the most innovative of contemporary linguists, stresses the relationship between his own work and that of Wilhelm von Humboldt (1767–1835) and of the rationalist philosophers of seventeenth-century France. But, if we want a boundary that will divide the stream of linguistic inquiry into 'history' and 'current affairs', as it were, then the beginning of our century will do very well.

The re-orientation that occurred about then was a shift from the 'historical linguistics', also known as 'diachronic linguistics' or 'philology', which had dominated nineteenth-century linguistic research – the investigation of the history of languages, the uncovering of their relationships, and the reconstruction of the lost 'proto-languages' from which families of extant languages descend – towards what became known as 'synchronic linguistics': the analysis of languages as communicative systems as they exist at a given point of time (often the present), ignoring (as their speakers ignore) the route by which they arrived at their present form.[1]*

It is never easy to appreciate novel ideas without some

*Notes (including definitions of technical terms) are on pages 243–58.

understanding of the climate of opinion existing when those ideas were formed, and against which they constituted a reaction. Accordingly, in this first chapter I shall sketch the intellectual trends which caused linguists of the nineteenth century to be preoccupied with the historical approach, as a prelude to considering in subsequent chapters the alternative views of language which have been advanced since that approach ceased to predominate.

It is easy for a newcomer to linguistics today to dismiss the philologers of the nineteenth century as pedants motivated more by a love of accumulating facts for their own sake than by a feeling for the excitement of scientific theory-construction. Such a judgement would be quite incorrect. It is true that the enormous effort devoted to the historical study of the Indo-European[2] language-family was inspired partly by personal taste, as opposed to considerations of rational scientific research strategy. The change of emphasis from 'classical philology' to the new subject of linguistics occurred first in Germany (indeed, throughout the nineteenth century linguistics was mainly a German pursuit); and the flourishing of Indo-European (in German '*Indogermanisch*') linguistic studies went hand in hand with the general intellectual and artistic movement of late-eighteenth to mid-nineteenth-century Germany known as Romanticism, with its rejection of the classical tradition and its emphasis on indigenous ethnic and cultural roots. (The link between linguistics and these wider intellectual and aesthetic currents is particularly clear in the work of such men as J.G. Herder (1744–1803), the leading figure in the *Sturm und Drang* movement in literature, collector of folk songs and relics of the early culture of the Germanic people, one of whose most influential works was his *Treatise on the Origin of Language* (1772), and Jacob Grimm (1785–1863), one of the founders of Germanic linguistics, and collector with his brother Wilhelm of a world-famous anthology of traditional German fairy-tales.) Since race, language and culture were assumed to be intimately related, reconstruction of the prehistory of the Germanic and other language-stocks was attractive to the Romantic temperament.

But there was much more to the situation than this: the history-centred outlook of nineteenth-century linguistic scientists was related to the general state of science at the time.

It is commonly the case in the history of science that at any given time there are a few outstandingly successful branches of science which are regarded as models of what a science should be, so that scholars attempting to investigate scientifically some new field of phenomena will almost inevitably imitate the methods and theories of the 'model' sciences. The modern philosopher of science Thomas Kuhn (1962) has coined the term 'paradigm' to suggest how, at a given period, thinking about a particular subject is commonly conditioned by some more or less coherent system of ideas which act, not so much as explicit tenets of a scientific theory, but as unspoken assumptions about the range of possible hypotheses which the scientist may entertain. For Kuhn, the most important scientific advances occur on the rare occasions when scholars manage to break out of these mental straitjackets by rejecting assumptions which their predecessors did not even feel the need to defend (as when Einstein responded to problems about the observed speed of light by suggesting that space, time, and mass might be observer-dependent rather than absolute quantities).[3] We may use Kuhn's term 'paradigm' also in a rather wider sense, so that the outlook of practitioners of a particularly successful science constitutes a paradigm not only for that science itself but also for less developed sciences. The nineteenth century contained two outstandingly successful scientific paradigms in this sense.

The first of these was mechanistic physics, according to which all phenomena could be described by simple, deterministic laws of force and motion – so that all future states of the world could in principle be inferred from a complete knowledge of its present state (the view classically expressed by Laplace in the preface to his *Théorie analytique des probabilités* (1820), and abandoned in our own century with the adoption of the quantum theory); the second was the biological theory of evolution by natural selection, which emerged from a great upsurge of interest in natural history during the eighteenth and nineteenth centuries, and culminated in Darwin's *Origin of Species* (1859) and the storm of controversy aroused by that book.

From physics, philologists took the notion of describing the history of sound-changes occurring in a language in terms of 'laws' which apply uniformly to whole ranges of examples, rather than discussing individual words in the anecdotal, case-by-case way in which a historian (in the ordinary sense) treats individual persons or events. One of the first such discoveries, for instance, was the Proto-Germanic consonant-shift commonly called Grimm's Law (though in fact stated first by the Dane Rasmus Rask in 1814), whereby Proto-Indo-European consonants changed in the Germanic branch in accordance with the following rules:

PIE		Germanic
voiceless stops [p t k]	>	voiceless fricatives [f θ x]
voiced stops [b d g]	>	voiceless stops [p t k]
voiced aspirates [bh dh gh]	>	voiced stops [b d g]

Since in other branches of Indo-European the consonants remained unchanged (or developed differently – thus PIE voiced aspirates become voiceless aspirates [ph th kh] in Classical Greek, which in turn become voiceless fricatives in Modern Greek), the Germanic consonant-shift produces many cases of words alike in meaning but containing distinct consonants in different languages: compare, for example, the initial consonants of Greek *thyra* and English *door*, Greek *genos* and English *kin*, Greek *pous* and English *foot*.[4] 'Grimm's Law' reduces many hundreds of cases like these to three simple formulae.

The term *Lautgesetz*, 'sound law', was first used by Franz Bopp in 1824 (Wechssler 1900, p. 400). (Bopp even offered what he called a 'mechanical' explanation for the Indo–European phenomenon known as 'Ablaut' – the alternation between different vowels in a morphological paradigm, of which we retain traces in the conjugation of English strong verbs such as *sing~sang~sung* – by invoking a 'law of gravity' in connection with the relative 'weight' of different syllables, cf. Delbrück (1880, pp. 68–9). If intended literally, however, this is surely a rather crude attempt to apply the findings of one discipline to the subject-matter of another.) Bopp's sound laws were only statements of general tendencies, and Bopp did not feel it necessary to provide explanations for cases which failed to follow the general rule; but, as the century grew older, the concept of 'sound law' took on more and more the rigorous character of genuine scientific laws such as those of physics: by the last quarter of the nineteenth century apparent counter-examples to a sound law were permissible only if they could be explained by a sub-law of their own.

While mechanistic physics provided one paradigm for linguistics, however, the influence of biology was certainly very much greater. As German scholarship came to distinguish between the *Naturwissenschaften* and *Geisteswissenschaften* – between the natural and moral sciences, or in modern terms between the 'sciences' and the 'arts' or 'humanities' – linguists were anxious to align themselves with the former: but, if linguistics is to be a natural science, then a 'language' must be some kind of entity which can be described objectively along with the rest of the furniture of the natural world. It will not be adequate to interpret the term 'language' as merely a convenient way of referring to various characteristics of the purely subjective intellectual life of a nation, as one adopting the 'humanities' rather than 'science' approach might be inclined to do. (This is perhaps not a very clear characterization of the 'humanities' view of language, and I am not sure that a clearer statement is possible at this point; but the problem of how 'languages' can be objects of scientific study remains a real one.) The solution of many nineteenth-century linguists was to regard languages as an order of natural organisms, on a par with plants and animals. Thus, Bopp (1827, p. 1) writes:

Languages must be regarded as organic bodies [*organische Naturkörper*], formed in accordance with definite laws; bearing within themselves an internal principle of life, they develop and they gradually die out, after, no longer comprehending themselves, they discard, mutilate or misuse ... components or forms which were originally significant but which have gradually become relatively superficial appendages.

Similar views are expressed by August Pott a few years later (1833, p. xxvii):

A language is in a constant state of change throughout its life: like every organic object [*organische Naturgegenstand*], it has its periods of gestation and maturation, times of accelerated and of slackened growth, its prime, decay and gradual extinction . . . .

It is difficult, now, to see how Bopp's 'no longer comprehending themselves' could ever have been more than a rhetorical flourish (although cf. page 27 below). For the rest, though, these remarks are by no means unreasonable, even though few would agree with them today. Although languages are in some sense a product of men's minds, they seem to have a life of their own, rather than being consciously created artefacts like a symphony or an aircraft design. Thus, it was clearly not by any process of conscious decision on the part of its speakers that the Old English of pre-Conquest days developed successively into Chaucer's English, Shakespeare's English and now the different varieties of modern English. Furthermore, groups of languages have 'family trees' just as groups of biological species do. As we saw above, French, Italian and Rumanian descend from Latin while English, German and Norwegian descend from 'Proto-Germanic', and Latin, Proto-Germanic and various other known or postulated ancient languages descend from a still more ancient Proto-Indo-European; this cannot fail to remind us of the situation in biology where, say, Man, chimpanzee and gorilla all descend from an extinct species of ape while cat, lion and tiger descend from an extinct proto-feline, and proto-ape, proto-feline, and others themselves share a common ancestor further back in geological time. Already at the beginning of the century scholars such as Friedrich von Schlegel (1808, p. 28) and Jacob Grimm (1819, p. xii) had suggested that the discipline most closely cognate with the new science of 'comparative grammar' was comparative anatomy. The *Stammbaum*, or 'family tree', theory of linguistic evolution was first formally expressed by August Schleicher (in his *Compendium*, 1861) almost simultaneously with the appearance of Darwin's *Origin of Species* (published in England in 1859, in German translation in 1860); Schleicher's friend Ernst Häckel (an important early evolutionist) drew his attention to Darwin's book, and Schleicher (who lived from 1821 to 1868) responded in 1863 by publishing a short treatise on *Darwin's Theory and Linguistics*, in the form of an open letter to Häckel, arguing strongly that linguistics should be regarded as one of the natural sciences to which Darwin's theory applies. (Schleicher did not say so, but it can be argued that, historically, Darwinism owed as much to linguistics as *vice versa*: cf. Hayek 1960, p. 59; Newmeyer 1975.) The linguist's language-families, languages, dialects, and idiolects[5] correspond to the biologist's genera, species, varieties, and individuals. Languages and language-families, like species, compete with one another in a 'struggle for survival' (consider, in the British Isles for instance, how English has spread at the expense of the Celtic languages: Cornish and Manx are extinct, Welsh and Scottish Gaelic live on but lose ground steadily to

English, Irish is kept alive artificially in a small Gaeltacht like a protected species in a game reserve); and, on a world scale, Schleicher saw the Indo-European language-family as having reached a dominant position linguistically, as Man has become dominant zoologically.

In one respect Schleicher even argued, with justice, that the validity of the evolutionary account can be confirmed more easily for language than with respect to the plant and animal kingdoms. For the biologist it is relatively difficult to establish that the ancestor-species which he postulates in order to explain the relationships between modern species ever really existed, since they have long ago disappeared, leaving only scanty and ambiguous traces in the form of fossils. Because the time-scale of change is so much shorter in the case of language, the relevant facts can often be studied directly rather than merely hypothesized. Thus, we possess plenty of documents not only in the modern Romance languages but in their ancestor-language, Latin, and in many of the intermediate stages; no one could claim that Latin is a figment of the linguist's imagination, as the notion of a common ancestor for Man and ape was pooh-poohed by opponents of the biological theory of evolution. (Indeed, Sir Charles Lyell (1863, ch. 23) had already used this argument to make evolutionary theory seem more plausible in biology.)

Even the standard objection to Schleicher's family-tree theory does not seem to me to have the force often ascribed to it. In 1872, Johannes Schmidt argued that the family-tree model failed to fit the facts of Indo-European for which Schleicher designed it. There were many cases where some trait was common to two language-groups, say A and B, lying relatively far apart on Schleicher's tree diagram, while being absent from other groups descending from the postulated common ancestor of A and B; but this situation could not be rectified simply by redesigning the tree diagram so as to make A and B adjacent, since in addition B shared some trait missing in A with group C, say. According to Schmidt, such findings could be explained only by abandoning the family-tree theory and seeing the process of linguistic change instead in terms of innovations originating at different geographical points and spreading outwards over arbitrary areas of territory, so that the resulting languages show a pattern of overlapping rather than hierarchically organized relationships. Certainly if we confine our attention to the most recent stages of the process, the diversification of modern languages into regional dialects, it is well known that dialect maps show many cases of isoglosses[6] crossing one another – contrary to what the family-tree theory might appear to predict (Bloomfield 1933, pp. 325 ff.). If Schmidt's 'wave theory' is incompatible with Schleicher's *Stammbaum* theory, then the analogy with biological speciation evaporates. But crossing isoglosses within the territory of one language do not damage Schleicher's theory: they are the analogue of various mutations which arose in individual members of a species being inherited by partially overlapping sets of descendants of those individuals, a situation which is perfectly normal and compatible with Darwinism. In 1876 August Leskien examined Schleicher's and Schmidt's theories and declared there to be no contradiction between them.[7]

Some readers may feel that to claim, as Schleicher did, that linguistics is literally a branch of biology alongside botany and zoology is self-evidently unreasonable. Languages are obviously not material objects: one can infer the existence and nature of languages, or even idiolects, only via the behaviour of speakers, not by direct observation as in the case of plants or animals. This might seem to rule out *a priori* the possibility of treating Darwin's theory as anything more than, at best, a suggestive metaphor for linguistics. But such a judgement would be quite wrong. What distinguishes life from non-life is still a deeply mysterious question; given that languages are describable entities at all, and given that, at a superficial level at least, they share a number of traits with living organisms of the standard classes, we have no right to deny the status of living organism to languages *a priori*: rather, we must look to see whether or not deeper study does indeed show languages to obey the same biological laws that operate in the animal and vegetable kingdoms. When it had come to seem clear that, after all, the laws of biology fail to apply to language – so that the only entities to fall within their domain are material plants and animals – some scholars (e.g Lane 1959, p. 315) 'charitably' reinterpreted Schleicher's equation of linguistics with biology as having been intended only metaphorically rather than literally, while others poured scorn on views like Schleicher's as if they embodied an obvious contradiction; thus Giuliano Bonfante

(1946, p. 295): 'Languages are historical creations, not vegetables.' But Schleicher and his contemporaries were not fools: they did not suppose that languages were tangible objects like carrots, even though it is true that they had not yet discovered the respects in which the laws governing the development of languages differ from those governing the evolution of vegetables.[8]

Until 100 years ago, then, the historical approach was the natural one for the study of language, and historical linguistics looked like one of the frontiers on which exciting new scientific advances could confidently be expected. As the nineteenth century neared its end, for a number of reasons this expectation came to seem less likely to be fulfilled.

The first problem had to do with the directionality of change. It is central to the evolutionary view of biology that the replacement of old species by new is not merely a process of random changes (even if the individual mutations on which evolution depends are random), but rather is a movement from lower to higher – mutations which succeed in spreading are those which give their possessor an advantage in the struggle for survival, while disadvantageous traits are eliminated. This notion that different forms of life occupy different points on a scale of degrees of development is by no means an original feature of Darwin's theory of descent with modification, of course; it had been familiar since Aristotle as the philosophical and theological doctrine of the Great Chain of Being, a concept which became particularly influential in the eighteenth century (Lovejoy 1936).

Nineteenth-century historical linguists in many cases took it for granted that linguistic change was similarly 'directional'. Thus, according to Rask (1818, pp. 35–6), languages became steadily simpler over time:

The language which has the most sophisticated grammar is the purest, most original, oldest, nearest to the source, because grammatical inflexions and endings are eroded in the development of new languages, and they require a very long time, and a certain mingling with other peoples, to evolve and organize themselves again. Thus Danish is simpler than Icelandic, English than Anglo-Saxon; and Modern Greek bears the same relation to Classical Greek, Italian to Latin, German to Gothic, and similarly in all cases known to us.

Rask's claim seems to be a statement of a purely empirical generalization about observed facts: it is certainly correct for the cases he cites (except that German is not now held to be a direct descendant of the extinct language called Gothic), and it is not clear whether Rask intended it as a strong hypothesis about all possible cases of language change – the clause about 'evolving and organizing themselves again' seems to allow for some cases of languages moving in the direction of greater complexity. As the biological analogy became increasingly persuasive, however, so the directional view of language-change came to play a more central role in linguists' theorizing. One strand in the directional view was the notion that languages could be classified into a small number of types, usually three: *isolating* languages, in which each word consisted of a single unchanging root (Chinese and Vietnamese being frequently cited examples); *agglutinating* languages, in which words include affixes as well as root, but the division of the word into root and affixes is clear (e.g. Turkish, where *sevişdirilmek* means 'to be made to love one another', and the word divides into *sev-* 'love', *-iş-* 'reciprocal', *-dir-* 'causative', *-il-* 'passive', and *-mek* 'infinitive'); and *inflecting* languages (e.g. Sanskrit, Classical Greek, Latin, and the other languages cited by Rask as relatively complex), where a single word includes a number of 'units of meaning' but one cannot assign these meaning-units to distinct portions of the entire word: thus, in Latin, *sim* is the first person singular present subjunctive of the verb 'to be', but one can hardly divide the word up into separate portions meaning 'be', 'subjunctive', 'present' or the like. (This last example is an extreme one – one often can split at least the root from the inflexional ending fairly unambiguously in Latin; but the three classes are intended as 'ideal types' of language, and it is recognized that real languages fall between the extremes provided by the scheme.) Otto Jespersen suggests that the three-way classification originated with Friedrich von Schlegel's brother August, who treated the inflecting type as the highest.[9] August Schlegel divided inflecting languages into two subclasses, *synthetic* and *analytic* languages – the former being inflecting languages in the fullest sense, the latter including some characteristics of the isolating type (prepositions in place of case-endings, subject pronouns in verb conjugations); and he treated the history of the Romance family of languages as a process of decay from synthetic Latin to analytic modern languages such as French.

August von Schlegel does not seem to have felt that the series isolating–agglutinating–inflecting represented a historical progression (the reason why he invents the notion 'analytic' rather than saying that the Romance languages are moving away from the inflecting towards the isolating type is presumably that he takes· it as axiomatic that membership of one of his three principal· types is part of the unchanging essence of a language-stock, so that no descendant of Latin *could* be isolating); and not everyone who discussed typology agreed that inflecting languages were *ipso facto* 'better' or 'higher' than isolating – Wilhelm von Humboldt (1836, section 24) suggests that both types have their advantages. By the mid-century, though, we find Schleicher (1848) claiming that the prehistory of languages involves a regular development from isolation through agglutination to inflexion, and that this is an evolution from less to more perfect.

There is a problem here: Rask claimed that the direction of language change was towards greater simplicity – i.e. from inflexion to isolation – while for Schleicher linguistic evolution proceeds from isolation to inflexion. But Schleicher solves the apparent contradiction by an argument which for him was inspired by Hegelian philosophy, but which also has a close parallel in (subsequent) biological theories.

According to this argument, we must distinguish in the evolution of Man between the period of prehistory, when Man is controlled by the same laws as the rest of animate and inanimate nature, and the historical period, when Man's intellect reaches the point at which he develops free will and thus rises above the blind laws of nature. Now, Schleicher argues (following Hegel 1837, pp. 62–3), the evolution of language presumably went hand in hand with the evolution of intellect, so that the perfection of language and of intellect would have occurred together: literature begins only when Man's intellect has fully evolved, so that the earliest forms of the classical languages are highly inflexional languages – we can infer that they were preceded by agglutinating and isolating stages only by *a priori* reasoning, and by comparison with the languages of tribes who are still pre-literate today. Once the historical stage is reached, intellect becomes autonomous and ceases to depend on the superficial form of language, and language is therefore free to regress to 'lower' forms: hence Rask's observation.

There are obvious and serious objections to this. If a race as intelligent as the Chinese can manage with a language which, in the historical period at least, has been near the isolating extreme, then how can we know that Man needed to develop inflecting languages in order to realize his intellectual potential? And to what extent can we assimilate linguistics to biology, if the recorded history of languages displays exclusively decay rather than improvement?[10] But the notion that the human mind is a development which cannot be explained within the framework of natural evolution, and which frees Man from the dictates of natural laws, is very reminiscent of Alfred Russel Wallace's objections, later in the century, to Darwin's theory as applied to Man (Wallace 1870; cf. Eiseley 1958, ch. 11); and the view that language decays once the achievement of free will liberates it from evolutionary laws is parallel to the widespread, and surely very plausible, idea that products of human intelligence such as medical knowledge, by suspending the law of the survival of the fittest, must lead to lower average levels of human physical excellence.

Furthermore, when Schleicher's view of linguistic development as perfection followed by decay was attacked by Wilhelm Scherer, Scherer explicitly appealed to contemporary biology as authority for his own view of language change. Until Lyell published his *Principles of Geology* in 1830–33, the existence of successive geological strata containing fossils belonging to different levels of organic complexity was explained by most geologists in terms of the 'catastrophist' theory associated with Georges Cuvier, which asserted that prehistory fell into a number of distinct epochs separated by destructive upheavals, after each of which new forms of life were divinely created *ex nihilo*. Lyell replaced this view with the 'uniformitarian' doctrine that the changes attested by geological evidence result from the same kinds of process that we can observe taking place in our own day; Scherer (1868, p. x) accordingly argues (as against Schleicher) for uniformitarianism also in linguistics:

We can hardly shut our eyes much longer to the realization that the distinction between evolution and decay, or – as it has also been put – between the nature and the history of language, rests on a fallacy. For my part, I have everywhere observed only evolution, only history.

Although discussions of linguistic evolution focused chiefly on morphology, directionality was argued also for phonological change. As late as 1893, Jan Baudouin de Courtenay (a Polish linguist of aristocratic French descent, who worked out his ideas at the university of Kazan', in Russia) argued that languages tend to replace sounds formed relatively far back in the mouth and throat with sounds formed nearer the teeth and lips: notice for instance that pharyngal and uvular consonants were common in the Semitic languages (which are among the earliest languages for which we possess records) but are rare in languages which emerged more recently, and compare the various fronting rules that have applied to velar consonants in the Slavonic languages. For Baudouin, this represents a 'humanizing' tendency, by which languages are losing the beastlike sounds that characterized their primaeval origins (Baudouin de Courtenay 1893).

There was thus a widespread acceptance of the view that language change is governed by fixed developmental laws (even if there was some disagreement about *which* direction languages moved in). In this respect, the biological paradigm fitted linguistics. Towards the end of the century, though, the directional view of linguistic change became much less popular. In the same work in which he argues for directionality of phonological development, for instance, Baudoin de Courtenay contradicts his predecessors by suggesting that morphological changes reveal only random 'oscillations' (Baudouin de Courtenay, p. 24). Certainly there are counter-examples to the view that languages in the historical period uniformly become less inflexional and more isolating. Modern French is arguably nearer the inflecting end of the scale than was Medieval French: consider, e.g., how plurality is indicated by vowel ablaut in phrases such as [lə garsõ̃] v. [le garsõ̃] 'the boy'/'the boys', as against the more agglutinative situation in earlier French [le garson] v. [les garsons]. Similar developments have occurred in Modern as against Middle Chinese and, apparently, in Coptic as against Late Egyptian (Hodge 1970). Moreover, it is easy enough to refute Baudouin's own claim about phonological directionality: consider, for instance, the replacement of apical by uvular *r* in Standard French, or the replacement of [t n] by [k ŋ] after most vowels in southern dialects of Vietnamese. Nowadays it is difficult to see the process of linguistic change at any level as more than a series of random movements in no particular direction; and, in that case, the analogy with biology falls to the ground. Some scholars kept faith with the directional view well into the twentieth century:

Holger Pedersen supported Baudouin's theory of 'humanization' of phonology in 1924 (Pedersen 1924, pp. 281–2), Otto Jespersen maintained his belief that natural selection makes languages steadily simpler as late as 1941. But few scholars would maintain such views today.[11]

If one gives up the idea that language change regularly proceeds in a particular direction, it becomes difficult to follow Schleicher in applying to language Darwin's concepts of 'natural selection' and 'struggle for survival': what, in language, will correspond to the biological notion of aptitude for survival? And in fact the expansion of certain languages at the expense of others seems to be explainable very adequately in terms of social factors, so that there is no room for an explanation referring to the intrinsic merits of the languages themselves. It might perhaps be that English is in some sense a 'simpler' or 'more advanced' language than Welsh; but the fact that English has been expanding and Welsh contracting is undoubtedly due to the fact that England has been a centre of power and wealth and Wales has not. Where the criterion of intrinsic simplicity and the criterion of social prestige conflict in determining which of alternative languages will spread, the latter almost invariably seems to be decisive: consider for instance the continued failure of Esperanto over ninety years to become a widespread second language, despite its extreme simplicity and the considerable concrete advantages that would follow from its universal adoption.

The abandonment of the directional assumption went hand in hand with a growing emphasis on the principle that language changes originate with individual speakers. Indeed, although I have written as if it was the empirical refutation of directionality which undermined the view of linguistics as a branch of biology, this is a *post hoc* rationalization rather than an accurate account of the theoretical developments of the late nineteenth century. It would probably be truer to say that the linguists of the time first adopted the general methodological approach that language must be treated in terms of the psychology of individual speakers, rather than in terms of a *Sprachgeist* having some kind of existence above and beyond individuals, and only subsequently noticed empirical evidence which tended to refute the view they were giving up. (Philosophers of science are familiar with the idea that relevant data are often noticed only *after* adoption of the theory for which the data are decisive: cf., for example,

Lakatos 1970, pp. 158–9.) Furthermore, although those who stressed individual psychology certainly believed that their approach was incompatible with the view of linguistics as biology, they seem to have been wrong in this – as I shall show shortly.

The point of stressing individual psychology was as a reaction to the views of earlier, Romantically-inspired linguists such as Grimm, who held that the nature of the language of a nation was determined by its *Sprachgeist* or *Volksseele* ('genius of the language', 'race-soul' – these and similar terms were used more or less interchangeably to denote some kind of spiritual entity embodying the aesthetic, moral, and intellectual values of a nation). It was his belief in a conscious *Sprachgeist* that allowed Bopp to write of languages 'ceasing to comprehend themselves' (cf. p. 17, above). This mystical but popular view was attacked already in 1858 by Rudolf von Raumer (1858, p. 374):

Whenever linguistic change, particularly sound change, is discussed, people are apt to appeal straight away to the '*Sprachgeist*' and its marvels. . . . But . . . the '*Sprachgeist*' does nothing of itself, separately from men, rather all changes in a language are brought about by men themselves.

The same point was hammered home repeatedly and forcefully by the group known as the 'neogrammarians' who dominated linguistic thought in the last quarter of the century. Thus Hermann Osthoff and Karl Brugman (1878, p. xii) hold

that language is not a thing, standing outside and above men and leading its own life, but has its true existence only in the individual, and that therefore all changes in the life of a language can originate only with individual speakers

and Hermann Paul, in his standard textbook *Prinzipien der Sprachgeschichte* (1880), writes (p. 11):

All psychic processes are executed in individual minds and nowhere else. Neither race-mind [*Volksgeist*] nor elements of the race-mind such as art, religion, etc. have a concrete existence, and consequently nothing can occur in them or between them. So away with these abstractions.

This last quotation makes it particularly clear that we are dealing here not with a modification of linguistic theory necessitated by the observation of awkward data, but rather with a very general shift in conceptions of the nature of social phenomena. However, from views such as those quoted it might well seem to follow that one cannot assimilate linguistics to biology as a science treating a class of natural objects. Paul (1891, p. 118) accordingly attacks Schleicher, 'who, being wedded to the view that linguistics is a natural science, was unable to succeed in forming any correct views about the nature of language development'. According to Kurt Jankowsky (1972, p. 147), 'For Hermann Paul linguistics was a historical discipline, not a natural science'.[12]

However, it is surely quite wrong to assume, because the *Sprachgeist* notion is admittedly nonsensical, that Schleicher's equation of linguistics with biology must necessarily be given up too. For Schleicher, a language corresponded to a biological species, and an idiolect in linguistics to an individual member of a species in biology. We do not accuse the biologist of mysticism because he recognizes as a theoretical construct the species 'carrot', even though all he tangibly observes are individual carrots. The analogue of the principle that linguistic changes originate in individual psychology is the claim that, in biology, it is spontaneous mutations in individuals which lead to the evolution of new species (rather than individual mutations being caused by the striving of the species as a whole towards some goal) – and this is a cardinal tenet of Darwinist theory.[13]

Apart from the lack of consistent direction in language change, another real problem for the evolutionist view of language had to do with the causation of changes. The difficulty here lay not so much in accounting for innovations in morphology, which might be explained with some plausibility as developments towards a simpler system, or as restoring intelligibility where unstressed case endings or the like had been eroded in rapid speech; the problem concerned rather the sound-shifts (such as Grimm's Law), which, by causing the pronunciations of words to diverge among different groups of speakers, seem to be quite arbitrary, unmotivated hindrances to communication. Sound-changes were law-like in the sense that they applied to all words containing the relevant sounds, *in a given language at a given point in time*; seen from a wider perspective, however, they were merely isolated, idiosyncratic events: Grimm's Law applied just to the Germanic dialect of Indo-European in a particular century, not to all languages at all times. One would scarcely be impressed by a physicist who invented one law of gravity for seventeenth-century Italy, another for modern England, and so on.

Certain scholars (particularly those, such as Hugo Schuchardt, who worked on Romance rather than Germanic languages) argued that sound-changes should be explained not in terms of scientific 'laws' but in terms of changes of taste or fashion in speech, with the corollary that such changes would spread sporadically from speaker to speaker and from word to word rather than occurring suddenly and 'across the board' (Iordan-Orr 1937). But, although this view might seem very plausible *a priori* and was adopted by the Italian school of 'neolinguists' (see, for example, Bonfante 1947), it was never taken seriously by the mainstream of German and, later, American historical linguistics; in 1946 R.A. Hall dismissed it as unworthy of serious consideration (R.A. Hall 1946, p. 280 n. 24).[14]

Quite a number of theories were advanced as to the causation of phonological change (see summaries in Oertel 1902, pp. 189ff.; Jespersen 1922, chs. 14, 15). One view was what would nowadays be called the 'substratum' theory: when a group of people adopt a new language (that of their conquerors, for instance), they are likely to carry habits of pronunciation over from the old language to the new. This theory is certainly correct in many cases: the Welshman's pronunciation of English is heavily influenced by the phonology of Welsh, even though most Welshmen today do not speak that language. But many sound-changes clearly happen within one language, independently of other languages: the Great Vowel Shift which occurred in English between the fifteenth and eighteenth centuries, for instance (the series of sound-changes which are responsible for the fact that the modern English pronunciation of the vowel-letters contrasts with their value in Continental languages), can hardly be explained by the substratum theory. Another possibility was to extend to phonology the theory that languages tend to become simpler: sound-changes might be caused by a tendency to greater ease of articulation. Again this explanation works well for some cases (e.g. elision of unstressed vowels or of consonants in consonant-clusters); but there are counter-examples. Thus, it is generally agreed that front rounded vowels are less natural (in terms of current phonological theory, more 'marked')

than back rounded vowels: yet French regularly developed front
rounded [y ø] from Latin back rounded [ū ō] (e.g.
lūnam > lune, *nōdum > nœud*). Since the language-families
that have been studied in depth appear to have undergone very
many sound-changes, the ease theory seems to imply that the
earliest languages must have been unusually full of difficult
sounds and sound-combinations – surely an implausible assumption.[15] And, of course, the ease theory says nothing as to why
particular ease-increasing changes happen when and where they
do. Thus, words spelled in English with initial *kn-* and *gn-* such
as *knee*, *gnaw* originally began with *k* and *g* sounds which later
dropped: in German, for instance, *Knie* 'knee' is still pronounced [kni:]. To quote Leonard Bloomfield (1933, p. 385):

> The English change of [kn-, gn-] to [n-] seems natural, after it has
> occurred, but why did it not occur before the eighteenth century, and
> why has it not occurred in the other Germanic languages?

Grimm himself explained the law that bears his name in terms
of the psychology of the Germanic race:

> ... from one point of view the sound-shift strikes me as a barbarity and
> a rejection of civilization, which other, more peaceable peoples avoided,
> but which is connected with the Germans' mighty progress and struggle
> for freedom which inaugurated the Middle Ages and was to lead to the
> transformation of Europe (1848, p. 417)

> The Roman Empire had decisively lost its strength after the end of
> the first century, ... and the invincible Germanic race was becoming
> ever more vividly aware of the unstoppability of its advance into all
> parts of Europe .... How could such a forceful mobilization of the
> race have failed to stir up its language at the same time, jolting it out of
> its traditional rut and exalting it? Does there not lie a certain courage
> and pride in the strengthening of voiced stop into voiceless stop and
> voiceless stop into fricative? (1848, p. 437)

Many of Grimm's contemporaries accepted this type of
explanation, and one still occasionally encounters similar
statements today (cf. Lane 1959, p. 321); but majority opinion
in the scholarly world has long disfavoured them. Some of the
same changes which Grimm took as symptomatic of courage and
vigour were treated by Karl Müllenhoff (1892, p. 197) as
indicating laziness or enervation, and subsequent research has
not established any empirical correlations between particular
sound-changes and particular psychological characteristics.

Others explained sound-shifts in anatomical terms. Quite late in the century, the neogrammarian Hermann Osthoff (1879, p. 16) claimed that 'modification of the vocal organs is in general the real cause of historical sound-changes in languages'; but, despite a number of unsubstantiated claims, there is very little evidence for anatomical differences between races correlating with different phonological systems, and the notion that phenomena as relatively frequent as sound-shifts might be triggered by the occurrence of biological mutations seems quite untenable (though cf. Brosnahan 1961).

A more plausible suggestion is that of Heinrich Meyer (1901), who suggested that phonetic changes of the kind represented by Grimm's Law might correlate with relatively energetic breathing, which could in turn be caused by living in a hilly region; Hermann Collitz (1918) took this idea up, and quotes several other cases of sound-shifts in different parts of the world which tend to confirm it. Again, however, Meyer's suggestion has failed to lead to an elaborated theory of geographical influences on phonology.

It would not be fair to say that the geographical theory of sound-change, or for that matter theories like Grimm's in terms of national psychology, have been decisively refuted. Scholars have simply given up working on such theories, and it is possible that they were mistaken to do so (cf. Catford 1974, p. 25). (Thus, the unpopularity of explanations which appeal to the concept of national psychology may have more to do with unpleasant memories of the most recent 'transformation of Europe' in the name of the Germanic race-soul than with considerations of rational research strategy.) On the other hand, one may well feel that 'the truth will out': scholars discussed various possible correlations of phonological changes with extraneous factors over a period of many decades, and if they did not end by producing a convincing theory of such correlations, then perhaps there are none to be found, and sound change really is random. Leonard Bloomfield (1933, pp. 385–6) certainly felt justified in drawing this conclusion from his survey of the field, and later scholars have not dissented. The neogrammarians of the late nineteenth century felt that sound 'laws', to be worthy of the name, must in principle be independent of particular times and places (cf. Jankowsky 1972, pp. 155–6); so that if one group of speakers applied Grimm's Law while others did not, there must have been some independently verifiable special circumstance applying to that group which regularly causes a sound-change of a similar kind whenever it occurs. Modern Chomskyan linguists, on the other hand, although they commonly dismiss most of their predecessors (including linguists of the nineteenth century) as mere collectors of facts who were not concerned to provide general explanations for the facts they collected, in most cases do not even feel a need for a theory of the causes of sound-shifts: thus Paul Postal (1968, p. 283) finds it clear that

... there is no more reason for languages to change than there is for automobiles to add fins one year and remove them the next, for jackets to have three buttons one year and two the next . . . .

(Postal thus accepts the 'neolinguistic' tenet that sound-changes are a matter of fashion rather than natural law – cf. page 29 above – *without* accepting the corollary that such changes are usually sporadic and incomplete.)

One must point out that failure to develop a theory of the causes of sound-change in a sense does not disturb the analogy with biological evolution. Darwin also had to treat the occurrence of modifications in the offspring of given parents as an unexplained axiom, and it was not until much later that people began to understand either the biochemical mechanisms by which the 'genetic blueprint' is transmitted from generation to generation, or the phenomena (such as radio-activity) which could lead to random modifications of that blueprint. However, Darwin's theory provided a satisfying explanation for so many other biological truths that people might be willing to take this gap in the argument on trust; while in linguistics, with no clear directionality of change and no clear analogue of 'fitness for survival', the failure to find causes for change was yet another factor making an evolutionary theory of language unattractive. It is also true that, between the 1860s and the end of the century, various counter-arguments (largely founded on what eventually turned out to be false assumptions about the unknown mechanisms of genetic inheritance) made Darwin's theory seem steadily less convincing, even to its author (see Eiseley 1958, pp. 209 ff., 233 ff.); and this is no doubt another reason why the equation of linguistics with biology was abandoned – by the end of the nineteenth century biology no longer appeared to offer such a prestigious paradigm as it had forty years earlier.

In 1880, Hermann Paul could still insist that the historical approach to language was the only scholarly method available for linguistic study (Paul 1880, p. 20). But then, despite his disagreement with Schleicher, Paul did still believe in the applicability of the concept of natural selection to language.[16] By the end of the century, however, the data for historical linguistics came to seem a mere assembly of sound-shifts which had occurred for no good reason and which tended in no particular direction; and the science to which linguists had looked as a model for their attempts to reduce this chaos to order had itself fallen on hard times. Some scholars continued to investigate language along the traditional lines; but now it really did begin to seem fair to regard these scholars as mere antiquarians studying individual quirks of particular languages for their own sake, rather than as serious scientists. I have suggested that the abandonment of the Darwinian paradigm for linguistics was in fact less well motivated than may have appeared at the time; but, at the turn of the century, it at least seemed clear that, if there was a scientific method available for the study of language, the historical approach was not it.[17] The time was ripe for the invention of synchronic linguistics.

2   Saussure: language as social fact

By the end of the nineteenth century – for reasons all of which seemed good at the time, and some of which remain cogent today – the equation of languages with biological species had largely been abandoned. This created a difficulty for the notion of linguistics as an academic discipline: if languages are not living species, in what sense are they 'things' that can be studied at all? The man in the street refers quite happily to 'French' as something which one can study, which possesses certain attributes, which resembles 'English' in some respects but differs from it in others; but, if 'French' is a thing, it is a very odd kind of thing. It obviously is not a concrete object like a table, or even like the stretch of terrain called 'France'. You cannot, strictly speaking, see or hear 'French' – the French language. You can hear Gaston the waiter saying '*Pas si bête* . . . '; you can see a line of print in a copy of *Le Monde*; but how does it make sense to hypostatize an entity called 'French' lying behind these and thousands of other concrete, observable phenomena? What *sort* of an entity could it be? The biological paradigm had treated the relationship between Gaston's speech and 'French' as akin to the relationship between a particular carrot and the species 'carrot': and, until the biological paradigm had to be given up anyway, this treatment seemed satisfying – even though one could see or eat only individual carrots, one appreciated that it made sense to talk about the species 'carrot' and to discuss, say, its genetic relationship with the species 'parsnip'. But, in the first place, the biological paradigm had fallen by the wayside; and, secondly, now that one thought about it that paradigm never really did offer a complete answer to the problem under discussion anyway. In biology, while species are abstractions, at least individuals of a species are concrete – few things are more tangible than a carrot. But the linguistic analogue of a biological individual is a person's idiolect: and this is almost, if not fully, as much of an abstraction as is the wider concept of a 'language'. We cannot *hear* 'Gaston's idiolect', as an entity; we can only hear examples of that idiolect – the comment he made when he noticed the tip we left, for example. This relationship between individual language, or 'idiolect', and example of that idiolect has no parallel in biology.[1] So, although it was not typically felt to be problematic by linguists of the nineteenth century, the question 'How does it make sense to postulate entities called "languages" or "dialects" underlying the tangible reality of particular utterances?' in fact remained open during that period. The man who answered it, in a way which satisfied his contemporaries and continues to satisfy many people today, was the Swiss scholar Ferdinand de Saussure.

Mongin-Ferdinand de Saussure, to give him his full name, was born in Geneva in 1857, son of a Huguenot family which had emigrated from Lorraine during the French religious wars of the late sixteenth century. Although nowadays one thinks of Saussure first and foremost as the scholar who defined the notion of 'synchronic linguistics' – the study of languages as systems existing at a given point in time, as opposed to the historical linguistics ('diachronic' linguistics, as Saussure called it to clarify the contrast) which had seemed to his contemporaries the only possible approach to the subject – in his own lifetime this was far from his main claim to fame. Saussure was trained as a linguist of the conventional, historical variety, and became outstandingly successful as such at a very early age: his *Mémoire sur le système primitif des voyelles dans les langues indo-européennes* (1878), published a few weeks after his twenty-first birthday while he was a student in Germany, remains one of the landmarks in the reconstruction of Proto-Indo-European. Saussure lectured at the École Pratique des Hautes Études in Paris from 1881 to 1891, before returning to a chair at Geneva; all his publications, and almost all his teaching, throughout his career dealt with historical rather than with synchronic linguistics, and indeed with detailed analysis of various Indo-European languages rather than with the general, theoretical discourse for which he is now famous.

In fact, although it is known that Saussure worked out his ideas on general linguistic theory as early as the 1890s (Koerner 1973, p. 29), he seems to have been very diffident about passing them on to others, and the story of how these ideas entered the public domain is a rather odd one. At the end of 1906 he was persuaded to take over responsibility for a course on 'General linguistics and the history and comparison of the Indo-European languages' from a scholar who had had to give it up after thirty-three years (presumably because of illness); Saussure taught such a course for the remainder of that session and in the sessions 1908–9 and 1910–11. In the first of these years Saussure limited himself exclusively to historical matters; but when he gave the course for the second time he included an introduction which dealt rather briefly with synchronic linguistics, and in the third course, finally, a full semester was devoted to theoretical, largely synchronic linguistics. And then not long afterwards, in 1913, he died, without having published any of this theoretical material. Several people had asked him to, but he always replied that the task of organizing his sketchy ideas into publishable form was too time-consuming to contemplate. Two of his colleagues, however, Charles Bally and Albert Sechehaye, who had been prevented by their own teaching duties from hearing Saussure's lectures on general linguistics, decided to reconstruct them from notes taken by students together with such lecture-notes as Saussure had left behind: the book they produced, the *Cours de linguistique générale* (Saussure 1916), was the vehicle by which Saussure's thought became known to the scholarly world, and it is in virtue of this one document that Saussure is recognized as the father of twentieth-century linguistics.

Before broaching what might be called the 'ontological question' – before, that is, we ask what kind of things Saussure thought languages are, if they are not living organisms as Schleicher and others had suggested – let us spend some time on the synchronic/diachronic distinction and on Saussure's reasons for thinking it so important.

The kind of linguistic publications with which Saussure's hearers were familiar were works which analysed some form or range of forms in a given language by tracing the stages through which they had evolved to reach their present state: and Saussure makes the point that, whatever other virtues such analyses had, they certainly told one nothing about how the language functions *from the point of view of those who use it* – since, for the speaker of a language, the history of the language does not exist (p. 81).[2] Consider, for instance, the fairly standard controversy in the description of English as to whether the affricate spelled *ch* should be analysed as a unit or as a combination of / t / followed by / ʃ /. There are arguments on both sides: the second solution is in a sense more plausible, since it suggests that an Englishman has fewer different sounds to learn, but on the other hand it implies a consonant cluster quite different in kind from the other clusters found in English (e.g. we have no / kʃ /, / pʃ /). What cannot be relevant, if phonological analysis is supposed to represent some truth about English as a vehicle of communication between contemporary English-speakers, is the fact that, historically, *ch* descends from a single sound, / k /, and never had anything to do with / t / + / ʃ /. Even an educated Englishman, unless he has made a special study of English philology, will be unaware that his *church* was originally identical to the Scot's *kirk*. In an analogy that keeps recurring throughout the *Cours*, Saussure compares a language with a game of chess (p. 89): what has gone before is quite irrelevant to the current state of play at any point. (Contrast chess with tennis, for instance, where the previous history of a match – as encapsulated in the score – may make all the difference to whether the point currently being played is a crucial one that must be battled for tooth and nail, or an unimportant one that the players can afford to relax on.)

One who describes a language 'from the outside', from the standpoint of observer rather than of participant, is free to adopt either the diachronic or the synchronic approach; but one who describes it 'from the inside', as it exists for its users, must describe an *état de langue* – a 'language-state' with no extension along the time dimension. But furthermore, according to Saussure there is an essentially *systematic* character to the synchronic facts of a language which he claims to be lacking in diachrony (p. 95). Historical linguistics is a relatively simple, even beguiling affair of describing one isolated event after another; synchronic description, by contrast, is a much more serious and difficult occupation, since here there can be no question of presenting isolated anecdotes – one either describes a complete *état de langue* or nothing at all. (It was largely because of the relative difficulty of synchronic linguistics as he envisaged it that Saussure was so reluctant to publish his ideas on the subject.)

What Saussure means by calling a synchronic *état de langue* 'systematic' is fairly easy to explain. Let us return to the chess analogy, and consider the problem of describing a given chess position. If we want to go beyond a mere listing of the location of various pieces on the board in order to say something more analytical about the situation the players are in, it is quite clearly no use considering individual pieces in isolation. For the black queen to be on one of the centre squares may be very advantageous to Black – but not if White is in a position to take it. Ultimately, in fact, the current value of any piece depends to a greater or lesser extent on all the others, and moving a single piece does not just change the potential of that piece but recasts the whole network of relationships between the pieces. In language, things are much the same.

Consider, for instance, the way that the words of a language stake out areas of meaning for themselves. Saussure's example was the English word *sheep*. Conventionally one says that English *sheep* is the equivalent of French *mouton*; but in English *sheep* contrasts with *mutton*, while French has no such contrast – so that the value of English *sheep* is rather different from that of French *mouton*, just as the value of a chess bishop may vary depending on what other pieces it shares the board with at the time. The point is perhaps better illustrated from more abstract parts of the vocabulary. Thus, what we understand when we read the word *high-handedness*, say, depends largely on the words with which it contrasts. The writer might have written *presumption*, but he did not; he might have written *arrogance*, but he did not – and so on; provided the writer is one who uses words carefully, the notion he indicates by *high-handedness* will be similar to the notions of *arrogance*, *presumption*, etc., but not quite the same as any of these. And if one of these words came to change its meaning radically, or to drop out of the language altogether (as words sometimes do), then rather than there remaining an empty slot of meaning, as it were, with no word to represent it, instead the other words would automatically reshuffle their meanings so as to take up the slack. (For a famous case-study, see Ullmann 1962, pp. 248–9.)

One can give further examples of the same idea from more technical aspects of linguistic structure. Thus, consider how one sound may play quite different roles in different languages. Both English of the RP variety[3] and Russian have a velarized lateral sound [lʷ] ('dark *l*'), but in RP this sound is merely a positional variant of the plain lateral [l] or 'clear *l*' (the plain lateral being used when a vowel follows, e.g. in *hilly*, while the velarized lateral occurs in other environments, as in *hill, hilltop* – the two sounds are said to be in *complementary distribution*); in Russian, on the other hand, these two sounds are independent 'phonemes' – words such as ['ugəlʷ] 'corner' and ['ugəl] 'coal' are perceived by Russian-speakers as contrasting in pronunciation and are spelled differently in consequence. However, while velarization does not 'matter' in English (it never affects the identity of the words uttered), in many varieties of English the precise area and duration of contact between tongue-tip and upper jaw in an *l* sound does matter, since if the contact is brief enough and over a small enough area the result will be perceived not as an / l / but an / r /: these are the criteria which distinguish e.g. *feeling* from *fearing* for many speakers of English, particularly Scots. In Japanese, by contrast, area and duration of contact is of no importance, and a Japanese would hear the words *feeling* and *fearing* as the same, since Japanese has only one rather than two phonemes in the area of our / r / and / l /.[4] Again, consider how a verb in the indicative in French will often carry a different implication from that borne by the equivalent verb in English because of the availability of a contrasting, subjunctive form in French but not in English: *J'attrape le ballon avant qu'il bondit* implies that, having caught the ball, I nevertheless let it bounce (since I could have written ... *avant qu'il bondisse* instead), whereas *I catch the ball before it bounces* is more likely to suggest that I prevent the ball bouncing by catching it first.

All these are of course only very limited examples, but perhaps they will serve to illustrate Saussure's concept of an *état de langue* as a network of relationships in which the value of each element ultimately depends, directly or indirectly, on the value of every other. Saussure (p. 112) invites us to picture a language, in terms of the diagram below, as 'a series of contiguous subdivisions marked off on both the indefinite plane of jumbled ideas (*A*) and the equally vague plane of sounds (*B*)' (see Figure 1, page 40).

A language comprises a set of 'signs' (represented by the divisions marked off by dotted lines), each sign being the union of a *signifiant* (a 'signifier', or portion of speech-sound) with a *signifié* (a 'signified', or portion of meaning); but individual signs cannot be considered in isolation, since both their

Figure 1

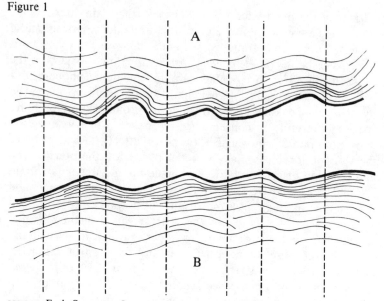

SOURCE: F. de Saussure, *Course in General Linguistics* (1916).

pronunciation and their meaning are defined by their contrasts with the other signs of the system – without the system provided by a given language, we have no basis for individuating sounds or concepts.

Why does Saussure say that diachronic linguistics lacks this 'systematic' character? In the first place, he is making a simple factual comment on the descriptive technique of historical linguistics as he knew it. A typical historical statement would be, say, that the sound [a] changed to [e] in such-and-such a language at some particular period; and a historical linguist would not, typically, have laid much stress on the question whether or not the language already had an [e] sound before the change occurred. But for Saussure this question is all-important. If there was no [e] previously, then all that has happened is that one of the phonemes of the language has modified its pronunciation, and from Saussure's point of view this hardly counts as a change at all. A state of play in chess is not affected in the slightest if we substitute a knight made of ivory for a wooden knight: similarly, in language, what matters is the *form* of the system, not the *substance* (in this case, speech-sound) by which the elements of that system are realized. (After all, English is still English whether we realize it as spoken sounds or as ink on paper.) If, on the other hand, the language already had an [e] identical to the new [e] from [a], then a change in the system has taken place. Two phonemes have merged into one; pairs of words that previously contrasted in pronunciation have become homophones, and this change in one part of the system will have repercussions throughout the system as a whole.

But Saussure meant more than just that his contemporaries neglected the systematic aspect of the phenomena they described: he felt that historical sound-changes are in a sense *intrinsically* independent of systems. Let me explain this by contrasting two hypothetical sound-changes that might occur at some future time in English. A fairly common type of sound-change is the dropping of consonants in word-final position: this has happened on a large scale in French, for instance, where very few of the final consonants that appear in the spelling are pronounced in modern French (although they were all pronounced at an earlier period). We could imagine two lesser changes in English: on the one hand, dropping of word-final labiodental fricatives / f v /, or, on the other hand, dropping of word-final alveolar fricatives / s z /. Now, from the phonetic point of view, there is little to choose between these two changes: they are very similar processes, equally simple to describe and equally plausible-sounding. But, in terms of their effect on English as a synchronic system, they are utterly different. Dropping of the final / f v / would be a minor change: a few groups of words (e.g. *leaf, leave, lee*) would become homophonous,[5] but most of the resulting ambiguities would be easily resolved in context and it seems unlikely that they would call for many compensatory changes elsewhere in the system. Dropping of final / s z /, by contrast, would be an enormous change: not only would groups of words such as *base, baize, bay* become homophones, but the distinction between singular and plural would disappear for the vast majority of nouns and verbs (*cat* and *cats*, (*he*) *walks* and (*they*) *walk* would sound the same), and the genitive would vanish completely (*John's* would sound the same as *John*). A high proportion of the inflexional morphology of English would be eliminated by this sound-change, and presumably very considerable compensatory changes would have to be introduced as a result, if the language were to continue functioning as an efficient medium of communication. Yet, according to Saussure, the changes which actually occur in the history of a language are in no way dependent on the effect they will have on the system: the dropping of final / s z / is no less (and no more) likely in English than the dropping of final / f v /. In chess, of course, moves are planned very much with an eye to the new state of play they will bring about. But, for Saussure, this is a point at which the chess analogy breaks down: we should rather compare a language with a game of chess played by a blind man, who makes his moves in ignorance of their consequences.

Saussure makes this statement about the random nature of diachronic processes as if it were a truism, needing only to be uttered to be accepted. This it is certainly not. It is entirely conceivable that historical changes might be determined, at least in part, by the effects they have on the synchronic system – so that, for example, changes which would create too much ambiguity simply do not occur. And indeed my use of the term 'compensatory change' has taken it for granted that some such controlling mechanism does play a part. Saussure does not, as far as I know, refer to this phenomenon, but there is little doubt that some historical changes come about in order to make up for undesirable effects of other changes: as when, for instance, the ambiguity resulting from loss of case-endings which existed in the classical European languages was compensated for by adoption of relatively fixed word-order in their modern descendants. At least, then, we must think of the chess game as played by two people, one moving blindly, the other using his eyes to react to the first man's moves.[6] Some might want to go further and deny even this great a role to the random element in language-change: not only do certain changes occur in order to compensate for earlier changes, they might claim, but even those previous changes will be to some extent predictable in terms of the synchronic state before they occur or the state reached after they occur, or both. We shall return to this question in later chapters; at this point I will simply say that, although Saussure's view of language-change as largely random is not the *a priori* truism he took it for, it does seem quite possibly correct as an account of the observed facts.

These, then, are the reasons why synchronic and diachronic description must be separated in the study of a language. On the one hand, the domains comprise facts of very different kinds, and impinge on each other only in a wholly unsystematic way; and on the other hand, a description which aims to analyse a language from the standpoint of those who use it must be a description which ignores the 'historical dimension.[7] Having got this material out of the way, let us now return to the question with which we began the chapter: what sort of entities did Saussure take 'languages' to be?

Saussure answered this question in terms of the new science of sociology. A language, according to Saussure, is an example of the kind of entity which certain sociologists call 'social facts'.

To a reader unversed in the theoretical writings of sociology this may sound as if Saussure was saying merely that languages are social phenomena, which would be a very uninspiring statement of the obvious. But the term 'social fact' carries considerably more force than this. The phrase was made a technical term by Saussure's French contemporary Émile Durkheim, the founder of sociology as a recognized empirical discipline: to understand what Saussure means by calling languages 'social facts', we must spend some time examining Durkheim's use of the term.

Durkheim propounded the notion of 'social fact' in his *Rules of Sociological Method* (1895). According to Durkheim, the task of sociology was to study and describe a realm of phenomena quite distinct in kind both from the phenomena of the physical world and from the phenomena dealt with by psychology, although just as real as these other categories of phenomena. Let me give an example (my own, rather than Durkheim's). Suppose that, on dressing one morning, I find that all my trousers happen to be at the cleaners or are otherwise unwearable – even the ones I wore yesterday have been ripped to pieces by the dog in a playful mood, let us say. If I am to go in to give my lectures at the University I must wear something; and, to a visitor from Mars, the answer might seem rather obvious – clearly the simplest solution is for me to borrow one of my wife's dresses and lecture in that. But the reader will not be surprised to learn that I should refuse absolutely to adopt this solution. I am subject to a kind of pressure forcing me, as a man, to wear trousers rather than skirts in public. This pressure is clearly not a *physical* force: from the physical point of view a skirt would serve as well as trousers to protect me against draughts inside the lecture room or inclement weather on the way to and from it. Nor is it a matter of my individual psychology: I may in fact feel that these arbitrary correlations between sex and type of clothing are very foolish, yet I knuckle under nevertheless. Rather, the pressure that prevents me wearing a skirt is a phenomenon which inheres in a *society* as an independent organism. Social facts, according to Durkheim, are ideas (*représentations*) in the 'collective mind' (*âme collective* or *conscience collective*) of a society. (Durkheim's notion of 'collective mind' is obviously closely akin to the Romantic notion of *Volksgeist* which we encountered in Chapter 1, though a Durkheimian collectivity is defined by a shared way of life rather than by common genetic descent.) The collective mind of a society is something that exists over and above the individual members of the society, and its ideas are only indirectly and imperfectly reflected in the minds of the people who make up that society. Some of the less reflective members of our society may never have consciously realized that there are rules prescribing distinctive clothes for the two sexes, but they obey these rules nevertheless.

(One might object, in this particular case, that in fact most members of our society *are* quite consciously aware of the rule against men wearing skirts. I doubt whether everyone is conscious of the rules in their full subtlety – for instance, it is far less acceptable for men to wear identifiably feminine clothes than *vice versa*, for some reason; but, to meet the objection, let me give a different example. Two people conversing face to face will stand a given distance apart, and this distance is constant for a given society but differs from one society to another (E.T. Hall 1959, ch. 10). The distance is less in the Middle East than in North America, for instance: one consequence of this is that a conversation between an Arab and an American will often involve a slow progress round a room, the Arab constantly moving forward to reduce the gap while the American steps back to increase it. It is quite likely that until recently *no one* knew these social facts, yet individuals' behaviour was none the less controlled by them.)

Notice that the lack of a physical or psychological basis for the prohibition of skirts for men does not prevent it being a real and very powerful force. If the worst comes to the worst and I really cannot lay my hands on a pair of trousers, I will phone

the University and claim to be ill sooner than appear there in a
skirt; yet I am, I believe, a reasonably conscientious man and
would cheerfully overcome quite a lot in the way of physical
obstacles (car breaking down, snow on the road, etc.) in order
not to miss a lecture.

The skirt case was intentionally chosen as a very simple
example of a social fact. Durkheim's idea is that a society
comprises a web of phenomena of this category, many of which
will possess much more complex structures. The legal system of
a society, for instance, is a relatively salient example of a highly
structured social fact which has effects, often very tangible ones,
on the lives of all the members of the society. John Smith signs
someone else's name on a cheque: as a consequence, in due
course other men lock John Smith into a room with bars at the
window. There is certainly a relationship of cause and effect
here, but the causal chain is not one about which a physicist
could say anything enlightening; and nor does it depend on the
psychology of the individuals involved. (Individuals differ greatly
in the extent to which they are familiar with the legal
framework within which they lead their lives, but that
framework is independent of the individuals' knowledge or
ignorance; and furthermore, in a good legal system, the effects
of the law will be independent of individuals' evaluative
judgements about the law – whether the judge personally
approves or disapproves of the law under which John Smith is
convicted should not affect the sentence he passes.) Since 'social
facts', whether laws or conventions of dress or conversational
behaviour, have concrete effects, according to Durkheim we
must admit that they are 'things' just as real as stones or
physical forces – though belonging, of course, to a quite
different logical category.

This gives Saussure the answer to the ontological problem
posed above. 'French' is not a thing in the same sense as a chair
or a table; but, if there is a category of 'things' which includes
legal systems and structures of convention, then languages surely
fit squarely into that category too. The data which a linguist can
actually observe are of course perfectly physical phenomena –
sequences of vocal sounds, printed texts and the like. But we
must draw a distinction between the physical facts which can be
tangibly observed – what Saussure calls *parole*, 'speaking' – and
the general system of *langue*, 'language', which those physical

phenomena exemplify but which is not itself a physical phenomenon. The concrete data of *parole* are produced by individual speakers, but 'language is not complete in any speaker; it exists perfectly only within a collectivity' (p. 14). That is, just as no one Frenchman possesses exhaustive knowledge of the French legal system, yet that legal system exists as a social fact independently of its more or less imperfect reflection in the minds of individual Frenchmen, so no one Frenchman possesses exhaustive knowledge of the French language, which exists independently of its more or less imperfect reflection in the minds and behaviour of individual French-speakers.

Durkheim's notions of 'collective mind' and 'collective ideas' are far from obviously correct. Durkheim made some remarkable sociological discoveries, notably in his work on *Suicide* (1897), which showed that despite the considerable year-to-year fluctuations in suicide rates there were some striking constancies in the relative frequency of suicide in various European nations. But it is possible to accept these empirical discoveries while rejecting the theoretical structure by which Durkheim accounts for them – in this case, the notion that different societies possess different quantities of a force which he called 'anomia', and that this force interacts with the particular circumstances of an individual in pushing him towards suicide. An alternative and perhaps more common-sensical approach to generalizations about societies – an approach that has come to be known as 'methodological individualism' as against Durkheim's 'methodological collectivism' (see, for example, O'Neill 1973) – holds that any such generalizations are really only abbreviations for large numbers of statements about the feelings, beliefs, habits, etc. of the individuals belonging to those societies: societies as such are merely convenient fictions, with no real existence or properties apart from those of the individuals they comprise. If I refrain from wearing skirts despite believing that our clothing conventions are arbitrary and foolish, then, rather than saying that my feelings are powerless against the force of the impersonal social fact, a methodological individualist will say that my lack of respect for the convention is outweighed by my (equally personal) desire not to be laughed at in public. Conventions of which those who obey them are not consciously aware, such as the convention about the distance between people talking to one another, are less difficult to explain individualistically now that we are familiar with the idea of unconscious mental activity.

This clash between two ways of thinking about the subject-matter of sociology was very much a live issue in the intellectual milieu within which Saussure's views on language were formed. At the time when Durkheim began propounding his views, the leading figure in French sociology was Gabriel Tarde, fifteen years Durkheim's senior. Tarde stressed that sociological generalizations hold only because individual human beings have a propensity to imitate one another, and he condemned Durkheim's theory of 'collective minds' as mystical (see, for example, Tarde 1894). The dialogue between Tarde and Durkheim was carried on in the journals over a number of years, with considerable passion on both sides: it culminated in a public debate between the two men at the École Pratique des Hautes Études in Paris (where Saussure had taught for ten years) in December, 1903, the year before Tarde's death.[8] While Tarde might seem to have had common sense on his side, in terms of acceptance by the general French intellectual world it was Durkheim who won a total victory (Clark 1969); indeed, although in later years Durkheim himself came to modify his extreme position, his followers seem to have remained faithful to the Durkheim of the Durkheim/Tarde controversy. The notion of a 'collective mind' independent of individual minds was a standard, uncontroversial notion by the time of Saussure's *Cours*: the French linguist Antoine Meillet, who had studied under Saussure in Paris and later worked with Durkheim, explicitly pointed out the relevance of Durkheim's concept of 'social fact' for linguistics in 1905 (Meillet 1905, p. 230). Although Saussure found Schleicher's idea of languages as biological organisms ridiculous (p. 4), he had no similar qualms about the concept of 'collective mind'.

I ought perhaps to make it clear here that I am *not* claiming that Saussure explicitly set out to expound Durkheimian sociological theory as it applied to language. Far from it: the name 'Durkheim' nowhere appears in the *Cours*, and although most of the *Cours* is infused with the Durkheimian view of social facts there is at least one passage (p. 5) where Saussure, having described language as 'a product of the collective mind [*esprit collectif*] of linguistic groups', appears to hedge his bet

('Certain metaphors are indispensable'). Although it has long been a commonplace that Saussure's ideas are related to Durkheim's, one scholar (Koerner 1973) has recently gone so far as to deny that Saussure was influenced by Durkheim, arguing that his intellectual forebears should rather be sought exclusively among linguists such as the American W.D. Whitney. This seems to me to miss the point, and to represent an impoverished notion of the history of ideas. Obviously a scholar of Saussure's calibre thought for himself; if he did not, no one would read him today. We know that Saussure followed the Durkheim/Tarde debates with interest (Doroszewski 1933, pp. 90–1; 1958, p. 544, n. 3); nobody is claiming that he adopted Durkheim's theories in slavish detail. What is claimed is that Saussure's discussion of language took for granted a general approach to the philosophy of society which was 'in the air' at the time and which Durkheim had done more than anyone else to create and to express; to deny this would strain credulity, in view of passages in the *Cours* already cited, or (to quote only one further example) in view of the passage on pages 99–100 which contrasts synchronic linguistics as 'concerned with the logical and psychological relations that ... form a system in the collective mind [*conscience collective*] of speakers' with diachronic linguistics as 'study[ing] relations that bind together successive terms not perceived by the collective mind'. It may be that Saussure never wholly faced up to the irreconcilability of and consequent need to choose between the collectivist and individualist positions, so that he saw no harm in making occasional remarks smacking of methodological individualism while embracing methodological collectivism in the bulk of his thinking, but I see no serious possibility of disputing that Saussure was essentially a methodological collectivist.[9]

In a sense my title, *Schools of Linguistics*, is less apt in connection with the present chapter than with my other chapters, since Saussure is not really the father of a school among other linguistic schools; with respect to the notion of a synchronic language-state as a system whose elements are defined by their contrasts, it is approximately true to say that we are all Saussureans now.[10] At most one might argue that Saussure's influence has been stronger in Europe than in America; and this may be why American linguistics typically differs from European linguistics in that Americans are more interested in syntagmatic relations (i.e. in the ways that linguistic units can be combined into longer constructions) while Europeans concentrate on paradigmatic relations (i.e. the relationships between elements that can substitute for one another in the same 'slot' in a linguistic structure). Saussure's argument that the value of a linguistic element depends on the elements with which it contrasts forces one to consider paradigmatic relationships: the word *high-handedness* contrasts with *arrogance* only because one word can substitute for the other in environments such as *I don't like his* ＿＿＿＿＿ (whereas *high-handedness* and *never*, on the other hand, cannot be substituted one for the other in any verbal environment, and correspondingly there is no direct way in which the meaning of *high-handedness* depends on the meaning of *never* or *vice versa*). As we shall see, Saussure had reasons of principle for paying less attention to syntagmatic relationships. There will be several points in this book at which we shall encounter instances of this difference in emphasis between American and European linguistics. But certainly most American linguists for several decades have read Saussure and have been broadly in sympathy with the bulk of Saussure's views, so that much of what he says, though strikingly novel when he said it, is almost uncontroversial today. The notion of a language as imposing an 'emic' system on intrinsically unstructured, 'etic' extra-linguistic reality (the terms are derived from 'phonemic' v. 'phonetic', but can be applied to the structuring of meaning as well as of sound) evolved independently in North America (as we shall see) and has long been a commonplace on both continents, although we shall encounter some dissentient voices.

It is Saussure's view of language as social fact and the related distinction he draws between *langue* and *parole* which form the most contentious elements of his structure of ideas. Perhaps surprisingly, for several decades these notions passed more or less unchallenged by linguists whom one might have expected to be relatively unsympathetic (I am thinking here of the American Descriptivist school, to be discussed in the next chapter).[11] In the last decade or so, however, Saussure's approach has again become a live issue because of a conflicting view put forward by Noam Chomsky.[12]

One of the most widely influential features of Chomsky's approach to language is the distinction he draws between *competence* and *performance*, a distinction somewhat reminiscent of Saussure's *langue* v. *parole*. Chomsky himself (1964, p. 10) actually identifies his notion of linguistic competence with Saussure's *langue*. But there is a crucial difference, which Chomsky seems not to appreciate. Chomsky's 'competence', as the name suggests, is an attribute of the individual, a psychological matter; he often (e.g. 1965, p. 4) defines competence as 'the speaker-hearer's knowledge of his language'. For Chomsky, as for his American predecessors, the individual's idiolect is primary; the 'language' of a wider community or nation is a secondary concept, a convenient way of referring to a large number of individual linguistic competences that are similar except for minor details. For Saussure, just the opposite is true: 'language . . . exists perfectly only within a collectivity'. What an individual Frenchman has in his head is not the definitive structure of his personal idiolect, but rather a good – but not perfect – command of the French language.

(It is interesting to speculate whether these contrasting attitudes might not have been reinforced by the different views of language held in French- and English-speaking societies. France has an Academy charged with the function of standardizing and maintaining the purity of the French language, French newspapers include regular features answering readers' queries about correct usage, and so on; Britain has no institutional equivalents, and Englishmen tend to take the line that 'I say it so it's English' – the tone of Fowler's *Modern English Usage* is very different from that of the ukases of the Académie Française. It is true that Chomsky is American and that linguistic self-confidence seems less common in American than in British society, perhaps because of the large proportion of Americans whose command of English is only a couple of generations old, but still the USA has not given itself the language-canonizing institutions of France.)

One might well feel that it is a mere matter of taste whether we choose to describe language as a communal property which each individual masters imperfectly, or as a highest common factor of individuals' idiolects. Saussure (p. 72) argues in favour of his approach by pointing out that 'speakers are largely unconscious of the laws of language'; but the question whether it is necessary to be explicitly aware of a norm of behaviour in order to conform to it (to which the answer, as we saw from the discussion of American and Middle-Eastern norms for face-to-face conversational distance, is no) is surely independent of the question whether the norms to which people's behaviour approximates inhere in them as individuals or in a 'collective mind'? (Admittedly, Chomsky commits a parallel error – as we shall see in Chapter 6, he infers, from the assumption that linguistic competence is an individual attribute, that individuals do in some sense know the structure of their language; and Saussure and Chomsky might jointly plead in their defence that it is difficult to see how a norm of behaviour could come into being and maintain itself as an influence on an individual's behaviour, if it neither exists outside the individual in his social environment nor has ever been consciously considered by the individual.) I am a Whig by temperament, suspicious of any tendency to accord to a collectivity precedence over individuals, and I naturally incline to the view according to which idiolects, as psychological entities, are central and which treats sociological generalizations of all kinds as merely handy, more-or-less accurate summaries of quantities of statements about individuals' beliefs, wishes, behavioural dispositions, and the like.

However, the philosopher Hilary Putnam has recently developed an argument (Putnam 1973, 1975) which seems to show that the issue is more than a question of taste and that at least one important aspect of language, namely semantic structure, must be regarded as a social rather than as a psychological fact. Despite my instinctive preference for Chomsky's approach to this question, I must admit that Putnam strongly vindicates Saussure as against Chomsky.

Putnam's argument is subtle and elaborate, and it is not possible to do full justice to it within the scope of this book. He begins with one of the grossly unrealistic, 'What would we say if . . . ?' hypotheses in which philosophers delight and of which the rest of us tend to feel suspicious (but the suspicion would be misplaced in this case – semantics is a subject which demands that we stretch our minds if we are to say anything worthwhile). Putnam invites us to suppose the existence of a planet elsewhere in the universe, say 'Twin Earth', which is closely similar to our own Earth (the inhabitants even speak English) except in one respect. The liquid in the rivers and seas of Twin Earth, which falls there as rain and which Twin Earthers drink and wash with, is not H_2O but some quite different chemical compound – 'XYZ', let us say. XYZ looks and behaves like water, and indeed Twin Earthers call it 'water', but a chemist could readily distinguish between XYZ and H_2O. 'Water', in English, means H_2O and not XYZ; 'water' in the Twin Earth language means XYZ and not H_2O.[13] Now, suppose meanings are 'in people's heads'; then, Putnam points out, since a Twin Earther's word 'water' means something different from our word, we would have to say that Twin Earthers and ourselves had different concepts of 'water' in our respective minds. But this is unreasonable; most of us have mental images of 'water' which depend on the superficial appearance of water (some of us may not know its chemical formula) and there is no reason why the same should not be true of Twin Earthers, in which case the 'concepts in individuals' heads' would be identical as between the two planets: yet the meaning, as we have agreed, would differ – so meanings cannot be things in people's heads.

Indeed, Putnam argues, one can make the same point with much more realistic examples. Putnam claims that, as a town-dweller, his own concept of 'beech' is in no way different from his concept of 'elm' – he thinks of each as deciduous trees and nothing more; yet it would be wrong to say that 'elm' and 'beech' are *synonyms* for Putnam, since he knows as well as anyone else that they are names of different species. (Here, though, it might be argued against Putnam that part of his concept of 'beech' is 'not elm' and *vice versa*, so that after all his concepts are not identical even though he does not know any of the specific differences between the two trees.)

The Twin Earth example depended on the fact that we chose, as representative speakers from the two planets, individuals who were not chemists: obviously an Earth chemist would have a concept of 'water' that *would* differ from a Twin Earth chemist's concept of what he called 'water'. This was a legitimate choice to make, since it would be ridiculous to suggest that 'water' was a specialized term restricted to chemists' jargon – it is a word that everyone uses, so if meanings are things in people's heads then the meaning of 'water' ought to be in everyone's head. But the fact that it mattered whether we chose to consider chemists or laymen illustrates Putnam's further point, that societies contain a 'division of linguistic labour' parallel to the division of real labour. To take another of Putnam's examples: it matters to many people that their wedding-ring is made of gold rather than a cheap alloy, but that by no means implies that they can tell the difference. In our society, some individuals have the 'job' of wearing gold wedding-rings, others have the job of buying and selling gold rings, and others again have the job of distinguishing between gold and other materials; but one cannot sensibly say that the word *gold* belongs to the language of only the last group. Rather, we must acknowledge that the semantic structure of a language is something which inheres in a linguistic community as a whole, and not in any one member of the community. As Putnam (1975, p. 146) sums up his argument:

there are two sorts of tools in the world: there are tools like a hammer or a screwdriver which can be used by one person; and there are tools like a steamship which require the cooperative activity of a number of persons to use. Words have been thought of too much on the model of the first sort of tool.

Since Putnam's argument is directed largely at linguists of the contemporary Chomskyan school, it is relevant to make a further point. I can conceive of ways in which the individualist approach could be defended against Putnam; but Chomsky and his followers are in a peculiarly awkward position from which to mount such a defence. A chief strand in their thought is the claim that psychology cannot be 'reduced' to physics – that the mind is an independent domain with laws of its own, and that statements about mental states and processes are not mere abbreviations of complex series of statements about brain cells and other material entities (cf. Fodor 1974, for instance). What Putnam (like Durkheim and Saussure before him) is maintaining, on the other hand, is that sociology cannot be reduced to psychology, as individualists claim it can. Now the arguments against reduction are much the same in either case. It requires a quite subtle argument to shore up the position that social facts reduce to psychological facts while the latter on the other hand do not reduce to physics, and there is little sign that Chomsky or his followers are prepared to offer such an argument. The bluff man of commonsense may find Chomsky's position attractive because the notion of an English or French 'collective mind' seems utterly mystical, while 'John Smith's mind' is straightforward – it is what keeps John Smith's ears apart. But the commonsense man naïvely ignores the very considerable mystery attached to the notion of an individual mind which is quite different in kind from but intimately related to the particular piece of matter we call a brain; if we can swallow this notion, *perhaps* we should not choke on Durkheim's 'collective minds'.

There is a further problem about the *langue/parole* distinction, and here Saussure's position is harder to defend. The stock of meaningful units – morphemes as we nowadays call them, though Saussure did not use the term[14] – with values defined by their paradigmatic contrasts, constitute the system Saussure called *langue*. When we speak, however, we string morphemes into sequences: words, phrases, sentences. Whereas it makes sense to think of a linguistic community as making available to its speakers a system of contrasting morphemes, it hardly seems that we could alternatively think of the community as making available a system of contrasting sentences; the sentences of a language do not form a limited set (as the vocabulary of morphemes does), rather there are innumerable possibilities and the individual speaker usually creates a novel sequence out of the fixed stock of morphemes each time he speaks, rather than selecting one from a range of sentences given in advance. So, to Saussure, it appeared that the construction of sentences – syntax – was a matter of *parole* rather than *langue*, and hence not part of the proper subject-matter of linguistics.

The trouble with this is that the syntax of a language is as much a matter of convention, which has to be learned by an infant before he can be regarded as a speaker of the language, as is the phonological structure or the vocabulary of the language. All (or most) individual sentences that we utter are novel, but still they conform to regular and conventional syntactic patterns – in English adjectives precede nouns, in French they follow; surely these patterns must be regarded as part of a *langue*? It is likely that Saussure was misled here partly because he simply did not see how it was mathematically possible for an endless variety of sentences to be defined in terms of a limited range of syntactic patterns. In Saussure's defence it can be said that the solution to this problem was never fully grasped by linguists until several decades after Saussure's death. One of Chomsky's chief positive contributions to the discipline is a clear exposition of this issue, and we shall see that syntax was not treated very successfully until after Chomsky began publishing in the late 1950s. However, the legacy of Saussure's view was that, as we have seen, European linguistic schools tended to ignore or de-emphasize not merely syntax but syntagmatic relationships in general.[15].

It is, again, interesting to speculate whether Saussure's feeling that the description of a language had no place for syntax may not have been reinforced by the linguistic attitudes of the society to which he belonged. It is a common belief among the French that their language is extremely 'logical', a view which seems to suggest that what has to be learnt (because it is arbitrary) is only the vocabulary – once one has mastered that, one puts words together in whatever ways make sense. This belief has no basis in reality (there are languages, such as Japanese, in which syntax is controlled by very simple logical principles, but French is far from being a language of that kind); and in any case Saussure's knowledge of other languages would have shown him the conventionality of syntax. But the pattern of a scholar's thought will often be influenced by presuppositions current in his intellectual milieu even though they involve beliefs which he would reject if he confronted them explicitly, and it seems possible that this may have been such a case.

Saussure's assignment of syntax to *parole* rather than to *langue* is linked in another way with the question of linguistic structure as social rather than psychological fact. As we have seen, Saussure argued that *langue* must be a social fact on the grounds that no individual knows his mother-tongue completely; and I suggested that this confused two issues – there are many patterns of behaviour which one 'knows how to' perform without necessarily 'knowing' much about them in the conscious, verbalizable, 'knowing that something is the case' sense of 'know'. For instance, I know how to ride a bicycle in the sense that I can do so in practice, but I could say next to nothing about how the complex balancing-act is achieved. Certainly speakers do not know the structure of their language in the 'knowing-that' sense (they cannot give a full and accurate description of it); but to deny that a language is a psychological fact is surely to deny that speakers know their language perfectly in the 'know-how-to' sense, which is a quite different and less obviously reasonable thing to say.[16] Notice, however, that it is specifically in the area of syntax that there is a clear disparity between what speakers know how to do and what they know to be the case. Any Englishman regularly utters faultless examples of English relative clauses or compound tenses, but not one in a thousand could accurately explain how such constructions are formed. When it comes to vocabulary, by contrast, on the whole speakers *can* with considerable success identify the words of their language and say what the words mean. The distinction between knowing-how and knowing-that seems to vanish or at least greatly diminish, here. So, from his own point of view, Saussure was not really confusing separate issues; and we have already considered Putnam's argument that the 'dictionary' aspect of a language must be treated as a social rather than a psychological fact. Saussure's sociological approach to language on the one hand, and his concentration on vocabulary on the other, thus turn out to be principles each of which supported the other. Because Saussure thought of a language as inhering in a society, he treated it as a system of signs rather than as a system of sentences – sentences seemed to be a matter of the individual speaker's use of the language, therefore a question of *parole* rather than *langue*. Conversely, because Saussure thought of a language as a system of signs, he was forced to think in sociological terms: it may make sense to describe the syntax of an idiolect, but no individual is master of the range of semantic relationships which determine the meanings of the words he uses.

At this point we leave Saussure. Such has been his influence on the discipline, however, that we shall find ourselves recurring again and again, in later chapters, to issues first raised in this chapter. We turn now to an almost exact contemporary of Saussure, Franz Boas, who independently evolved in America a linguistics which in many specific points is closely similar to Saussure's, while as a whole having a very different flavour.

3 The Descriptivists

During the years at the end of the nineteenth and beginning of the twentieth centuries when Saussure was working out his ideas in Europe, synchronic linguistics was emerging independently, and in a very different style, in America under the leadership of the anthropologist Franz Boas. Boas set a direction for American linguistics which turned out to be enormously fruitful, and which was never seriously disputed until Noam Chomsky appeared on the scene in the late 1950s. I use the term 'Descriptivist linguistics' for the school founded by Boas, for reasons that will be discussed shortly. Since, throughout the twentieth century, the great majority of synchronic linguists have been Americans, it has often seemed that Descriptivist linguistics *was* linguistics.

Franz Boas (1858–1942), born in Westphalia, began his academic career as a student of physics and geography, and it was through the latter subject that he came to anthropology. The key to Boas's thought lay in the realization, borne in to him on his first field trip (to Baffin Land in 1883–4), that, contrary to what he (like many of his contemporaries) had supposed, anthropology is not a branch of geography – that is to say, the culture of a community is not simply a function of its material circumstances, and the human sciences are quite distinct both in content and in methods from the physical sciences. Once Boas appreciated this, it was the human sciences which attracted him; and, among the various aspects of a culture which the anthropologist can attempt to understand and describe, language came to seem especially important to Boas. This was not only because language was the key to the other aspects of culture, but (significantly in view of later disputes between Descriptivists and Chomskyans) because people are normally unconscious of the principles on which their language operates, while when it comes to other aspects of their culture they commonly have their own erroneous but firmly-believed rationalizations which hinder rather than help the anthropologist who seeks to understand how the system really hangs together (cf. Boas 1911, section iv, especially p. 63).

Boas specialized in the anthropology of North America, and, after a short period teaching in Berlin, he settled in the USA in the late 1880s. What made Boas not just an isolated scholar interested in language but the founder of a large and productive school of linguistic research was his work as organizer, under the aegis of the Smithsonian Institution, of a survey of the many indigenous languages of America north of Mexico. The *Handbook of American Indian Languages* was published in 1911. Boas's Introduction to it contains what is still a good summary of the Descriptivist approach to language. Several of the chapters on individual languages were written by Boas, and he trained the men who investigated the other languages; for decades subsequently, all the great names of American linguistics learned their subject from Boas at first or second hand.

The nature of the languages dealt with was one of the chief differences between the Boasian and Saussurean traditions. Saussure had seized the attention of the scholarly world by inventing a new way of looking at phenomena which had been so familiar for so long that it seemed impossible for them still to hold any surprises. He illustrated his theoretical discussion by reference to his own tongue, French, and to the other widely-spoken European languages – the vehicles of the great civilizations of the West, worked over for centuries by philologists and historical linguists, and taken for granted by anyone who was educated enough to encounter Saussure's ideas. The interest in what Saussure said lay in his abstract conceptual analysis rather than in the facts to which the analysis applied. Thus, the idea of treating the sounds of a language as a system of phonemes whose current identity and interrelationships might be at odds with their ancestry was a novel one; but, once one had the idea, it appeared unnecessary to spend much time in identifying the phonemes of French – they seemed to be reasonably obvious. Boas and his colleagues, on the other hand, were faced with the severely practical problem of working out what the current structure of various utterly alien languages was like. They had no need to worry about being misled by history, since neither they nor the speakers of these languages knew anything about the route by which the languages had reached their current state; but on the other hand it was so difficult to get to grips with the brute facts of these exotic languages that the Descriptivists had little time to spare for drawing elegant logical distinctions between *langue* and *parole* or the like. Hence the name 'Descriptivist': for this school, in a way that is true of no other group discussed in this book, the description of an individual language was an end in itself, or a necessary first step towards understanding the wider culture of a particular community. (Following the tradition initiated by Boas, linguistics departments in American universities have usually budded off from departments of anthropology, rather than, as in Europe, from modern-languages departments.)

The Descriptivists tended to think of abstract linguistic theorizing as a means to the end of successful practical description of particular languages, rather than (as Chomsky does, for instance) thinking of individual languages as sources of data for the construction of a general theory of language. It is true, of course, that the most eminent of the Descriptivists are well known because they did theorize about language in general; but in all cases their general theories were backed up by intensive research on the detailed structure of various exotic languages, and many of their less famous colleagues and followers preferred to take the theories for granted and concentrate on the data. (Later, during the Second World War, the practical orientation of American linguistics was reinforced as linguists were called in by their government to organize teaching programmes in the languages of distant countries with which the USA had suddenly become involved. Much solid linguistic analysis sprang out of this war effort.)

The fact that Boas was a purely self-taught linguist was an advantage rather than a hindrance in dealing with American Indian languages, since it was necessary in approaching them to discard any presuppositions about the nature of language inherited from a European background. (This was a real problem; during the early part of Boas's career, more orthodox linguistic scholars sometimes flatly refused to believe the results he was publishing.) A characteristic of the school founded by Boas was its relativism. There was no ideal type of language, to which actual languages approximated more or less closely: human languages were endlessly diverse, and, although the structure of a language spoken by some primitive tribe might strike us as very 'arbitrary' and irrational, there was no basis of truth in such a judgement: our European languages would appear just as irrational to a member of that tribe. Boas was at pains to argue, as against the nineteenth-century Romantics who thought of language as embodying the soul of a race, that race in the genetic sense, language and (other components of) culture are three separate issues which by no means necessarily go together (see, for example, Boas 1897). There are many known cases where, because of the vicissitudes of history, groups belonging to the same race speak unrelated languages, or a single language is spoken by men of great ethnic diversity; and similarly speakers of one family of languages sometimes belong to very diverse cultural groups and *vice versa*. Therefore, although one may recognize that the peoples of the technologically advanced West are in some sense superior to the inhabitants of many other parts of the world (whether that superiority is purely cultural, as it has become fashionable since Boas's time to believe, or is partly also genetic), one is not entitled to infer that the languages of different peoples can similarly be classified as 'advanced' versus 'primitive' – and in fact they cannot.

We have already seen Saussure arguing that a language imposes an arbitrary structuring on the intrinsically unstructured domains of sound and meaning; Boas showed how this phenomenon produces a false appearance of primitiveness in languages which are in fact fully comparable with our own. Thus, it was often felt in the nineteenth century that while European languages used definite ranges of fixed sounds corresponding fairly consistently with the letters of the alphabet, the sounds of primitive languages on the other hand were vague and variable, so that a given word would now be pronounced with this sound, now that. In his first linguistic article, in 1889, Boas showed what lay behind this notion. In the first place the human mouth can make many more different sounds than the Roman alphabet has letters; if an exotic language contains a sound falling between two sounds familiar to a European, he will hear the alien sound as alternating between these two. Secondly, exotic languages, like European languages, have groups of allophones in complementary distribution (as velarized [lʷ] and plain [l] are in complementary distribution in R P); whereas each of us has learned to ignore the differences between allophones in his own language, we notice such differences in alien languages because they often correspond to distinctions which are phonemic for us, and thus we perceive the alien language as confusing separate sounds in an irrational way. But each of these sources of misunderstanding betwen the speakers of European and exotic languages is perfectly symmetrical; speakers of an American Indian language would equally hear English as containing alternating sounds.

What is true of sound systems is just as true of the syntactic and semantic aspects of language. Two points are often claimed to be characteristic of 'primitive languages'. On the one hand they are said to be vague; thus, many languages fail to distinguish singular from plural. On the other hand, they are claimed to deal only in the concrete and not to tolerate the formation of abstract concepts: for instance in Kwakiutl (a language of British Columbia studied by Boas) a noun can occur only with an inflexion indicating the possessor, so that one can speak of 'my love' or 'his love' but not of 'love' as a general phenomenon. The two criticisms cancel each other out – over-specificity is the opposite of vagueness. As Boas explains, the truth is that in *every* language there are certain logical categories which must obligatorily be expressed whether relevant to a particular message or not. For English the distinction between one and more-than-one is among these obligatory categories, so that if we wish to be non-committal about number we have to resort to awkward turns of phrase such as 'person or persons unknown'; but the identity of the obligatory categories differs from language to language, so that a speaker of language A will find language B vague when some category obligatory for language A is optional for language B, and over-specific when the reverse is true. Again the situation is perfectly symmetrical; and it would be very difficult to argue seriously that the range of categories which happen to be obligatory in the familiar European languages are intrinsically more important than those which other languages have chosen to make obligatory. As Boas suggests, it might be an excellent thing if our newspapers could adopt the Kwakiutl verbal system in which, while time of action (which is normally obvious from the context) is left unmarked, it is obligatory to use an inflexion showing whether the narrator personally witnessed the action reported, or, if not, whether he knows of it by evidence or by hearsay, or whether he merely dreamed it!

Boas furthermore makes the very apposite point that abstract terms are created when philosophers bend a language to their purposes; since philosophy is a minority interest this is always a somewhat artificial procedure, but it need be no more artificial for languages in which no one has yet philosophized than it is for the classical languages of philosophy. Logical terms such as *quality, essence*, now commonplace in the languages of Europe, were wholly artificial when first coined ('how-ness', 'be-hood'); and similarly, when Boas tried as an experiment to speak about the general notion of 'love' shorn of any possessive in Kwakiutl, his Kwakiutl informants agreed that the discussion made sense even though it was quite unidiomatic (Boas 1911, pp. 65–6).

Boas must unquestionably take pride of place in any account of the Descriptivist school; he created the tradition which moulded the work of all other members of the school. But the man who is nowadays taken as principal representative of the Descriptivist school, and is read by many more linguists than read Boas today, is Leonard Bloomfield (1887–1949).[1] Leonard Bloomfield was a nephew of a leading American historical linguist, Maurice Bloomfield. Leonard Bloomfield himself studied linguistics in the traditional style, spending a year in his twenties at Leipzig and Göttingen working with some of the great figures of the neogrammarian movement, and his teaching responsibilities at various Mid-Western universities were concerned with Germanic philology (until in 1940 he became Professor of Linguistics at Yale). However, from an early stage in his career Bloomfield took up the study of American Indian languages of the Algonquian family, and of certain languages of the Philippine Islands, and he also wrote at length on general synchronic linguistic theory. The book by which he is best known, *Language*, appeared in 1933. But, while Bloomfield did much to promote and codify the Descriptivist tradition of linguistic analysis (and much also to organize linguistics as a profession: thus Bloomfield was the prime mover behind the foundation of the Linguistic Society of America in 1924), it is fair to say that his theoretical work does not contain a great deal of innovation. The main points of Bloomfield's theories of language description can already be found in Boas, though they are often stated more explicitly and with more elaboration by Bloomfield.

What was new in Bloomfield was a philosophically sophisticated emphasis on the status of linguistics as a science. Bloomfield came to scholarly maturity at a period when philosophers attributed a peculiarly lofty position to science *vis-à-vis* other intellectual pursuits, while at the same time they were exceptionally fastidious about what they were prepared to count as scientific. The 1920s and 1930s were the years when the Logical Positivism of Rudolf Carnap and the Vienna Circle flourished. For the logical positivists, there were only two basic kinds of meaningful statement: logical propositions such as 'Either P or not P', and reports of simple sense-data, e.g. 'I am now seeing a patch of red', which (they believed) were verified by immediate experience with no room for dispute. All of science, even the most abstract theoretical principles, could according to the positivists ultimately be reduced to quantities of statements about simple sense-data linked together logically, and scientific theories were true or false according as the sense-data statements which they abbreviated did or did not correspond to experience. Furthermore, scientific theories were for the positivists the only category of discourse that told us anything at all. Mathematical truths could be reduced to truths of logic like 'P or not P', and these, though meaningful, were merely tautologous; while any statement that could not be reduced to sense-data and/or logic was just nonsense. Aesthetic, ethical, religious discourse – all this was strictly meaningless, an atavistic hangover from our pre-scientific past, and fit only for the flames.

Nowadays, philosophers of science are much less puritanical. They have realized that even the 'hardest' of sciences contains, and must always contain, much that is neither logic nor pure sense-data statements (if, indeed, there are such things); and they have realized furthermore that what is not science need not be nonsense, but may often be a different kind of sense. But one can easily understand that, while its intellectual hegemony remained unchallenged, logical positivism exerted a strong pressure on the 'social scientist' to establish that his subject was a genuine science and to weed out any elements that might endanger its scientific status.

Bloomfield was not merely passively influenced by logical positivism but (after a flirtation in his twenties with very different views) became an active proponent of positivist ideas as they applied to the study of human behaviour, including language. He contributed a monograph on 'Linguistic Aspects of Science' (1939) to the first volume of the *International Encyclopedia of Unified Science*, a project under the editorship of Otto Neurath which was intended ultimately to form a systematic reconstruction according to positivist canons of the foundations of all human knowledge. It will be obvious that positivism was wholly incompatible with notions such as 'collective mind' on which the view of linguistics as sociology seems to depend; for Bloomfield linguistics was a branch of psychology, and specifically of the positivistic brand of psychology known as 'behaviourism'. Bloomfield's theorizing about language was heavily behaviouristic; he had the behaviourist psychologist Albert Weiss (a colleague of Bloomfield's) contribute an article on 'Linguistics and Psychology' to the first issue of *Language*, the journal of the Linguistic Society of America (1925).

There is a good side and a bad side to behaviourism. In its good aspect, behaviourism is a principle of scientific method: a rule which says that the only things that may be used to confirm or refute a scientific theory are interpersonally observable phenomena, rather than, say, people's introspections or 'intuitions' – some of which may appear unchallengeable to their 'owners', but all of which are intrinsically private to an individual and unsharable. It is obviously tempting for a psychologist in particular to proceed by introspection, and psychologists in the early years of the twentieth century commonly did. But since introspections are private, if one man's introspectively based theory clashes with another's there is no principled way available to resolve the issue; and, of course, clashes of this kind arose frequently (see, for example, Broadbent 1961, pp. 18 ff.). Thus psychologists came at about the time of the First World War to acknowledge the behaviourist method as the only way of giving their discipline a sound, scientific foundation. To forsake introspection was to give up the possibility of formulating any theory at all about many aspects of our mental life; but that was accepted by psychologists as a price that had to be paid in exchange for the reliability of the theories which remained. When, rather later, the behaviourist method had entered linguistics via Bloomfield's writings, it manifested itself in slogans such as 'Accept everything a native speaker says in his language and nothing he says about it'. That is, a linguistic description was reliable insofar as it was based on observation of unstudied utterances by speakers; it was unreliable if the analyst had resorted to asking speakers questions such as 'Can you say so-and-so in your language?'

In some ways it was in fact easier for linguists than for psychologists to accept behaviourist methodology. In the first place, it is less immediately obvious in the case of language than in the case of psychological topics such as emotion or perception that there are questions which cannot be answered from observational evidence alone. Perhaps more importantly, an introspectionist psychologist could at least regard himself as producing theories which were new, even if they rested on shaky foundations; but every human community is interested in its mother tongue and has evolved a system of well-entrenched beliefs about it which are handed down from generation to generation, so that a linguist who allows himself to treat the native-speaker's beliefs as authoritative can rapidly find himself reduced to doing little more than retailing, in slightly more systematic form and with a veneer of modern jargon, a description which in all its essentials had been worked out long before the linguist arrived on the scene. (It may be, as Boas held, that people have fewer explicit beliefs about their language than about other aspects of their culture, but they certainly do have plenty of beliefs about their language.) When a linguist works with an exotic language it is relatively easy to ignore native-speaker theories about it, since learning such theories requires some positive effort; but Descriptivists who worked with familiar languages sometimes resorted to extreme measures in order to avoid contamination of their descriptions by pre-scientific inherited prejudices. Thus Charles Fries's grammar[2] of English (1952) eschews completely the use of traditional part-of-speech terms like 'noun' and 'verb', talking instead of 'Class 1 words', 'Class 2 words', and so on; and this is not as pedantic as it might seem, since, as Fries points out, although the classification he evolves to handle his corpus of examples of contemporary spoken American English is similar to the classification implied by the traditional terms, nevertheless the two turn out to disagree in a number of respects.

Behaviourism in this methodological sense is wholly desirable. Although I have pointed out, above, that logical positivism is no longer the reigning philosophy of science, the arguments for behaviourist method are unaffected by the fall of positivism. We now recognize that the generalizations of science cannot be reduced to conjunctions of statements about individual observations: a theory is not an abbreviation of a set of observation statements, but rather a guess which can never be ultimately proved right by any finite series of observations no matter how protracted. But that does not mean that anything other than observation is relevant for corroborating or refuting a theory: once allow theories to be answerable to opinion rather than to observation, and one opens the door wide to controversies which can be settled only by shouting-matches. This problem is just as real for linguistics as for psychology: people sometimes have startlingly erroneous beliefs about even such elementary properties of their own speech as whether some simple construction occurs in it (see Labov 1975, section 2.3, for a striking example). The folklorist may be interested in Englishmen's beliefs about English; the linguist must concentrate rather on how Englishmen speak when they are not thinking about their language. Furthermore, although modern philosophers of science acknowledge that what is not science (nor logic or mathematics) need not therefore be nonsense, it remains true that subjects which can be treated scientifically should be. Ethical discourse may be valid though unscientific, but then ethical principles do not pretend to be reports about matters of observable fact. There is no excuse, on the other hand, for the use of speakers' opinions in defence of a syntactic analysis, since the analysis concerns phenomena which are open to observation.

Many behaviourist psychologists, however, confused the methodological issue with a matter of substantive belief. They took the wrongness of introspection to imply that there was nothing to be introspected. This is clearly a *non sequitur*; the proper move to make is to admit that introspection gives each of us privileged access to a rich and subtle programme of mental activity, while resigning oneself to the fact that this category of phenomena cannot be studied scientifically and must be left to the philosopher and the poet. But behaviourists often wrote as if belief in the existence of minds and mental activity were on a par with belief in the existence of a water-god who is angry when the sea is rough.

This attitude on the part of some (not all) behaviourists is illogical, and laughable when, as sometimes, it leads to the spectacle of the psychologist heroically trying to convince himself that he really is the mindless zombie which he thinks he ought to be. It has more serious consequences when it causes psychologists to claim to be able to explain phenomena which they cannot explain. What we can observe about human beings are the inputs to them (the sights they are in a position to see, the sounds they hear, the blows or caresses they receive) and their outputs – what they do, consciously or unconsciously (including, of course, what they say). Now the common-sense view is that inputs to us will often affect our internal mental organization, and that the activities of our mental organization will in turn determine many of our outputs; but, since minds are enduring and enormously complicated phenomena, there is not likely in most cases to be much *direct* relationship between individual inputs and individual outputs. What I do may in a sense be a function of what is done to me; but, if so, it is a function not exclusively of what was done to me in the last five minutes but rather of a countless variety of things that have been done to me at different times throughout my whole life.[3] Therefore, if our only data are observations of inputs and outputs, we are very unlikely in practice to be able to produce a theory which shows how outputs are related to inputs. Behaviourists who commit the fallacy just described are unwilling to admit this; since they disbelieve in minds, they feel that human inputs and outputs must be related in some fairly straightforward fashion. In a few cases they are right: the input of a tap below the knee is followed immediately by a jerk of the leg. By dint of emphasizing this kind of example at the expense of the categories of behaviour which ordinary folk think of as more characteristically human, some behaviourists have succeeded in convincing themselves that the task of stating the relationship between human inputs and human outputs is already accomplished, all but for the filling in of some matters of detail. This view is very explicit in the work of B. F. Skinner, one of the last and most outspoken of the group of psychologists I am criticizing (and Skinner has been very properly rebuked on this count by Noam Chomsky).

Up to a point it does not matter for linguistics whether a 'good' behaviourist commits the fallacy which turns him into a 'bad' behaviourist. Speech is a richly patterned category of observable output (from the speaker) and input (to the hearer); much of the interest of linguistics involves working out the nature of the patterns, and for this it is unnecessary to appeal to hypothetical mental activity. (Psychologists not oriented towards language, on the other hand, tend to be dealing with categories of input and output which are in themselves fairly simple and uninteresting, so that the whole point of the work is to establish the input/output relations.) The branches of linguistic description called phonology, morphology, and syntax are all concerned with different types of patterning observable in speech data.

Where the fallacy becomes relevant is in connection with semantics, since to talk about the meanings of utterances is not to talk about patterns the utterances display but rather to talk about the effects they have on the minds of those who hear them. When Leonard Bloomfield wrote about meaning he very openly and clearly committed the behaviourist fallacy. For Bloomfield, to analyse meaning in a language is to show what stimuli evoke given utterances as responses, and what behavioural responses are evoked by given spoken stimuli. The paradigm case in Bloomfield's discussion of semantics (1933, pp. 22 ff.) concerns a story according to which sight of an apple beyond a fence conjoined with secretion of gastric juices causes a girl, Jill, to utter a sentence such as *Please fetch me that apple* to her more agile companion Jack, and the stimulus of hearing this utterance in turn causes Jack to climb the fence and bring the apple to Jill. The problem with this story is obvious: 'People very often utter a word like *apple* when no apple at all is present' (ibid., p. 141). Bloomfield calls the latter situation *displaced speech*, and he tries to assimilate its explanation to that of the Jack-and-Jill case; for a speaker to use the word *apple* when he is not currently being stimulated by the perception of an apple is for the speaker to 'respond . . . to some obscure internal stimuli of a type which was associated at some time in [his] past with the stimuli of an apple' (ibid., p. 143). But anyone who is not prejudiced by attachment to the fallacious version of behaviourism will recognize that 'displaced speech' is the norm and cases like the Jack-and-Jill story are exceptional. An evening chat round an English sitting-room fire might concern anything from traditional Chinese architecture to the economics of the motor industry; if it restricts itself to the contents of the sitting-room it is likely to be a desperately dull conversation. Bloomfield's appeal to 'obscure internal stimuli' either refers covertly to mental activity under another name, or else is just mere hand-waving in defence of the indefensible: Bloomfield is convinced because of his theoretical assumptions that there must be some potentially observable stimuli preceding the utterance of 'displaced speech', but he has observed no such stimuli and we have no real reason to believe that there are any to be observed.

However, although Bloomfield was quite wrong here, the

mistake did no harm. For phonology, morphology and syntax, only the 'good', methodological aspect of behaviourism was relevant. In these areas Bloomfield's behaviourism had a desirable influence in causing linguists to purge their analyses of appeals to intuition or inherited folk-wisdom, so that the analyses (whether right or wrong) became genuinely scientific rather than a bastard mixture of statements testable against observation versus statements that had to be taken on faith. In semantics, Bloomfield's reasoning led him to conclude that the statement of meanings was in practice impossible, and would remain so 'until human knowledge advances very far beyond its present state' (1933, p. 140) – for instance, science would have to lay bare the 'obscure internal stimuli' that impinge on a man just before he utters a sentence such as *I hear that apples will be cheaper next year*. Bloomfield was mistaken in supposing that such stimuli exist; but we have seen that even a behaviourist of the 'good' variety must agree that the observable data are in practice insufficient to permit the construction of models of the interaction between observable speech and unobservable mind. Indeed, philosophical considerations which we shall take up in Chapter 6 suggest that scientific description of meaning is impossible not just in practice but in principle. Thus Bloomfield's conclusion that semantic analysis is impossible was sound, even if his reasoning was defective.

There is a sense in which it is difficult to say a great deal about the Descriptivists' theories of language. A theory is by definition something which concentrates on the relatively constant factors in the range of phenomena with which it is concerned, while ignoring the many features that are peculiar to single individual instances. Meteorology tells us that cumulus clouds are formed by convection currents; it ignores the fact that this cumulus cloud is shaped rather like a duck while the one over there looks more like a galleon. But Boas and his Descriptivist successors emphasized the diversity found in human languages. This assumption of limitless diversity was in the first place a sensible research strategy for the Descriptivists – one will not get far with the analysis of an alien language if one starts by assuming that its structure is much like that of English or Latin, and the Descriptivists' need was to overcome their inherited presuppositions about what languages must be like, not to erect new presuppositions. But the Descriptivists went further: limitless diversity was for many of them not just a heuristic principle but a substantive belief. Bloomfield wrote (1933, p. 20) that 'Features which we think ought to be universal may be absent from the very next language that becomes accessible'; and, while this says only that if there are any universals of language they are likely to be different from what our prejudices suggest, Martin Joos stated the position unequivocally when he wrote with approval of 'the American (Boas) tradition that languages could differ from each other without limit and in unpredictable ways' (Joos 1957, p. 96). In other words, for the Descriptivists the true theory of language was that there was no theory of language; which, as I say, makes it difficult to write at length about their theory.

This unlimited-diversity principle was more than a mere confusion of heuristic strategy with theoretical tenet. For Boas the point was that languages are creations of the human mind rather than of physical circumstance, so there will be no more limitations on the diversity of languages than on the diversity of men's imaginings. Bloomfield turned 'mind' and 'imagination' into taboo terms, but he would probably nevertheless have approved of some version of that idea once it had been translated into behaviourist vocabulary. However, while there were respectable grounds for holding the unlimited-diversity principle, it did lead to certain characteristic confusions in Descriptivist thought. Because they held the principle, Descriptivists supposed that when they wrote about general linguistics they were merely discussing *techniques* of analysis which made no substantive presuppositions about the nature of the systems to be analysed. But this is a contradictory notion – any analytical technique in any domain must depend on some assumptions about the nature of the things analysed. The result was that the Descriptivists found it very difficult to recognize what had gone wrong when their analytical practice threw up refutations of their implicit assumptions.

Consider, for instance, one of the problems of Chinese phonology discussed by Y.-R. Chao in an influential article on 'The Non-Uniqueness of Phonemic Solutions of Phonetic Systems' (1934). Mandarin Chinese has an alveolo-palatal fricative, [ɕ], with very restricted distribution: it occurs only before close front vowels, [i ɪ y ʏ].[4] Other Mandarin consonants, e.g. [p] or [l], are found before a much wider range of vowels. A Descriptivist faced with these facts will immediately suspect that [ɕ] may be one allophone of a phoneme which as a whole has a distribution similar to that of the more versatile consonants (just as, in English, the union of the distributions of the [l] and [lᵚ] sounds is more 'normal' than is the distribution of either allophone taken singly); and he will therefore hunt around for another Mandarin consonant phone in complementary distribution with [ɕ]. The problem is that Mandarin has not just one such phone but three: the alveolar, retroflex, and velar fricatives [s ʂ x] each occur before almost all vowels *other* than close front ones. Thus we find, for example, [sū] 'Soviet' contrasting with [ʂū] 'book' and with [xū] 'to exhale', but no *[ɕū]; and, for example, [ɕī] 'west' but no *[sī], *[ʂī], *[xī]. So which is the other member of the phoneme which has [ɕ] as one of its members? We cannot link [ɕ] phonemically with more than one of the three other fricatives, because the latter contrast with each other; thus if, for instance, we were to say that [ɕ s ʂ] all belong to a single phoneme for which we might write / s /, then we would have only one phonemic spelling / sū / available for the non-homophonous words for 'Soviet' and 'book' – which violates the basic principle of phonemic transcription, namely that it should record any phonetic differences which are distinctive in the language. On the other hand we can hardly treat the four fricative phones as four separate phonemes, since the very purpose of phonemic transcription is to reduce the number of units of sound to be recognized by ignoring all differences of sound which are *not* distinctive, and the difference between [ɕ] and the other three fricatives is certainly not distinctive. We may narrow the field somewhat by appealing to a criterion of phonetic similarity between the members of a phoneme; that would presumably rule out the choice of [x] to be linked with [ɕ], but it hardly seems decisive as between [s] and [ʂ] which are made with articulatory positions about equidistant from that of [ɕ]. Just to confuse the issue further, if we bring historical evidence into the picture we find that [ɕ] derives from a merger of [s] and [x] before close front vowels (modern [ɕī] 'west' comes from older [sī], but its modern homophone [ɕī] 'rare' comes from [xī]); and Chao gives evidence that native speakers perceive [ɕ] as a variant of [x], the fricative which it least resembles phonetically!

Faced with problems of this sort, Descriptivist linguists tended to react in one of two ways. Some of them took the tack that linguistic analysis was a matter not of *discovering* structure that

existed independently of linguists' researches, but rather of
inventing structure which the linguist imposed on the language
under study – they saw linguistics as concerned with 'hocus pocus'
rather than 'God's truth', to use F. W. Householder's labels. For
the hocus-pocussers, choice between alternative analyses was a
matter of mere personal taste and certainly not of correct versus
incorrect; there was no 'right answer', so it was pointless to worry
about cases such as the one cited. The trouble with this attitude is
that it is scarcely possible to maintain it consistently and still want
to do linguistics. If a description of a language can really never be
anything more than an arbitrary fiction invented by linguists for
linguists, then why bother? And furthermore the hocus-pocus
position implies that the *real* nature of a language is somehow
ineffable, which seems strange. If the suggestion is merely that
linguists tend to describe languages as if they were much neater
and more systematically structured than they really are (which is
undoubtedly true), then this means not that there is no such thing
as correctness of linguistic description but rather that the
descriptions produced by linguists are as a matter of fact all
incorrect and should be replaced by descriptions more faithful to
the inelegant 'God's truth' – which is a very different thing to say.
One suspects that the hocus-pocussers may have been happy
enough to regard linguistic descriptions as true so long as the
descriptive techniques worked unproblematically, and that they
simply held the hocus-pocus position in reserve to be used if they
encountered an *impasse* such as the Chinese case described
above. That is rather like saying 'Who cares about silly games
anyway?' when, after a hard struggle, one realizes that one's
position on the chess-board is hopeless.

The alternative reaction to this kind of *impasse* was to seek
solutions by suggesting refinements to the battery of analytic
techniques. A Descriptivist might ask whether, perhaps,
native-speaker intuition ought after all to be admitted to resolve
stalemates such as the case cited, and if so just what kind of
elicitation techniques were permissible and in what precise
circumstances was it legitimate to resort to such data? What
weight, if any, should be given to the historical evidence? Or
perhaps statistics about the frequency of the various sounds
should be brought in – if, say, [ʂ] were noticeably less common
in Mandarin than [s] or [x], then it might make sense to link [ɕ]
with [ʂ] to give the phoneme as a whole a more normal frequency.

(I do not in fact remember encountering the last proposal in the literature, but it is in the general spirit of the sort of suggestions that were made in problematic cases.)

In the Mandarin case, none of these proposals are satisfactory. The arguments already discussed against giving any weight at all to history or to native-speaker intuition in scientific synchronic analysis are sound arguments; and criteria such as phonetic similarity or statistics of frequency do not solve this particular problem. The move which seems correct in this case is one that a Descriptivist would have been unlikely to make: viz., to acknowledge that the Mandarin case refutes the phoneme theory. The notion that sounds are grouped into 'phonemes' involves an empirical assumption about human language in general, namely that whenever the respective ranges of contrasting sounds which occur in two phonetic environments in a given language are not identical, the two ranges will at least have the same number of members so that they can be paired off with one another. There is no logical reason why this should have to be so, but there does appear to be a strong tendency for languages to conform to the principle – which is presumably how the notion of phonemic analysis was able to arise in the first place. One does not often encounter languages in which, say, eighteen different consonants contrast before [i], four before [e], eleven before [a], and so forth. To hold that phonemic analysis is the proper mode of phonological description for any language is to hold that the principle is more than just a tendency but actually a fixed universal of human language, which it is not – as the Mandarin example and many other cases show. Therefore, if one insists on sticking to phonemic analysis, one will inevitably have to make arbitrary choices, such as linking Mandarin [ç] with [ʂ] for no better reason than that they both sound to an Englishman somewhat like his [ʃ]. One ought rather to seek some more sophisticated format for phonological description which would respect the principle described as a statistical tendency without trying to turn it into an absolute law.[5]

The Descriptivist would not have made the move of rejecting phoneme theory, because he did not think of linguistics as embodying a set of theories about human language in general which might be right or wrong, and it was therefore difficult for him to recognize what had happened when he met a counter-example to one of the beliefs which were tacitly implied by his analytic practice. Nowadays, as we shall see in Chapter 6, linguists consciously strive to produce theories about linguistic universals; accordingly they take great pains to make explicit the assumptions lurking behind their formal descriptive techniques and to point out that these assumptions are in no sense necessary truths. For the Descriptivist, this was not the job of linguistics. His concern was with the production of correct theories about individual languages; it would have been merely embarrassing for him to recognize that general linguistic theorizing pre-empted some of the choices available to him when describing a particular language by making gratuitous assumptions that all languages were alike in certain respects.

The Descriptivists, then, thought of general linguistics more as a body of techniques of description than as a body of beliefs about the nature of language. (I am speaking now about a general atmosphere of thought shared by very many practising American linguists of the 1930s, 1940s and 1950s, rather than about the explicit statements of individual scholars.) Sometimes, as with phonemic analysis, Descriptivists overlooked the fact that the appropriateness of any particular descriptive technique implies that some general characteristic runs through the objects described. Often, though, they approached alternative techniques of description in a more catholic way, seeing them as alternative tools to be pulled out of the toolbag when needed – one language, or one aspect of a language, might call for one technique, another for a different technique, as some jobs need a spanner and others need a drill.

Consider, for instance, the alternative approaches to morphological and syntactic description christened by Charles Hockett (1954) the *item-and-arrangement* and the *item-and-process* models – 'I A' and 'I P'. We can illustrate the difference between the two by considering how they would handle the alternation between masculine and feminine forms of French adjectives, as exemplified below:

Masculine	Feminine	
ver	vert	'green'
blã	blãʃ	'white'
gri	griz	'grey'
blø	blø	'blue'

(I have deliberately limited myself to examples that raise only one of the many problems that would arise if the full range of French adjectives were considered.) The I A approach says, roughly, 'A French adjective in the singular consists of an adjectival root morpheme, e.g. / ver /, / blã /, / gri /, / blø /, ..., followed in certain circumstances (which need not be specified in detail here) by a suffix morpheme that we may call 'Feminine'. The morpheme Feminine has many allomorphs according to environment: thus it is realized as / t / after / ver / (and many other roots, such as / pla / 'flat', which I shall not list), / ʃ / after / blã / (etc.), / z / after / gri / (etc.), zero after / blø / (etc.), ... ' (In a full statement other allomorphs of Feminine would have to be listed with their respective environments.) An IP description on the other hand will take the feminine forms of the adjectives as basic, and will say: 'A French singular adjective consists of an underlying form such as / vert /, / blãʃ /, / griz /, / blø /, ..., to which in certain circumstances (the converse of those specified in the I A description) the following instruction is applied: "Delete the last phoneme provided it is a consonant".' In this particular case the I P description happens to be considerably more elegant and Hockett cited similar examples in order to suggest that the usefulness of I P description should not be lost sight of in the enthusiasm for IA current among linguists at that time. But Hockett did not mean to argue that I P was *better* and that I A should be abandoned; he explicitly argues that both models should be developed, and indeed he alludes briefly to a third model ('word-and-paradigm' or 'W P') which, he feels, deserves equal consideration with the other two. It is easy to think of languages (Chinese is one) in which I P has virtually no applicability at any level of description; for Sanskrit, on the other hand, I P seems almost indispensable.

The view of general linguistics as technique rather than theory was laudable insofar as it reflected a desire on linguists' part to free themselves from prejudices about necessary characteristics of language stemming from traditional doctrines or from the nature of their own mother-tongue. However, it manifested itself in a less desirable way in the work of some scholars writing during the later years of the Descriptivist period, who held that the purpose of formalization in linguistics was to express procedures which could be applied to derive the correct grammar of a language from a corpus of observed data in a purely mechanical way. As awareness of electronic computers spread in the 1950s, some of these linguists came to feel that an – if not the – appropriate goal for general linguistics was to devise explicit 'discovery procedures' which, when translated into a computer-programming language, would enable the machine to process raw observed data about any language into a completed grammar of that language without intervention by the human linguist. The fullest and most interesting expression of the 'discovery procedure' approach to linguistics is a book, *Methods in Structural Linguistics* (1951), by Zellig Harris of the University of Pennsylvania. Harris gives very detailed and explicit rules for moving from a collection of utterances recorded in phonetic transcription step by step to a phonemic analysis, a morphemic analysis, and finally to a registration of the syntactic patterns. (Harris's book is noteworthy also as being one of the most serious attempts before Chomsky to deal with syntax; many Descriptivists concentrated chiefly on phonology and morphology, with only fragmentary descriptions of syntax.)[6]

The objection to the discovery-procedure approach was expressed in a well-known passage by Chomsky (1957, section 6). To write a grammar of a language is to formulate a set of generalizations, i.e. a theory, to account for one's observations of the language. No established scientific discipline has ever supposed that its aim was to provide rules of thumb for arriving at correct theories about its subject-matter; for instance, when Einstein contradicted Newton by putting forward his Special Theory of Relativity he did so as a result of creative inspiration, and it seems absurd to suppose that there might be a mechanical technique which could render inspiration redundant in such matters. To work out the rule governing ordering of adjectives in Choctaw (say) is a less momentous achievement than Einstein's, but the principle is the same; only a creative leap of the imagination can take us from a collection of observed examples to a general rule which accounts for those examples, and the point of formalization is not that it replaces imagination in discovering the theory but rather that it makes the theory, once discovered, explicit and precise enough to test against the data and to compare with alternative theories.

The history of the discovery-procedure controversy has been a curious one. The idea that linguistics is about discovery procedures stems from the idea that general linguistics consists of techniques rather than theories about language, and this belief in turn derives from the view that there is no limit to the diversity of human languages (and hence no room for theories about language in general). Nevertheless, there is a tension within the Descriptivist school between the principle of unlimited linguistic diversity and the view that linguistics should consist of mechanical rules for processing data into grammars. The latter view can be plausible only provided one feels sure about what the general shape of the grammar for any language must be like; someone who sincerely believed that 'features which we think ought to be universal may be absent from the very next language that becomes accessible' could hardly be very confident about the ability of his computer program to analyse as yet unknown languages without requiring modification. For Chomsky, on the other hand, there is no such tension. Chomsky, as we shall see, believes that children succeed in mastering their mother-tongue only because they are born with complex genetically inherited mental equipment geared specifically to the task of acquiring a language of a well-defined kind; and for Chomsky (1965, pp. 24 ff., 30 ff.) a chief task of linguistic theory is to model the functioning of that equipment. Chomsky's approach to linguistics, in other words, *is* a discovery-procedure approach; and, fifteen years after Chomsky came to prominence via a book in which the argument against discovery procedures formed one of the most quoted sections, he published a brief, inexplicit, and somewhat ungracious footnote (1972b, p. 120 n. 7) which in effect retracted what he originally said and argued that Descriptivists were after all right to aim at discovery procedures.

To my mind, Chomsky's first thoughts on this issue were best. Sauce for the Einstein is sauce for the infant. If one agrees that advances at the frontiers of human knowledge happen because some humans have a greater than average ability to produce explanations for what they observe by making creative, unregimented leaps of imagination, then surely the most straightforward account of the human ability to learn a first language will treat this too as a consequence of the modicum of imaginative ability which even we ordinary non-Einsteins possess. That seems simpler than to suppose that we learn a language by following a set of mental tramlines programmed into our brain from birth, a notion which entails the awkward consequence that our ability to learn our mother-tongue must be quite separate from our ability to master the countless other skills and ideas which various ordinary humans acquire – each of which would by parity of reasoning require its own set of innate tramlines. Chomsky has been unwilling to acknowledge the possibility that imagination rather than innate discovery procedures might explain children's acquisition of language. However, he also has positive arguments for his position on this issue, and we must defer consideration of these until Chapter 6.[7]

I have made a number of criticisms of Descriptivists' views in this chapter. However, it lies in the nature of a book such as this that it must deal more with the writings in which linguists propound their theoretical principles than with the writings in which those principles are applied in analysis of data – which in the case of the Descriptivist school formed the great bulk of their output. The Descriptivists in particular are put at a disadvantage by this procedure; since one of their key principles implied that no general theory of human language was likely to be both non-trivial and true, their touch was least sure when they did theorize, and they were seen at their best in actual analytic practice. It is with the Descriptivist school that the present author's allegiance lies, or more precisely with its unlimited-diversity wing rather than with the discovery-procedures wing. The Descriptivists' practice, it seems to me, was essentially what linguistics ought to be. They were confused about some issues and wrong about others, but their errors were of very little consequence by comparison with the errors of their successors.

Unfortunately, the Descriptivist tradition rather decisively lost its hold on the American linguistic community at some point in the 1960s.[8] There are still many people who are more concerned to describe than to theorize, and who see general linguistics as a toolkit rather than as an end in itself; but the ethos of the discipline has changed. Nowadays, as soon as 'data-oriented' people such as I have just described come into contact with academic linguistics, it is made clear to them that if they wish their descriptive work to be taken seriously they must begin by mastering a particular, very specific and complex range of grammatical formalisms, and then regiment the data which interest them in terms of these formalisms as best they can. If there are points in their data which cannot naturally be expressed in terms of the given formalisms, it is better to leave those points

out of the description than to make up one's own descriptive
framework. True, modifications to the standard formalisms are
permissible and indeed in a sense desirable; but any such changes
require the approval of a sort of self-appointed linguistic
Academy, most of whose immortals have fairly limited
acquaintance with or interest in any languages much more exotic
than French or Russian. I do not say that this attitude was never
found in the Descriptivist camp: it was. But the ideas of the best
Descriptivists militated against it; the ideas of the best of the new
men, although those ideas are held for respectable reasons,
unwittingly encourage it.

Descriptivism has not died out, although it has been edged from
the centre of the stage deep into the wings. In the first place,
some men work in the old style on aspects of language which
happen hardly yet to have been touched by the new orthodoxy:
Dwight Bolinger on intonation, for instance. Apart from such
special cases, some scholars have stood firm against, or have
simply ignored, the tide of fashion. Thus Charles Hockett of
Cornell University (b. 1916), who like Boas came to linguistics
via anthropology, has never seen any reason to accept the
hegemony of Chomskyan linguistics; his *State of the Art* (1968) is
required reading for anyone who is prepared to regard the
fundamental assumptions of the Chomskyan school as open to
question – Hockett raises objections which have never been
answered by the Chomskyans (if indeed they have been
understood).

Possibly the most significant continuing segment of the
Descriptivist tradition is that represented by the work of the
Summer Institute of Linguistics, under the academic leadership of
Kenneth Pike. Some might argue that Pike and his followers
merit a chapter to themselves, if only because they have a special
name for their technique of linguistic analysis – 'tagmemics'. It is
true that the tagmemicists have their own fairly esoteric symbolic
format for writing grammars; but to my mind (and not to mine
alone: cf. Hockett 1968, p. 33) the novelty of tagmemic formulae
lies more in their superficial appearance than in any theoretical
innovations they represent, and the abstract theoretical writings
of Pike and others of this group seem the less valuable aspect of
their contribution. What matters is that they maintain
the Descriptivist approach of subordinating theory to the task of
analysing unfamiliar languages, and their analytical work has a

very concrete practical purpose: to aid the conversion of the heathen by enabling the Holy Scriptures to be given to every human in his own mother-tongue. The Sumner Institute of Linguistics provides linguistic training for the missionaries of the Wycliffe Bible Translators, Inc., founded in 1942, who are working with the very numerous and wholly alien vernacular languages of large parts of Central and South America and of the Western Pacific area. Such languages invariably lack a writing system, let alone any pedagogical tradition, so that a great deal of linguistic analysis has to take place before any translation is possible. I have heard it estimated that even today, when Chomskyan linguistics is a much more fashionable academic subject than Descriptivist linguistics ever was in its heyday, the greater part of the work of actually describing languages that is going on in the world is occurring under the aegis of the Summer Institute. Happily for linguistics, there would appear to be little likelihood of this work coming to an end in the near future, judging by the title of a book (Wallis and Bennett 1959) about the Wycliffe Translators: *Two Thousand Tongues To Go.*

4 The Sapir–Whorf hypothesis

The subject of this chapter is not so much a geographically or chronologically distinguishable school of thinkers, as an idea which has held a perennial fascination for linguists of diverse schools, and indeed for very many people who have never been students of language in any formal sense. This idea – that a man's language moulds his perception of reality, or that the world a man inhabits is a linguistic construct – although in one form or another a very old one, has become associated with the names of the Americans Edward Sapir (1884–1939) and Benjamin Lee Whorf (1897–1941), and more particularly with the latter.

The work of these writers might well have been treated in the last chapter, since it fell squarely within the tradition initiated by Boas. I have chosen to discuss Sapir and Whorf in a separate chapter, because the aspect of their work which we shall examine represents a rather special development within the Descriptivist school, and one which conflicted fairly sharply with the thought of many other members of that school. Sapir and Whorf fully shared the relativism of Boas and his Descriptivist successors, with its emphasis on the alienness of exotic languages, while never being influenced by the behaviourism (in either 'good' or 'bad' senses) of Bloomfield. (Behaviourism was an element which Bloomfield imported into the Descriptivist tradition rather than finding it already there – Boas, and indeed Bloomfield himself in his early writing, were happy to discuss meanings and spent little time worrying about the logical status of linguists' data. But Bloomfield succeeded in taking most of his colleagues with him in his conversion to behaviourism, which is why I say that there was a conflict between the ideas summarized as the 'Sapir–Whorf hypothesis' and the ideas of other Descriptivists.)

Sapir studied languages of the Pacific coast of North America, and began his career in charge of anthropological research at the Canadian National Museum; in 1925 he moved to the University of Chicago, and in 1931 to Yale. Much of his work was quite comparable to that of other Descriptivist linguists, though he differed from the behaviourists in stressing that patterns revealed by linguistic analysis were patterns in speakers' minds (it is significant that the collection of his papers published in 1949 bears the title *Selected Writings in Language, Culture, and Personality*), and Sapir took it for granted that if one wants to know how a language is structured for its speakers it is appropriate to ask them.[1] Sapir's independence of his American colleagues' assumptions is particularly obvious in his notion of linguistic 'drift': behind the more-or-less random fluctuations which make up the detailed history of any language, Sapir thought, there was a long-term tendency for that language to modify itself in some particular direction, as the coming and going of waves on a beach masks a steady long-term tidal movement (Sapir 1921, ch. 7). This idea comes very close to implying that a language has a life of its own in some more than metaphorical sense, and it would clearly have been anathema to a methodological individualist such as Bloomfield.

On the issue with which this chapter is concerned, Sapir was by no means single-minded. The occurrence of his name in the term 'Sapir–Whorf hypothesis' is perhaps due more to the fact that Whorf took his general approach to linguistics from Sapir than to Sapir's being one of the most active proponents of that hypothesis. (The term was introduced by J. B. Carroll (Whorf 1956, p. 27).) In his popular book *Language*, indeed, Sapir suggests that differences between languages are merely differences in modes of expressing a common range of experiences, rather than corresponding to differences in the experiences themselves (Sapir 1921, p. 218). Later, though, Sapir changed his mind. Consider, for example, the following passages:

Human beings do not live in the objective world alone, nor alone in the world of social activity as ordinarily understood, but are very much at the mercy of the particular language which has become the medium of expression for their society. It is quite an illusion to imagine that one adjusts to reality essentially without the use of language and that language is merely an incidental means of solving specific problems of communication or reflection. The fact of the matter is that *the 'real world' is to a large extent unconsciously built up on the language habits of the group.* No two languages are ever sufficiently similar to be considered as representing the same social reality. The worlds in which different societies live are distinct worlds, not merely the same world with different labels attached. [1929, p. 209; my italics]

Language ... not only refers to experience largely acquired without its help but actually *defines experience for us* by reason of its formal completeness and because of our unconscious projection of its implicit expectations into the field of experience.... Such categories as number, gender, case, tense,... are not so much discovered in experience as imposed upon it because of the tyrannical hold that linguistic form has upon our orientation in the world. [1931; my italics]

These remarks might be interpreted as mere truisms, but if taken literally they are strong statements. The special contribution of Whorf was, by means of detailed analysis of certain American Indian languages, to make as convincing a case as has ever been made for believing that we must acknowledge the view expressed by Sapir as true in a quite radical, untrivial sense.

Benjamin Lee Whorf, a descendant of seventeenth-century English emigrants to Massachusetts, was in his scholarly work an outstanding example of the brilliant amateur. After taking a degree in chemical engineering he began a successful career as a fire-prevention inspector with an insurance company in Hartford, Connecticut, and despite several offers of academic posts he continued to work for the same company until his death at the age of 44. (Whorf learned lessons from his professional work which encouraged his belief that world-view is moulded by language. In analysing a large number of reports of how fires had started, Whorf tells us (1941a, p. 135), he began by assuming that only physical factors would be relevant but came to realize that language often played an important role: for instance, people behaved cautiously near what they categorized as 'full petrol drums' but carelessly near 'empty petrol drums', although the 'empty' drums contained explosive petrol vapour and were thus even more dangerous than the full ones.) Whorf's linguistic interests were originally rather diverse; when in 1931 Sapir moved to Yale University, only thirty-odd miles from Hartford, Whorf became a regular collaborator of his and began to focus his attention mainly on Hopi, a language of

Arizona. Much of Whorf's writing discusses the special, very un-European world-view which he believed to be implied by various features of Hopi grammar.

Whorf makes the point that only certain grammatical categories in any language are marked overtly, as, for example, the distinction between present and past tense is marked in every finite verb which occurs in English. There exist also numerous 'covert' categories, or 'cryptotypes' as Whorf sometimes calls them. For instance, in English the names of countries and towns form a 'cryptotype' because, although they outwardly resemble other nouns, they cannot be reduced to pronouns after the prepositions *in, at, to, from* (Whorf 1945, p. 92). Thus one can say *I live in it* when 'it' refers back to a phrase such as *that house* or *the basement*, but not when it refers to *Kendal* or *Bulgaria* – even though *I live in Kendal, I live in Bulgaria* are perfectly correct. Whorf felt that such covert categories were more telling than the overt categories of a language in establishing the world-view of its speakers, on the ground that the use of overt markers may be merely learned by rote but 'cryptotypes' can be manipulated consistently only if the categorization which they imply is real for the speaker. (If all country-names and town-names ended in some special suffix, say *-ia*, then an Englishman could simply remember 'nouns ending in *-ia* may not pronominalize after a preposition', but since they in fact have no special form we must think of them as a semantic class.) In Hopi rain-prayers, it seems that clouds are spoken of as if they were alive. Whorf points out that from this alone one cannot know whether the usage 'is some metaphor or special religious or ceremonial figure of speech', or whether the Hopi actually believe that clouds are living beings. However, the distinction between animate and inanimate exists as a covert category in Hopi. Any noun used to refer to a living being is pluralized in a special way (even when the noun is not basically animate, so that, for example, the Rolling Stones in Hopi would take the animate plural of 'stone'); and the word for 'cloud' is invariably pluralized in the animate way, which demonstrates that the Hopi do indeed believe clouds to be alive (Whorf 1956, p. 79).[2]

Although this neatly illustrates Whorf's point about the importance of covert categories, it is not a particularly good example of the differences Whorf claims to exist between Hopi and European world-views: in this case the *categories* animate/inanimate are perfectly normal for a European, and the only question concerns the status of clouds with respect to these categories. (We shall consider a better example of Whorf's thesis about linguistic diversity shortly.) Nevertheless, even here it is possible to take a sceptical stance. Thus, suppose that we encounter another tribe in which sex is a 'covert category', so that, say, all nouns referring to females evoke special suffixes in words modifying them; and suppose further that many words for inanimate objects, such as 'stone', 'water', 'moon', belong to the female cryptotype, while others, such as 'iron', 'fire', 'sun', behave like the words for males. Clearly Whorf would have to conclude that this tribe holds some sort of animistic view of Nature, according to which everything that exists is alive and has a sex. But there is such a tribe: they live just across the Channel from Dover, and if there is one thing the French are not it is surely animists. Whorf did not in fact apply his notions to differences between the familiar European languages; he felt that these all presupposed the same world-view because of the long period in which Europe had shared a common culture, and he referred to them collectively as 'Standard Average European'. It is perhaps appropriate to be cautious, at least, in accepting a theory which says that certain communities see the world in ways startlingly different from ours, but which is illustrated almost wholly by reference to primitive tribes about whose beliefs we have little independent evidence. The non-European language with which the present writer is best acquainted is Chinese; although traditional Chinese ideas about the world differ greatly from European ideas, the two intellectual systems do not seem to possess quite the same quality of mutual incommensurability that Whorf alleges to occur with Hopi *vis-à-vis* 'Standard Average European'. One cannot help wondering whether this may be because Chinese civilization, although, like that of the Hopi, quite independent of Europe, has been articulate enough to refute the flights of fancy in which a Whorf might be inclined to indulge on the basis of formal characteristics of Chinese grammar.

In fact, the various contrasts in world-view for which Whorf argues differ greatly in the extent to which they are surprising or controversial. Boas had already made the point that, for instance, where English has the one word *snow* Eskimo has separate basic roots for snow falling, snow on the ground, drifting snow, and so forth; at this relatively concrete level disparities between the conceptual schemes of different languages are fairly familiar, and there is no doubt that they influence perception – it can be shown that people's perceptions of their surroundings are modified by the conceptual categories their language happens to provide (Lenneberg and Roberts 1956, p. 31; cf. Herman *et al*. 1957; Hanson 1958). Whorf discusses cases of this kind, but they are not what he is primarily interested in. 'What surprises most', Whorf rightly says, 'is to find that various grand generalizations of the Western world, such as time, velocity and matter, are not essential to the construction of a consistent picture of the universe' (1940, p. 216). Hopi, in particular, 'may be called a timeless language': the language does not recognize time as a linear dimension which can be measured and divided into units like spatial dimensions, so that for instance Hopi never borrows spatial terms to refer to temporal phenomena in the way so common in European languages (*before the door* ~ *before noon, between London and Brighton* ~ *between 9 and 10 a.m., in the box* ~ *in the morning*), nor does Hopi permit phrases such as *five days* since daytime is not a thing like an apple of which one can have one or several. Furthermore, Hopi verbs do not have tenses comparable to those of European languages. And since there is no concept of time, there can be no concept of speed, which is the ratio of distance to time: Hopi has no word for 'fast', and their nearest equivalent for 'He runs fast' would translate more literally as something like *He very runs*. If the Hopi rather than Europeans had developed sophisticated scientific theories, Whorf suggests, modern physics would be very different from what it is, though it might be equally self-consistent and satisfactory.

One objection to this interpretation of Hopi thought, voiced, for example, by Max Black (1959), is that Whorf's claim is untestable and therefore vacuous. It might be that the Hopi have much the same concept of time as we have, but simply use somewhat exotic turns of phrase in talking about matters of time – *He very runs* is just their way of saying 'He runs fast', and they mean by their sentence just what we mean by ours. After all, an Englishman calls a huntsman's coat 'pink' but that does not imply that he sees it as other than red. Whorf admits that 'the Hopi language is capable of accounting for and describing correctly, in a pragmatic or operational sense, all observable phenomena of the universe' (1956, p. 58); could any evidence then force us to conclude that the difference between Hopi and English ways of talking about time is more than a difference in formal modes of expressing a common range of ideas? (Philosophers will recognize that Willard Quine in *Word and Object* (1960) and subsequent writings has argued, essentially, for a negative answer to questions of this kind.)

There may be a reply to this objection (as it relates to Whorf's claims – not to the more general point made by Quine). In the first place, it may be that there are indeed observable aspects of Hopi behaviour which correlate with their 'timeless' outlook on life; cf. Whorf (1941a, pp. 148, 153). I have read that Indians on reservations in the US Southwest (unfortunately I do not remember whether this was said specifically of Hopi) have difficulty in holding jobs in the white man's economy because they cannot get into the habit of catching commuter buses and generally keeping to a timetable, and this might be evidence in favour of Whorf's ideas. True, the sceptic could point out that some individual Englishmen have similar problems, and we do not usually ascribe this to causes so lofty as a non-standard philosophy of time. But if the sceptic argues that the reason for American Indians missing buses is mere idleness or fecklessness rather than a special view of time, it would perhaps seem an awkward coincidence that the communities in which this idleness is unusually widespread are also communities which speak languages that treat time in an odd way.

Furthermore, even if independent evidence did little to corroborate Whorf's claims, I am not sure that Black's objection need be fatal. It is perhaps wrong to suppose, because of the word 'hypothesis' in the standard name for Whorf's idea, that it is to be interpreted as a scientific theory which makes testable predictions about observable data. It might be more appropriate to interpret Whorf as giving a philosophical account of alternative conceptual frameworks, which could not be confirmed or refuted by facts observed from within any one of those frameworks. (To give a parallel: we can contrast the mediaeval system of arguments from authority with the modern 'scientific method' of proposing and testing falsifiable hypotheses, but we cannot usefully cite evidence showing that the latter method of discovering truth is superior to the former, since the question whether it is appropriate to cite evidence for one's beliefs is exactly what is at stake.) Ludwig Wittgenstein in his later writings argued a view very similar to Whorf's (though without Whorf's knowledge of exotic languages) about the interdependence of world-view and language, and Wittgenstein was quite clear that he could only ask his readers to 'see' that his account was correct, he could not demonstrate it to be so; ironically, while Black attacks Whorf's 'hypothesis' for untestability he strongly supports Wittgenstein's frankly untestable philosophy.

Where Whorf (although not Wittgenstein) does fall down badly is in his apparent inability to allow for the radical changes of world-view which occur within a given linguistic community. Since we are discussing time and space, the obvious example to quote here is Albert Einstein. Einstein's new account of the 'grand generalizations' of physics seems fully as alien, from the standpoint of received views, as the Hopi approach; yet Einstein spoke a Standard Average European language. The history of science over several centuries has been a history of repeated radical changes of world-view, almost all of which occurred within the Standard Average European linguistic framework. Whorf (1941a, p. 153) supposes that Newton's physics was given to him ready-made by his language, but this idea that Newtonian physics is just common sense rendered explicit is an illusion deriving from the long period in which Newtonian physics has been accepted as true. As Black points out (1959, p. 254), Descartes, although also a 'Standard Average European' speaker, had worked out a very different structure of spatial concepts from those later evolved by Newton, and Newton's account was preferred not because it conformed better to men's commonsense ideas but because it turned out to be closer to the truth. Rather than saying that if the Hopi had developed physics then physics would look very different, it might be more appropriate to say that if the Hopi had developed physics then the Hopi world-view would have changed (and, by the same token, presumably the Hopi language is unsuitable for discussing bus timetables because the Hopi have not had much to do with buses, rather than *vice versa*).

Of course it is true that each of us accepts many inherited presuppositions, and such presuppositions may well be reflected in our language; but none of our inherited prejudices are sacrosanct, and human thought consists of a constant process of individuals questioning received presuppositions and replacing them by new and better ideas, which then become later generations' 'commonsense' until another individual has a still better idea. As the German philosopher J. G. Hamann wrote in 1760, 'a mind which thinks at its own expense will always interfere with language' (quoted by Cohen 1962, p. 10). Certainly the language of a community and the thought of individual members of the community each influence the other, but what ultimately counts is the individual's influence on the language; the influence of language on individual is a purely negative matter of the individual's failure to examine critically all the ideas of various earlier individuals. Sapir and Whorf write as if language exerted a positive influence, and one with far more power than the reverse influence: Sapir writes of individuals being 'at the mercy of' their language, which exerts a 'tyrannical hold' over their mind (cf. pages 82–3 above), Whorf writes of speakers being parties to an 'absolutely obligatory' agreement to conceptualize the world in a certain way (1940, pp. 213–14). It seems to me that this 'tyranny' is of the same order as the 'tyranny' to which my body is subjected early on a Monday morning by my bed. Sapir's and Whorf's account of the situation may not be too inaccurate in practice, but that is only because many people are mentally very lazy. To quote Imre Lakatos (1976, p. 93 n.): 'Science teaches us not to respect any given conceptual–linguistic framework lest it should turn into a conceptual prison – language analysts have a vested interest in at least slowing down this process [of conceptual change].'

There is a further problem that arises when Whorf's hypothesis is taken in its most radical interpretation: it may actually be self-contradictory. The most fundamental component of any semantic structure, deeper even than the 'grand generalizations' of physics, is its logical apparatus – in English, the use of words such as *not, if, all* and so forth. One might take the Whorf hypothesis to mean that even logic is relative to language, so that, say, if Aristotle had been a Hopi then modern logic as well as modern physics would have developed quite differently. There are hints in Whorf's writings (e.g. 1941b,

p. 241) that he meant to go as far as this, and other linguists have put the point plainly: see for example Sommerfelt (1938, p. 9), Benveniste (1958), Hjelmslev (1963, p. 121). If these writers mean only that formal characteristics of language have influenced the explicit systems of logic which philosophers have devised in their fallible attempts to *describe* publicly the patterns of our (largely unconscious) thought-processes, they are no doubt right. If, though, they mean that those thought-processes in their logical aspects are themselves a function of our language, then their notion must be rejected on *a priori* grounds.

To see this, let us turn to a predecessor of Sapir and Whorf who argued for the view that I regard as untenable perhaps more fully than anyone else has done, namely the French anthropologist Lucien Lévy-Bruhl (1857–1939). Lévy-Bruhl's view of the relation between language and thought was in general similar to Whorf's (Lévy-Bruhl 1910, ch. 4), except that he did not share Whorf's relativism: rather than thinking of Standard Average European as one among a diverse range of alternative conceptual frameworks, Lévy-Bruhl believed that the thought-patterns of all primitive peoples were similar as contrasted with the thought-patterns of civilized men. Lévy-Bruhl did not suggest that the distinction between savages and civilized men was a sharp one, but for him different men's minds occupied different points on a single scale. The most important aspect of the distinction in mental type was a matter of logic: according to Lévy-Bruhl, the primitive mind does not acknowledge the law of non-contradiction.[3] That is, whereas a civilized man regards any statement of the form 'P and not P' as self-evidently false, a primitive man will regard many such statements as true and will see no difficulty therein. (It is true that all of us make statements such as 'I want to go and I don't want to go', but these are intended to be understood in ways which make them non-contradictory, e.g. as 'There are reasons why I should like to go and other reasons why I should not'. We succeed in interpreting such statements correctly just because we do recognize the law of non-contradiction and therefore know that they cannot mean what they appear to mean. Lévy-Bruhl argues that primitive men, on the other hand, believe contradictions in which each half is understood literally and unequivocally.)

To quote one of many pieces of evidence which Lévy-Bruhl

cites in favour of this claim, the Bororó of northern Brazil are said by Karl von den Steinen to believe that they are red parakeets (although, one must presumably add to get the 'not P' side of the contradiction, they can obviously see that they are not red parakeets):

This does not merely mean that after their death they become parakeets, nor that parakeets are metamorphosed Bororó, and must be treated as such. It is something quite different. 'The Bororó', says von den Steinen, who was reluctant to believe it, but finally had to give in to their explicit affirmations, 'give one rigidly to understand that they *are at the present time* parakeets . . . . ' [Lévy-Bruhl 1910, p. 77, quoting – somewhat loosely, it should be said – von den Steinen 1894, p. 352]

I find Lévy-Bruhl's explanation for findings such as von den Steinen's a quite unsatisfactory one, for one thing because it could so easily be turned round against the 'civilized' mentality. One can well imagine a Bororó who had visited Europe announcing to a meeting of the Bororó Anthropological Association, with a superior smile, that the wise men of that region claim with every appearance of sincerity that coal and diamonds are the same substance: 'this does not merely mean that they have a method of making diamonds out of coal, or anything of that sort; the white men give one rigidly to understand that a lump of coal consists of the same stuff as a diamond *at the present time*, but I found their attempts to explain the nature of this identity quite impossible to follow (sniggers in the auditorium); clearly the whites do not recognize the law of non-contradiction.' What distinguishes the Bororó, as described by von den Steinen, from the European is surely not a matter of logic but of beliefs about fairly abstract matters of fact: each community holds certain sophisticated theories which are only very indirectly connected with observable reality, and these theories cannot be merely *translated* but must be *taught* at length to members of the other community, just as they must be taught to young members of the community which has evolved them. We have no more right to call the Bororó mentality 'pre-logical' because of their theory about parakeets than they have to call us pre-logical because of Western chemistry or the doctrine of the Trinity. (It *may* be that our doctrines are truer than theirs, but a false belief is not necessarily an illogical belief.) Granted that no man is what Bertrand Russell calls a 'logical saint' – none of us works out all the innumerable implications of his beliefs and weeds out all the sources of contradiction which his beliefs contain – still Lévy-Bruhl gives us no reason to think that savages are greater logical sinners than we.

It is difficult to know exactly what Lévy-Bruhl means by calling savages pre-logical – he hedges his bets to some extent, and in later writings he abandons the notion of a 'pre-logical mentality' entirely in response to criticisms similar to mine. But suppose I am right in interpreting him as saying that savages will typically believe certain statements which translate into English as 'P and not P' (for some statement P). I have shown that the kind of evidence Lévy-Bruhl gives does not *require* us to accept this: let me show that no conceivable evidence could even *allow* us to accept it.

Let us say that the savage shows signs of assenting to a sentence which in his own language runs *P ka bu P*, and an anthropologist claims that *P* translates into some simple English statement, that *ka* means 'and', and that *bu* means 'not'. How does the anthropologist know how to do the translation? For some words the translation can be worked out by observation of the external world: if the savage points to a parakeet and says *Arara!* it is likely (though far from certain) that *arara* means 'parakeet'. In the case of more abstract words, the evidence of observation is less helpful: if the savage uses the word *vekti* to explain why he hands over some of his goods to a man who comes to the door, we may at first suppose that *vekti* means 'tax', but when that assumption forces us to translate a subsequently heard remark as 'Nobody is required to pay tax' or as 'It gives one a good feeling to pay tax' we are likely to change our mind and translate *vekti* as 'charity'. In other words, an important part of what makes a system of translation 'correct' is that it translates sentences which speakers of the source-language regard as true into truths of the target-language, that it translates falsehoods into falsehoods, nonsense into nonsense, tautologies into tautologies, and so on. We cannot expect perfect matching: it might be that the French hold the sentence *La Concorde, c'est l'avion de l'avenir* to state a truth while the English regard 'Concorde is the aeroplane of the future' as false, and this is clearly not enough to show that the two sentences mean different things. But, if the *majority* of translations which are generated by the system we learn at school for turning French into English turned out to have truth-values which contrasted with those of the original sentences, then we would have to conclude that the traditional system of translation embodied a serious misunderstanding of the French language. (Clearly this is not in fact so: cases of the 'Concorde' type are a small, though interesting, minority among all accepted translations between the two languages.)

Now logical words like 'not' and 'and' are words whose meanings are ascertained exclusively from 'internal' evidence of this sort, rather than by observation of the external world (one can show someone a parakeet, but one can hardly show them 'and'). Furthermore, unlike the case of 'charity', for 'not' and 'and' the relevant internal evidence is very simple and straightforward. To say that a word means 'not' is to say that the word changes a truth into a falsehood and *vice versa*; to say that a word means 'and' is to say that the complex sentence formed by inserting it between two simpler sentences is true if and only if both the simple sentences are true. (Cases where 'and' links elements which are not sentences, *e.g. John and Mary* . . . , may be ignored here.) From this it follows that to say that some sentence means 'P and not P' is to say that the sentence as a whole cannot be true, irrespective of the meaning of P (since if 'P' is true 'not-P' must be false, and therefore the sentence as a whole must be false; and if 'P' is *not* true then the sentence as a whole is not true).

In other words, evidence that the savage believes *P ka bu P* to be true *is itself the best possible evidence* that that sentence does *not* mean 'P and not P'.

It is senseless to claim that a savage (or anyone else) believes an explicit contradiction, because to believe any proposition entails understanding it, and to understand a contradiction *is* to recognize that it is necessarily false. Probably all of us hold beliefs which lead to contradictions at the end of chains of inference which we have not worked out, but that is a different matter. It is conceivable that one might encounter a community speaking a language which was wholly untranslatable, in the sense that *no* systematic scheme for translating its sentences into sentences of a European language generated more matches between truths and truths, falsehoods and falsehoods, tautologies and tautologies, etc., than would occur if translations were chosen at random. (It is interesting that no such language has ever been reported, since there is no obvious reason in logic why such a language might not exist.) What is excluded *a priori* is a language for which there is a 'correct' system of translation, but whose speakers disagree with us not just on specific matters of fact but on basic principles of logic.

I do not suppose that von den Steinen or Lévy-Bruhl erred by mistakenly translating some Bororó word as 'not' or 'and'. Much more probably, they correctly translated a standard Bororó assertion as, say, 'We are red parakeets', and mistakenly supposed that observation of their own bodies would force the Bororó (as it forces us) also to believe 'We are not red parakeets' – but Bororó theories are such that this does not follow, just as our theories are such that the sight of a diamond does not force us to the conclusion 'This is not the same substance as coal'. But whatever Lévy-Bruhl meant by calling the primitive mind 'pre-logical', the general point is made. The deeper and more abstract are the aspects of a 'world-view' which are claimed to be a function of language, the more compelling becomes the argument that alleged differences in world-view result from misinterpretation of language. Concepts of space and time are already distant enough from immediate observation to make Whorf's claim very difficult to substantiate; in the case of logical concepts, the argument for mistranslation is certain to succeed. Whorf is on much firmer ground with cases such as the Eskimo's several words for types of snow, because words of that sort are linked relatively closely to observable reality, and the possibility of mistranslation is accordingly remote. But this means that the Sapir–Whorf hypothesis is most plausible where it is relatively trivial.

I say that the hypothesis is 'trivial' insofar as it refers to differences in the categorization imposed by various languages on concrete, observable phenomena, because examples of such differences are familiar to many people and this aspect of the hypothesis was until recently quite uncontroversial. In the case of colour, for instance, it is well known that various languages cut the visible spectrum up in different ways: thus Welsh subsumes our 'blue' and 'green' under a single word *glas*, while Russian uses separate words, *sinij* and *goluboj*, for our 'light blue' and 'dark blue', respectively. H. A. Gleason's popular elementary textbook of linguistics gives the following diagram as its very first illustration of the differences between linguistic structures (Gleason 1969, p. 4):

Figure 2

English

purple	blue	green	yellow	orange	red

Shona (a language of Rhodesia)

cips^{w}uka	citema	cicena	cips^{w}uka

Bassa (a language of Liberia)

hui	z̃iza

SOURCE: H.A. Gleason, *Introduction to Descriptive Linguistics* (New York: Holt, Rinehart & Winston, 1969).

(Note that the Shona system has three, not four, terms – our orange, red, and purple are all *cips^{w}uka*; note also that *citema* covers black as well as blue and blue-green, and *cicena* covers white as well as yellow and some greens.)

Colour is in fact a particularly favourable arena for the Whorf hypothesis, possibly the most favourable of all. It is an immediate property of observed sense-data: to find out whether *vekti* meant 'tax' or 'charity' we had not only to observe but also to investigate speakers' beliefs about *vekti*, but a red patch is a red patch irrespective of the beliefs of the man who sees it. And, among perceptual variables, that of colour is one in which we are physically capable of making a very large number of distinctions (there are estimated to be at least 7,500,000 discriminable shades of colour), so the question how these are grouped into classes in any given language is very far from trivial. Furthermore, physics provides us with a neutral, objective standard against which to compare the terminologies of different languages; and, most important, the world of colour appears to have no natural boundaries – it seems a featureless steppe on which colonists must draw their frontiers where they will, rather than a continent which Nature has already parcelled up by means of mountain ranges and wide rivers. So, if Whorf's hypothesis applies anywhere, it should certainly apply to colour; and linguists have long taken it for granted that it does.

Against this background, two anthropologists of the

University of California at Berkeley, Brent Berlin and Paul Kay, caused a considerable stir in 1969 by publishing a book, *Basic Color Terms*, which argues, on the basis of copious evidence, against linguistic relativism in the very field where it seemed so secure. Berlin and Kay belong to the new movement in linguistics which holds that human languages are all cut to a common pattern which is determined by psychological structuring innate in our species (we shall return to this notion in later chapters). While they have no quarrel with Whorf's claim that the nature of a language and the world-view of its speakers are intimately connected, they object to the other half of the Whorfian hypothesis, namely that language structures (and their associated world-views) are highly diverse. Berlin and Kay obviously recognize that there do exist differences between the colour terminologies of various languages, but they argue that the differences are relatively superficial matters which mask certain deep underlying principles common to the colour terminologies of all languages.

Berlin and Kay begin by investigating the colour terminologies of twenty languages from widely scattered areas of the world, using native-speakers' judgements of how to label various portions of a large standard colour chart. For each language, they set out to establish a class of most-basic colour words, excluding terms for finer shades (e.g. for English *red* is included, *vermilion* rejected because it is a subdivision of *red*); they use several formal clues to help in this, thus a colour term is probably non-basic if it is morphologically complex (e.g. *yellowish, sky-blue*) or borrowed from another language (e.g. *maroon* from French *marron*) or if it also refers to a thing of the relevant colour (e.g. *silver* or *chocolate* – though they are forced to admit exceptions, such as *orange* in English). After analysing the results of this stage of the research, they supplement their data by using the patterns that emerge from the analysis to interpret published descriptions of the colour terms of a further seventy-eight languages for which they had no access to native informants.

In analysing their results, Berlin and Kay first make the very astute remark that previous writers erred in concentrating on the *boundaries* of the domains of various colour terms, while what matters are the *focal points* or 'best examples'. (Concentration on boundaries was clearly encouraged by

Saussure's 'structuralist' approach to semantics – cf. Figure 1 (page 40) – but is not really an essential principle of the Saussurean and Boasian semantic relativism which Berlin and Kay aim to refute.) To continue with our metaphor of the colour terms of a language as rival colonies dividing up a continent, we should think of the colonies not as territories with formal frontiers, but as city-states whose control over the surrounding land diminishes gradually with distance, so that there are many border areas of doubtful allegiance. One knows how hard it is to decide whether certain shades are 'green' or 'blue' – many people would call the official colour of Cambridge University light green; there is much less disagreement about what shade is the 'greenest green' or 'bluest blue'.

Berlin and Kay then investigate the distribution of 'focal colours' as identified by the informants on their standard colour chart, which is a two-dimensional array of 320 samples at forty steps along the hue dimension and eight steps on the tone dimension. (Hue is the perceptual variable corresponding to wavelength, i.e. position in the rainbow spectrum; tone is the lightness or darkness of a colour, thus all hues vary along the tone dimension from white through pale, mid, and dark shades of that hue to black. The distinction in English between *pink* and *red* is mainly a distinction of tone. Berlin and Kay supplement the main 40 × 8 chart with a series of nine neutral greys of various tones.)

When the focal points for various colour terms in various languages are all plotted on a single copy of the chart, they turn out to cluster in certain quite limited areas, rather than being scattered randomly over the whole chart (as Whorf might predict). For instance, one particular sample in the yellow area was chosen as the focal point of a colour-term for eight languages, and its neighbouring samples also scored well, although, since the twenty languages investigated at first hand had 127 basic colour terms between them (ignoring words for black, white and grey) and the colour chart included 320 samples, an 'average' sample would have scored only 0.4. Berlin and Kay therefore identify eleven smallish areas of the chart as 'universal colours' (the phrase is mine, not theirs), corresponding to the English words *red, pink, orange, yellow, brown, green, blue, purple, black, white, grey*.

Not every language investigated codes each of the eleven

'universal colours'; languages with words for all eleven tend to be languages of technologically advanced civilizations, while primitive tribes have far fewer colour-names.[4] But Berlin and Kay go on to show that there is considerable patterning in which of the 'universal colours' are coded in simple systems. The minimal system ('Stage I'), naturally enough, has just two terms whose focal examples are black and white (although, in such languages, 'black' and 'white' cover dark and light shades, respectively, of every hue). None of the twenty systems which Berlin and Kay themselves studied was as simple as this, but they cite reports by colleagues and others of several such languages, mostly spoken in New Guinea. If a language has three colour names, the focal point of the third will be red. (Shona, as described by Gleason – cf. Figure 2, page 95 – is an example of this 'Stage II', three-term system. From Gleason's description it is impossible to tell whether or not his other language, Bassa, fits Berlin and Kay's analysis, since Gleason does not explain how Bassa treats black and white.) A four-term system will have black, white, red and either green or yellow; and a five-term system will have the first three together with green *and* yellow. Only a system with at least six terms will have blue; a seven-term system will add brown; and finally purple, pink, orange, and grey may occur in any combination in languages which also have all seven of the earlier universal colours. Languages with, say, a four-term system of black, white, red, and blue simply do not exist.

All in all, Berlin and Kay appear to have dealt a severe blow to the notion of linguistic relativism. If even this area of semantics manifests such constancies between widely-separated cultures, are there likely to be many areas in which people's world-views really are free to differ?

However, a closer examination of Berlin and Kay's work reveals a number of problems which, taken together, leave one in some doubt as to what, if anything, they have demonstrated.

In the first place, Berlin and Kay write as if the second-hand evidence they cite from published reports on seventy-eight languages corroborates the results they worked out from their first-hand data for twenty languages, but that claim can scarcely be taken seriously. As they themselves point out, the published reports hardly ever specify the focal point of a given exotic colour term, but rather list English words describing the total area covered by the term. Thus a four-term system might have a word glossed 'blue, green'; since Berlin and Kay believe that blue occurs as a *focal* colour only in systems of six or more terms, they count the word in question as meaning basically 'green' and claim the language as another instance of their 'Stage III' (black, white, red, green-or-yellow) of colour-term evolution – thus assuming what they set out to prove. A particularly flagrant example occurs in their analysis of the very restricted colour terminology of Homeric Greek, where the word *glaukos*, normally regarded as meaning 'gleaming, silvery' in the Homeric period and 'blue-green, grey' later, is said by Berlin and Kay to mean 'black', apparently for no better reason than that their theory demands a word for black and for some reason they have overlooked the existence of the standard Greek word for black, *melas* (despite the fact that this is actually by far the commonest single colour-word in the Homeric texts).[5] Clearly we must ignore the 'evidence' of the seventy-eight 'second-hand' languages and assess Berlin and Kay's theory exclusively on the data of the twenty languages which they examined in person.

But even their analysis of these languages contains many questionable points, for instance with respect to decisions (often crucial for their theory) as to whether some word is 'basic' in a given language or not. Frequently they seem to be led into error by ignorance. For instance, Berlin and Kay eliminate terms as 'non-basic' when they can be seen to be borrowed from other languages; but, while they are able to detect borrowings into various languages from English and Spanish, they appear not to realize that many terms which they list as basic for Vietnamese are borrowings from Chinese. If the Chinese borrowings were eliminated, Vietnamese would be left with words for black, white, red, brown, purple and grey, which would be a disaster for their theory. (Similarly, in discussing the language of Murray Island, New Guinea, which is one of the seventy-eight 'second-hand' languages, they eliminate many colour expressions on the ground that they are reduplications of nouns for objects having the colour in question – e.g. *bambam* 'orange, yellow', from *bam* 'turmeric'; but when it comes to *golegole*, 'black', which they need as a basic term, they dismiss as 'suspicious' the claim made by their published source that this derives similarly from *gole* 'cuttlefish' – Berlin and Kay perhaps do not know about the black ink secreted by cuttlefish.)

In other instances their decisions seem merely capricious. Thus, one of the traditional 'Five Colours' in Chinese thought, *ch'ing*, is commonly glossed 'green, blue, the colour of Nature'; Berlin and Kay list it as a basic term for the Cantonese dialect of Chinese and for Vietnamese and Korean (both of which borrowed the word from Chinese), in all three cases with the focal example in the same small area of the chart (a deep blue-green), but they count it as meaning 'blue' in Korean, 'green' in Cantonese and Vietnamese, and in Mandarin Chinese they ignore it altogether while including *lan* for 'blue', a word which etymologically referred to the indigo plant and is usually regarded as a subdivision of *ch'ing* (and which they explicitly omit for those reasons in their discussion of Cantonese).

Furthermore, Berlin and Kay seem not to appreciate the extent to which common traits in modern colour terminologies are influenced by the spread of a common technology with its range of pigments and dyestuffs, colour-coded electrical wires, traffic lights and the like. This effect is likely to have been particularly important in their research, since all but one of their twenty languages were studied through informants who lived in or near San Francisco. Noriko McNeill (1972) makes a relevant point here: she explains that the 'standard' eleven-term system which Berlin and Kay describe Japanese as possessing dates only from Japanese contact with the West, beginning in the 1860s, and that the traditional Japanese system of colour names has five terms whose foci are black, white, orange, turquoise, and yellow. This system is very awkward for Berlin and Kay's theory, but it is explained by the fact that the colours other than black and white correspond to natural dyes occurring in Japan.

Considerations of this sort go a long way also to explaining the ordering of the 'universal colours' described by Berlin and Kay. Thus, one puzzling feature of their ordering is the 'recessiveness' of blue: it is claimed to occur only in sixth place, after red, green, and yellow. At first sight this seems a quite surprising, unpredictable fact, if true, and thus a fact which counts heavily against the Whorf hypothesis; after all, blue is a primary colour, and one might suppose it merited a name as much as red, green, and yellow. But how many blue things are there in the environment of a primitive culture? Sky and sea; but everyone knows their colour, so there is no point in discussing it. A few flowers perhaps, but flowers are of little practical importance; and the edible parts of plants, which do need to be discussed frequently, are never blue. Even in our own generation with its sophisticated chemical technology, blue is recognized by the manufacturers of commercial pigments as a difficult colour to create; it is small wonder that many primitive civilizations have got along without a special word for blue.

I have not yet dealt with the most striking of the facts presented by Berlin and Kay, namely that colour foci of diverse languages cluster in very limited areas of the colour chart. However, the explanation of this finding, which was provided by George Collier (1973), constitutes the most damning criticism of all.

The fact is that the variables of hue and tone are not the only variables relevant to colour. There is also the variable of 'saturation', which measures the extent to which a shade of a given hue and tone departs from the grey of the same tone. When we call a colour such as pillar-box red 'bright' or 'vivid' we normally mean not that it is light in tone but that it is highly saturated; 'old rose' would be an example of a low-saturation red. (In fact there is at least one other relevant variable besides hue, tone, and saturation, but we may ignore this.) Now the human eye is physically capable of perceiving greater saturation for some hue/tone combinations than others; a red of medium tone can be very saturated indeed, but even the 'brightest' light blue will not be too different from a light grey. Other things being equal, a language will obviously have names for the most vivid, noticeable colours rather than for colours in which high saturation is impossible. In other words, the continent which colonies divide between them is not a featureless steppe after all, but contains small areas of lush valley land alternating with wide, barren uplands. Quite naturally the first colonies will be founded in the best areas, subject to the constraint that no two colonies will be too close (it would be inefficient to have separate names for very similar shades of colour in a language which has few colour terms in total); only if there are many colonies will the middle slopes be occupied, and the highlands will always remain as tributary areas. Comparison of a chart of attainable saturation at different hue/tone combinations with Berlin and Kay's chart of the distribution of focal colours shows the two to coincide almost perfectly.[6]

Taken in conjunction, these arguments seem to undermine Berlin and Kay's theory fairly completely. I have no doubt that the traditional, common-sense Descriptivist view of semantic variation is correct: where a fairly concrete domain of meaning contains no natural boundaries or specially salient features, nothing in our minds forces us to analyse it in one way rather than another, and languages will differ randomly in the way they categorize such domains. Cases such as the physics of space and time are very different. After all, most people recognize that the question 'How many colours are there?' is meaningless unless asked in the context of some particular principle for individuating colours, while we certainly do not regard the search for correct ideas about space and time as a meaningless activity, even though we may recognize that Mankind has not yet completed this search (and perhaps never will complete it).

So long as Sapir and Whorf claim only that our mother tongue provides an arbitrary but convenient set of pigeonholes for categorizing experience, on which we tend to rely whenever it appears to matter little what particular scheme of categorization we use, they are surely right. No doubt they are right, too, to argue that the decisions which we allow our language to pre-empt in this way sometimes matter more than we realize. But when they suggest that we are the helpless prisoners of the categorization scheme implied by our language, Sapir and Whorf underestimate the ability that individual men possess to break conceptual fetters which other men have forged.

5 Functional linguistics: the Prague School

We have seen that the impetus towards synchronic linguistics, as opposed to traditional philology, originated independently with Saussure in Switzerland and Boas in the USA. A third impulse in the same direction came from Vilém Mathesius (1882–1945), a Czech Anglicist who studied and subsequently taught at the Caroline University of Prague. Saussure's lectures on synchronic linguistics were given in 1911, and that year also saw the publication of Boas's *Handbook*; coincidentally, it was in 1911 too that Mathesius published his first call for a new, non-historical approach to language study (Mathesius 1911).

Around Mathesius there came into being a circle of like-minded linguistic scholars, who began to meet for regular discussion from 1926 onwards, and came to be recognized (until they were scattered by the Second World War) as the 'Prague School'. The Prague School practised a special style of synchronic linguistics, and although most of the scholars whom one thinks of as members of the school worked in Prague or at least in Czechoslovakia, the term is used also to cover certain scholars elsewhere who consciously adhered to the Prague style.

The hallmark of Prague linguistics was that it saw language in terms of function. I mean by this not merely that members of the Prague School thought of language as a whole as serving a purpose, which is a truism that would hardly differentiate them from others, but that they analysed a given language with a view to showing the respective functions played by the various structural components in the use of the entire language. This differentiated the Prague School sharply from their contemporaries, the American Descriptivists (and it differentiates them equally sharply from the Chomskyan school which has succeeded the Descriptivists). For a linguist working in the American tradition, a grammar is a set of elements – 'emes' of various kinds in Bloomfield's framework, 'rules' of various sorts for a Chomskyan; the analyst seems to take much the same attitude to the linguistic structure as one might take to a work of art, in that it does not usually occur to him to point to a particular element and ask 'What's that for?' – he is rather content to describe and to contemplate. Prague linguists, on the other hand, looked at languages as one might look at a motor, seeking to understand what jobs the various components were doing and how the nature of one component determined the nature of others. As long as they were describing the structure of a language, the practice of the Prague School was not very different from that of their contemporaries – they used the notions 'phoneme' and 'morpheme', for instance; but they tried to go beyond description to explanation, saying not just *what* languages were like but *why* they were the way they were. American linguists restricted themselves (and still restrict themselves) to description.

One fairly straightforward example of functional explanation in Mathesius's own work concerns his use of terms commonly translated *theme* and *rheme*, and the notion which has come to be called 'Functional Sentence Perspective' by recent writers working in the Prague tradition. Most (or, at least, many) sentences are uttered in order to give the hearer some information; but obviously we do not produce unrelated pieces of information chosen at random, rather we carefully tailor our statements with a view not only to what we want the hearer to learn but also to what he already knows and to the context of discourse which we have so far built up. According to Mathesius, the need for continuity means that a sentence will commonly fall into two parts (which may be very unequal in length): the *theme*, which refers to something about which the hearer already knows (often because it has been discussed in immediately preceding sentences), and the *rheme*, which states some new fact about that given topic. Unless certain special effects are aimed at, theme will precede rheme, so that the peg may be established in the hearer's mind before anything new has to be hung on it.

Very often, the theme/rheme division will correspond to the syntactic distinction between subject and predicate, or between subject-plus-transitive-verb and object: we may say *John kissed Eve* because we have been talking about John and want to say what he did next, or because the hearer knows that John kissed someone and we want to tell him who it was. However, it might be that the hearer knows that Eve was kissed and we want to say who kissed her: in other words, we want to make *John* the rheme and *kissed Eve* the theme. But theme normally precedes rheme. In an inflecting language, such as Czech, this is no problem: we simply put the grammatical subject at the end of the sentence and say *Evu políbil Jan* – the accusative *-u* and absence of feminine ending on the verb shows that Eve was kissed rather than kisser. However, English uses word-order to mark grammatical relations such as subject and object, and so is not free to permute the words of *John kissed Eve* so simply. Instead, we solve the problem by using the passive construction, *Eve was kissed by John*, which reconciles the grammatical demand that the subject stand first with the functional demand that the kisser, as rheme, be postponed to the end, by means of a special form of the verb which signals the fact that the grammatical subject is not the 'doer' of the action. In Czech the passive construction is rare, and particularly so when the actor is mentioned in the equivalent of a *by*-phrase. Even in English the passive has a second function: it enables us to reconcile the occasional wish not to be explicit about the identity of the actor with the grammatical requirement that each finite verb have a subject, so that we can say *Eve was kissed* if we are unable or unwilling to say who kissed her. (The passive construction, in sentences such as *Adoption of the proposal is felt to be inadvisable*, is beloved by bureaucrats aiming to disclaim responsibility for their decisions.) But English is unusual in the frequency with which 'full' passives with *by*-phrases occur; the notion of Functional Sentence Perspective shows us a job which such constructions do in English and which is carried out by other means in other languages. (That is not to say that the job is always and only done by means of the passive in English, e.g. it is possible to mark *John* as rheme rather than theme in *John kissed Eve* by stressing it; but that is normally reserved for contradicting an expectation that someone else did the kissing.)

It would be inaccurate to suggest that the notion of Functional Sentence Perspective was wholly unknown in American linguistics; some of the Descriptivists did use the terms 'topic' and 'comment' in much the same way as Mathesius's 'theme' and 'rheme'. But, apart from the fact that the Prague scholars developed these ideas rather further than any Americans ever did, I believe it is fair to say that the Americans never dreamed of using the ideas to explain structural differences between languages, such as the frequency of the passive construction in English as opposed to many other languages. In the case of the Descriptivists this was understandable, since these explanations make unavoidable use of concepts (such as 'the wish not to identify the actor explicitly') which do not correspond to observables and are therefore illegitimate by behaviourist standards. Descriptivists, indeed, tended to be suspicious of questions beginning with the word 'why', regarding them as a relic of childhood which mature scientists should have learned to put behind them (cf. Joos 1957, p. 96). The modern Chomskyan school, however, lays great stress on the need for linguists' statements to 'explain' rather than merely 'describe', and it has no objection to the postulation of unobservables; yet a Chomskyan grammar will simply list the syntactic 'transformations', such as Passive, which a given language contains, and will give no hint as to why the language needs them, or why one language possesses some particular construction which another language lacks or uses very rarely.

A related point is that many Prague linguists were actively interested in questions of standardizing linguistic usage: see e.g. Havránek (1936). Such an interest was perhaps natural for Czechs, whose language is marked by unusually extreme divergence between literary and colloquial usage, and had in the inter-war period only just become the official language of an independent State; but it was certainly encouraged also by the functional approach of the Prague School. The American Descriptivists not only, quite rightly, drew a logical distinction between linguistic description and linguistic prescription, but furthermore left their followers in little doubt that prescription was an improper, unprofessional activity in which no respectable linguist would indulge: cf. the title of R. A. Hall's *Leave Your Language Alone!* (1950). This latter attitude is wholly irrational; a high culture needs conventional norms of linguistic usage (though such norms are surely better evolved through informed debate than imposed from above by an Academy), and presumably training in linguistics ought to be a help rather than a hindrance in formulating appropriate standards. But certainly one cannot talk sensibly about which usages are worthy of acceptance and which are not, unless one sees language as a tool or set of tools for carrying out a range of tasks more or less efficiently.

The theory of theme and rheme by no means exhausts Mathesius's contributions to the functional view of grammar; given more space, I might have included a discussion of his notion of 'functional onomatology', which treats the coining of novel vocabulary items as a task which different languages solve in characteristically different ways (see, for example, Mathesius 1961). Let us turn instead, though, to a consideration of the functional approach to phonology, as exemplified in the work of Trubetzkoy.

Prince Nikolai Sergeyevich Trubetzkoy (1890–1938) was one of the members of the 'Prague School' not based in Czechoslovakia. He belonged to a scholarly family of the Russian nobility; his father had been a professor of philosophy and Rector of Moscow University. Trubetzkoy began at an early age to study Finno-Ugric and Caucasian folklore and philology; he was a student of Indo-European linguistics at his father's university, and became a member of staff there in 1916. Then came the revolution, and Prince Trubetzkoy had to flee: first to Rostov on the Don, where (after the servants had taken him for a tramp and had tried to thrown him out of the Rector's house) he was given a chair at the local university; and, when the Whites lost Rostov in 1919, to Constantinople. In 1922 he was appointed to the chair of Slavonic philology at Vienna, and he became a member of the Prague Linguistic Circle when it came into being under Mathesius's aegis a few years later. (Prague is only some 150 miles from Vienna, and separated from it by a political boundary which was then very new.) Trubetzkoy remained in Vienna until he died a few months after the 1938 *Anschluss*, from a heart condition brought to a crisis by Gestapo interrogation (he had been a public opponent of Nazism). We know Trubetzkoy's ideas today chiefly through the book, *Principles of Phonology*, which he struggled to finish (and all but succeeded in finishing) in his last weeks of life.

Trubetzkoyan phonology, like that of the American Descriptivists, gives a central role to the phoneme; but Trubetzkoy, and the Prague School in general (as I have suggested is characteristic of the European style of linguistics), were interested primarily in the paradigmatic relations between phonemes, i.e. the nature of the oppositions between the phonemes that potentially contrast with one another at a given point in a phonological structure, rather than in the syntagmatic relations which determine how phonemes may be organized into sequences in a language. Trubetzkoy developed a vocabulary for classifying various types of phonemic contrast: e.g. he distinguished between (i) *privative* oppositions, in which two phonemes are identical except that one contains a phonetic 'mark' which the other lacks (e.g. / f / ~ / v /, the 'mark' in this case being voice), (ii) *gradual* oppositions in which the members differ in possessing different degrees of some gradient property (e.g. / ɪ / ~ / e / ~ / æ /, with respect to the property of vowel aperture), and (iii) *equipollent* oppositions, in which each member has a distinguishing mark lacking in the others (e.g. / p / ~ / t / ~ / k /). In some cases a given phonemic opposition will be in force only in some environments and will be suspended or 'neutralized' in others, for instance the German / t / ~ / d / opposition is neutralized in word-final position (only / t / occurs word-finally, and roots which end in / d / before a suffix replace the / d / by / t / when the suffix drops, e.g. / 'baːdən / *baden* 'to bathe' v. / baːt / *Bad* 'bath'); in such cases we can speak of the occurrence of the *archiphoneme*, that is the highest common factor of the phonemes whose opposition is neutralized. Trubetzkoy's 'archiphoneme' idea is useful in dissolving pseudoproblems. For instance, in English also the / t / ~ / d / opposition is neutralized, after / s / (there is no contrast between e.g. *still* and **sdill*); but, unlike in the German case, the sound which occurs in the environment of neutralization is identical to neither member of the opposition (the sound written *t* in *still* is unaspirated like / d /, though it is voiceless like / t /). A Descriptivist would have to assign the sound arbitrarily either to the / t / phoneme or to the / d / phoneme; the archiphoneme concept allows us to avoid this arbitrary choice.[1] Trubetzkoy, in the *Principles*, establishes a rather sophisticated system of phonological typology – that is, a system which enables us to say what *kind* of phonology a language has, rather than simply treating its phonological structure in the take-it-or-leave-it American fashion as a set of isolated facts. (Typology was another distinctive preoccupation of the Prague School; Mathesius (1928; 1961) worked on what has been rather inelegantly translated as 'linguistic characterology', which aimed to enable one to discuss what kind of grammar a language has. Americans, on the other hand – with occasional exceptions such as Sapir or Hockett (1955) – tended to treat the synchronic structures of various languages as globally different examples of a single genus of thing; this was perhaps part of their inheritance from the German neogrammarians, who had suggested that the only interesting way of classifying languages was in terms of their historical relationships.)

What is particularly relevant to our present discussion is that Trubetzkoy distinguished various functions that can be served by a phonological opposition. The obvious function – that of keeping different words or longer sequences apart – he called the *distinctive function*, but this is by no means the only function that a phonological opposition may serve. Consider the opposition between presence and absence of stress, for instance: there are perhaps rather few languages in which this is regularly distinctive. In Czech (in which every word is stressed on the first syllable) or Polish (in which words normally bear penultimate stress), stress has no distinctive role but it has a *delimitative function*: it helps the hearer locate word-boundaries in the speech signal, which is something he needs to do if he is to make sense of what he hears. In languages with more variable stress position, such as English or Russian, stress has less delimitative function and scarcely any distinctive function (pairs such as *súbject* (n.) ~ *subjéct* (v.), which are almost identical phonetically except for position of stress, are rare in English); but it has a *culminative function*: there is, very roughly speaking and ignoring a few 'clitics' such as *a* and *the*, one and only one main stress per word in English, so that perception of stress tells the hearer how many words he must segment the signal into, although it does not tell him where to make the cuts. Nor is it only suprasegmental[2] features such as stress which fulfil these subsidiary functions. Thus Trubetzkoy points out that, in German, while the opposition between / j / and other consonant phonemes has a distinctive function (*verjagen* 'expel' contrasts with *versagen* 'deny', for instance), / j / also has a delimitative function in that this consonant occurs only morpheme-initially (*verjagen* is morphemically *ver+jag+en*). Conversely, English / ŋ / has a 'negative delimitative function': when we hear that sound we know that there cannot be a morpheme boundary immediately before it, because / ŋ / never begins an

English morpheme. In English, consonant clusters such as / ts /, / ps / signal an intervening morpheme boundary (in all but a few very exceptional cases such as *tsetse, lapse*); Finnish on the other hand has no initial or final consonant clusters, and permits only / n t s / as final consonants, so that the clusters in *yksi* 'one' or *silta* 'bridge' signal absence of morpheme boundary.

In the American tradition there is no room for such statements. The Descriptivists thought of all phonological contrasts as 'distinctive' contrasts in Trubetzkoy's sense. In the case of the fixed stress of Czech, for instance, a Descriptivist would have said either that it never keeps different words apart and is therefore to be ignored as non-phonemic, or else (if pairs of word-sequences can be found which differ only in position of word-boundaries and hence of stresses, e.g. *Má melouch* ['ma:'meloux] 'He has a job on the side' v. *Máme louh* ['ma:me'loux] 'We have lye') that there is a phonemic contrast between stress and its absence which is fully on a par, logically, with the opposition between / p / and / b / or / m / and / n /. Trubetzkoy's approach seems considerably more insightful than either of these alternatives.

Each of the three phonological functions discussed so far has to do, ultimately, with enabling the hearer to work out what sequence of words has been uttered by the speaker. But Trubetzkoy, like other members of the Prague School, was well aware that the functions of speech are not limited to the expression of an explicit message. In analysing the functions of speech Trubetzkoy followed his Viennese philosopher colleague Karl Bühler, who distinguished (Bühler 1934) between the *representation function* (i.e. that of stating facts), the *expressive function* (that of expressing temporary or permanent characteristics of the speaker), and the *conative function* (that of influencing the hearer). I find Bühler's three-way distinction rather too neat and aprioristic to merit the somewhat exaggerated respect which many have paid it, but it does serve to make the point that there is more to language than the 'representation function'. Trubetzkoy shows that Bühler's analysis can be applied in phonology. A phonetic opposition which fulfils the representation function will normally be a phonemic contrast; but distinctions between the allophones of a given phoneme, where the choice is not determined by the phonemic environment, will often play an expressive or conative role. For instance, in London the diphthong / au / has a range of allophones differing in the degree of initial openness – one encounters pronunciations ranging from [ɑʊ] through [æʊ] to [ɛʊ] (together with differences in the off-glide which I ignore here); and this allophonic gradient correlates with or 'expresses' a variable of social status: roughly speaking, the less open the beginning of the diphthong, the lower the speaker's prestige. (In the diphthong / ai / , on the other hand, the correlation is reversed: the 'rough' speaker who has [ɛʊ] in the first case will have something like [ɒɪ] for the latter, while a 'well-spoken' individual will have something like [ɑʊ] and [aɪ] respectively.) In a Mongolian dialect (Trubetzkoy, 1939, p. 17) frontness of vowels 'expresses' sex: back vowels in men's speech correspond to central vowels in women's speech, and male central vowels correspond to front female vowels. As an example of the conative function in phonology, we might take the use of duration in American English vowels. Vowel duration is a respect in which RP and standard American English differ markedly in their phonological structure. In RP, vowel duration is phonologically determined: the 'checked' or 'lax' vowels, such as / ɪ / , are short, and other vowels are long or short depending on their phonemic environment. In American English, on the other hand, vowel duration has no 'distinctive' function and is always free to vary, and length is used to engage the emotions of the hearer: thus an American making an appeal on behalf of a charity might wind up his peroration with a phrase like 'I want you to put your hands in your pockets and gɪ::v', with an ultra-long vowel in *give* where an Englishman would be bound to use a short vowel.[3] Again, statements of these kinds tell us considerably more about how a language works than do phonological analyses in the American style. For a Descriptivist, alternation between allophones of a phoneme is either phonologically determined (as is the case with plain versus velarized / l / in RP) or else is said to be in 'free variation'. But this latter phrase merely dodges the issue: cases of truly random allophonic variation which correlates with *no* other factors either internal to or outside the language are vanishingly few and far between.

Another manifestation of the Prague attitude that language is a tool which has a job (or, rather, a wide variety of jobs) to do is the fact that members of that School were much preoccupied with the aesthetic, literary aspects of language use (Garvin

1964 provides an anthology of some of this work). Many American linguists, both Descriptivists and, even more so, those of the modern Chomskyan school, have by contrast maintained an almost puritanical concentration on the formal, logical aspects of language to the exclusion of more humane considerations. This aspect of Prague School thought lies somewhat outside the purview of the present book. Suffice it to say that the Prague group constituted one of the few genuine points of contact between linguistics, and 'structuralism' in the Continental (nowadays mainly French) sense – a discipline whose contemporary practitioners often appeal to the precedent of linguistics in their approaches to literary criticism without, in many cases, really seeming to understand the linguistic concepts which they cite.

If American linguists ignored (and still ignore) the aesthetic aspects of language, this is clearly because of their anxiety that linguistics should be a science. Bloomfieldians and Chomskyans disagree radically about the nature of science, but they are united in wanting to place linguistics firmly on the science side of the arts/science divide. The Prague School did not share this prejudice; they were not interested in questions of methodology, and it seems likely that, say, Mathesius in discussing the 'characterology' of English would, if asked, have thought of his work as more akin to that of a historian than to that of a physicist.

There have, however, been certain developments whose roots lie in Prague School thought but which have come to be fairly clearly scientific in their nature; it happens that in each case the conversion into a fully fledged empirical theory took place away from Prague.

The first of these is what may be called the therapeutic theory of sound-change. Mathesius, and following him various other members of the Prague School, had the notion that sound changes were to be explained as the result of a striving towards a sort of ideal balance or resolution of various conflicting pressures; for instance, the need for a language to have a large variety of phonetic shapes available to keep its words distinct conflicts with the need for speech to be comprehensible despite inevitably inexact pronunciation, and at a more specific level the tendency in English, say, to pronounce the phoneme / e / as a relatively close vowel in order to distinguish it clearly from / æ /

conflicts with the tendency to make it relatively open in order to distinguish it clearly from / ɪ /. At any given period the phonology of a language will be in only imperfect equilibrium, and changes are to be expected at the points of asymmetry. For instance, before the seventeenth century the phoneme / ʒ / did not occur in English, but the sound involved no un-English phonetic features: most of our obstruents were found in voiced/voiceless pairs and only / ʃ / was unpaired, so / ʒ / was a 'vacant slot' waiting to be filled by a phoneme at no extra cost to the language – and sure enough / ʒ / has now entered English, both through coalescence of / zj / sequences (as in *leisure*) and by remaining unchanged in words borrowed from foreign languages (e.g. *rouge*). While / ʒ / was a 'vacant slot', / h / on the other hand might be called a 'sore thumb' – it is an isolated sound not fitting into the overall pattern of English phonemes; and many English dialects (although not RP) have abandoned the / h / phoneme (Cockney is by no means the only regional variety of English in which it is usual to 'drop one's aitches'). Since languages are immensely complex structures and since new factors are constantly coming into play as human life evolves, this therapeutic process will never reach a conclusion: a change which cures one imbalance will in turn create tensions elsewhere in the system (as a move at chess removes one danger only to bring about another), so that linguistic change will continue indefinitely.

It is worth noting that this view of sound-change is somewhat at odds with Saussure's approach to linguistics. Saussure, remember, contrasted synchronic linguistics, as the study of a system in which the various elements derive their values from their mutual relationships, with historical linguistics as the description of a sequence of isolated, unsystematic events.[4] As a description of the kind of historical linguistics current in Saussure's day, this latter characterization is fair; but the Prague School is in effect arguing that the atomicity which Saussure attributes to 'diachronic' linguistics is not an intrinsic property of historical as opposed to synchronic linguistics but only of a particular school of linguists, who happened to be interested in historical rather than synchronic linguistics for reasons independent of their atomistic approach. The Prague School argues for system in diachrony too, and indeed it claims that linguistic change is determined by, as well as determining, synchronic *état de langue*. To pursue the chess metaphor, for the Prague School no player is blind, although one might say, perhaps, that the players do not foresee all the indirect consequences of their moves (any more than real chess-players do). We shall see, later in this chapter, that recent work in the Prague tradition has tended to undermine the synchronic/diachronic distinction in other ways too.

The scholar who has done most to turn the therapeutic view of sound-change into an explicit, sophisticated theory is the Frenchman, André Martinet (b. 1908). Martinet himself never lived in Prague; he was appointed to the École Pratique des Hautes Études in Paris in 1938 but spent the war years interned as an army officer, becoming head of the linguistics department at Columbia University (New York) in 1947 and returning in 1955 to the École des Hautes Études. However, Martinet (who is unusual, and admirable, in his appreciation of diverse trends in linguistic thought) was heavily influenced by Prague thinking from an early stage in his career, and nowadays it seems fair to describe him as the chief contemporary proponent of mainstream Prague ideas. The book in which Martinet set out his theories of diachronic phonology most fully is significantly entitled *Économie des Changements Phonétiques* (1955). The therapeutic view of sound-change is indeed reminiscent of the economists' doctrine of the invisible hand, according to which the various countervailing forces in an economy tend (in the absence of governmental interference) towards an ideal equilibrium.[5]

One of the key concepts in Martinet's account of sound-change (borrowed by him from Mathesius) is that of the *functional yield* of a phonological opposition. The functional yield of an opposition is, to put it simply, the amount of work it does in distinguishing utterances which are otherwise alike. Thus the opposition between the English phonemes / θ / and / ð / is of unusually low functional yield, since there are very few minimal pairs of the kind *wreath* ~ *wreathe* (and furthermore this particular pair could normally be distinguished in context by the syntax even if they were pronounced alike); the yield of / f / ~ / v / is higher, because there are quite a number of minimal pairs, such as *foal* ~ *vole*, in which genuine confusion is possible. Because we can imitate one another's pronunciation only inexactly and because we have no linguistic analogue of the pianist's tuning-fork by reference to which a community can preserve the identity of a sound over time, Martinet argues, the pronunciations of similar phonemes will overlap and will tend to merge. This tendency towards merger will be opposed by the need to preserve distinctions in order to communicate, but the strength of that countervailing force will depend on the functional yield of the opposition in question. Therefore phonological developments should be predictable from statistics of functional yield.

This notion is of course rather more complex than it looks. Martinet is well aware that he leaves many questions open: for instance how much weight, in estimating the yield of the / f / ~ / v / opposition, should be given to the fact that *foal* and *vole* are not merely both nouns but both names of animals and are therefore that much more likely to occur in similar contexts? It is unclear even what category of phonological oppositions are relevant; there is no observable tendency for / θ / and / ð / to merge in English, but we could explain this by saying that what distinguishes e.g. *wreathe* from *wreath* is presence v. absence of voice (in the final segment), and the yield of the voiced/voiceless distinction in the language as a whole is enormous even though, in the special case of interdental fricatives, it happens to be low. Martinet certainly does offer a number of persuasive examples for which his principle seems to account neatly. Thus, in a conservative style of French, we find a distinction of duration between, for example, [mɛtr] *mètre* and [mɛ:tr] *maître*; but there are few minimal pairs, and duration is not distinctive in other vowels (except that some speakers distinguish a long and a short *a*, but again this opposition has a low yield): as predicted, younger speakers pronounce words such as *mètre* and *maître* alike. Again, among French nasal vowels the opposition between / œ̃ / and / ɛ̃ / (e.g. *brun* 'brown' ~ *brin* 'sprig') has a far lower yield than that between / ɔ̃ / and / ɑ̃ / (*long* ~ *lent*, *don* ~ *dent*, etc.); and an innovating style of speech has abandoned the former distinction by replacing / œ̃ / with / ɛ̃ /.

Unfortunately, despite the attraction and plausibility of this hypothesis about sound-change, further examination does not seem to have borne it out. Even the examples cited from Martinet himself seem somewhat inconsistent; English / θ / and / ð / remain distinct because what matter are oppositions between phonetic features rather than between phonemes, but on the other hand (since the rounding which distinguishes / œ̃ /

from / ɛ̃ / is also what distinguishes / ɔ̃ / from / ɑ̃ /, which show no sign of merging) the nasal-vowel example seems to work only if we think in terms of phonemes rather than of phonetic features. King (1967) and Wang (1967a; 1969, p. 10 n. 3) have tested the hypothesis by evolving explicit, numerical measures of functional yield and comparing the known histories of certain languages with the predictions which follow from these statistics; their results have been rather clearly negative.

It is of course possible to defend the functional-yield hypothesis by arguing that King and Wang have formalized the notion in an inappropriate way. We have seen that there are various conceivable ways in which functional yield could be measured (and any measure that could be applied in practice would presumably be only a crude approximation, at best, to the variable which is in fact relevant); it might be that a more sophisticated measure would give better results in the cases King and Wang discuss (cf. Weinreich *et al*. 1968, p. 134; Kučera 1974). But the onus is on proponents of the hypothesis to show this, and in any case there are phenomena in the history of the world's languages which seem so radically incompatible with Martinet's hypothesis that no reformulation could conceivably avail against them. The history of Mandarin Chinese, for instance, has been one of repeated massive losses of phonological distinctions: final stops dropped, the voice contrast in initial consonants was lost, final *m* merged with *n*, the vowel system was greatly simplified, etc. In Chinese, morphemes and syllables are co-terminous, but modern Mandarin has so few phonologically distinct syllables that on average each syllable is ambiguous as between three or four etymologically distinct morphemes in current use (and most morphemes, as is to be expected in the language of an ancient culture, display a more or less wide range of meanings). A case such as English / faul / (*fowl* or *foul*, and the latter morpheme ambiguous between moral and sporting senses) would be unusual in Mandarin not because it permits alternative interpretations but because the number of alternatives is so small. The language has of course compensated for this loss of phonological distinctions – if it had not, contemporary Mandarin would be so ambiguous as to be wholly unusable. What has happened is that monomorphemic words have to a very large extent been replaced by compounds – in many cases compounds of a type, very unusual in European languages, consisting of two synonyms or near-synonyms. (Cf. English *funny-peculiar* v. *funny-ha-ha*; although the analogy is a poor one, first because the ambiguity of *funny* is a case of polysemy rather than of homonymy – i.e. the two senses of *funny* are alternative developments of what was once one unambiguous word, rather than two words having fallen together in pronunciation – and secondly because in the English expressions only the first half is ambiguous, whereas in a Chinese synonym-compound the two halves disambiguate one another.) But, unless we interpret Martinet as saying merely that a language will *somehow* maintain its usability as a means of communication, then Mandarin must surely refute him; the distinctions it has lost were of great functional yield (while on the other hand the sound [ɽ], from Middle Chinese [ɲ], has remained distinct despite being a 'sore thumb' in terms of the overall phonological pattern and despite the very low functional yield of the oppositions between this sound and the similar sounds [l], [n]). In other words (to stretch the chess metaphor to breaking point) the player making moves on the Chinese board seems to be not merely blind but incapable of distinguishing by touch between pawns and queen. Mandarin strikingly vindicates Saussure's view of the difference between diachronic and synchronic linguistics.[6]

Perhaps this obituary for Martinet's theory of sound-change is premature; one can think of ways in which some sort of rearguard action might be mounted in its defence. (For instance, although I think it is improbable, one might conceivably be able to demonstrate that replacement of monomorphemic words by compounds in Chinese took place before rather than as a consequence of the major losses of phonological contrasts, and that would rob Chinese of much of its force as evidence against Martinet's theory.) But even if the therapeutic theory of sound-change has indeed to be given up, one can say in its favour that Martinet put it forward very explicitly as an empirical, testable hypothesis (Martinet 1955, p. 34). Sir Karl Popper has taught us that the first duty of a scientist is to ensure that his claims are potentially falsifiable, because statements about observable reality which could be overturned by no conceivable evidence are empty statements. Martinet's defeat is therefore an honourable one.

The situation is rather different in the case of another theory

evolved out of Prague School doctrines, namely Jakobson's
theory of phonological universals.

Roman Osipovich Jakobson (b. 1896) is a scholar of Russian
origin; he took his first degree, in Oriental languages, at
Moscow University. From the early 1920s onwards he studied
and taught in Prague, and moved to a chair at the university of
Brno (capital of the Moravian province of Czechoslovakia) in
1933, remaining there until the Nazi occupation forced him to
leave. Jakobson was one of the founding members of the Prague
Linguistic Circle. He spent much of the Second World War at
the École Libre des Hautes Études which was established in
New York City as a home for refugee scholars from Europe. In
1949 Jakobson moved to Harvard, and since 1957 he has been
associated also with the next-door institution of MIT, which was
to become the focus of the modern revolution in linguistics.
Jakobson in fact represents one of the very few personal links
between European and American traditions of linguistics; and,
as will become apparent in the course of the following chapters,
his ideas have had much to do with the radical change of
direction that has occurred in American linguistics over the last
twenty years.

Jakobson's intellectual interests are broad and reflect those of
the Prague School as a whole; he has written a great deal, for
instance, on the structuralist approach to literature. However, in
terms of influence on the discipline of linguistics, by far the
most important aspect of Jakobson's work is his phonological
theory. Here Jakobson is recognizably a member of the Prague
School – like Trubetzkoy he is interested in the analysis of
phonemes into their component features rather than in the
distribution of phonemes; but his views represent a special
development which takes to their logical extreme ideas that are
found only briefly and tentatively adumbrated in the work of
Trubetzkoy and other members of the School. The essence of
Jakobson's approach to phonology is the notion that there is a
relatively simple, orderly, universal 'psychological system' of
sounds underlying the chaotic wealth of different kinds of sound
observed by the phonetician.

Let us begin by defining some terms. Speech-sounds may be
characterized in terms of a number of distinct and independent
or quasi-independent *parameters*, as we shall call them. Thus the
height within the oral cavity of the highest point of the tongue is

one articulatory parameter (a vowel may be 'close' or 'open'), and the position of this point on the front/back scale is another parameter (vowels may be 'front' or 'back'). These two parameters represent choices which are to some extent independent of one another, but not wholly so: the more 'open' a vowel is – that is, the more the tongue is depressed into a flat mass in the bottom of the mouth – the less meaningful it is to speak of a particular 'highest point' and hence the less difference there is between front and back vowels. Position of the soft palate is a third articulatory parameter, and this is more independent of the two former parameters than they are of each other: any vowel (and many consonants) can be 'nasal' or 'oral', though the independence is not absolute – there is a tendency, because of the way in which the workings of the relevant muscles interact, for nasal vowels to be relatively open rather than relatively close. We may call the range of alternative choices provided by any single parameter the *values* of that parameter: thus [e] differs from [ɛ] in having a different value of the aperture parameter, and [e] differs from [ẽ] in having a different value of the parameter of nasality (i.e. position of soft palate). The word 'feature' is used ambiguously by various writers to mean either 'parameter' or 'parameter-value' (and Bloomfield (1933, p. 79) even used it in a third sense when he defined a phoneme as a 'minimum unit of distinctive sound-feature', which suggests that for him a 'feature' was a bundle of simultaneous parameter-values); discussion will therefore be much clearer if we avoid using the word 'feature' in what follows.

One of the lessons of articulatory phonetics is that human vocal anatomy provides a very large range of different phonetic parameters – far more, probably, than any individual language uses distinctively. In English, for instance, the various alternative airstream mechanisms play no part whatsoever in the phonological system – all our sounds are made with air forced out of the lungs by the respiratory muscles; and the wide range of possible vocal-chord actions are only marginally exploited, for the simple voiced/voiceless distinction and for the use of pitch in stress and intonation, the latter being relatively peripheral matters in English phonology. Furthermore, parameters differ considerably in the number of alternative values they may take. Nasality, arguably, is a simple binary choice: the soft palate is either raised or lowered, and thus a sound is either oral or nasal. The open/close and front/back parameters for tongue position, on the other hand, represent continuous ranges of values: the highest point of the tongue may be anywhere between the highest and lowest, furthest front and furthest back positions which are anatomically possible. The system of cardinal vowels divides up these continua in a discrete fashion: thus it provides for just four equidistant degrees of vowel aperture; but this is simply a convention invented for ease of description, and the cardinal parameter-value 'half close' is no more 'special' phonetically as compared to adjacent non-cardinal values than the line '54 degrees North' is special geographically as compared to the territory immediately to the north and south of it. The articulatory phonetician would be much more inclined to say that parameters which appear *prima facie* discrete are really continuous rather than *vice versa*. Thus, physiologically speaking, the soft palate can be lowered to a greater or lesser extent rather than being simply up or down; and, though the perceptual differences between sounds with different degrees of soft-palate lowering are very slight, there is claimed to be at least one language which distinguishes three values on the nasality parameter (Ladefoged 1971, pp. 34–5).

The Descriptivists emphasized that languages differ unpredictably in the particular phonetic parameters which they utilize distinctively, and in the number of values which they distinguish on parameters which are physically continuous. Many languages exploit the contrasts in airstream mechanisms and vocal-chord actions which English ignores, while making no use of contrasts which are important in English: the voiced/voiceless distinction, for example, which is central in the phonology of English and even more so in some other European languages, is non-distinctive in Chinese, while that language makes heavy use of pitch to distinguish words in a way quite alien to all European languages, including the few sometimes called 'tonal'. English distinguishes three degrees of aperture in pure vowels, as in *pit/pet/pat*; French has four distinctive aperture values, none of which are identical to any of the English values, as in *rit/ré/raie/rat*; Tswana is said to have six (Cole 1955). The Descriptivists' approach to phonology might be described metaphorically as 'democratic', in that they tended to see all phonetic parameters and all sounds as intrinsically equal in their potential for use in a language. Descriptivists tended to be reluctant to admit that any sound which can be found in some language might nevertheless be regarded as a relatively 'difficult' sound in any absolute sense: if an Englishman thinks of the [a] of French *rat* as a more 'straightforward' vowel than the [y] of French *rue*, for instance, this is only because English, as it happens, has vowels which are similar (though admittedly not identical) to [a] but completely lacks front rounded vowels such as [y].

Jakobson, on the other hand, is a phonological Tory. For him, only a small group of phonetic parameters are intrinsically fit to play a linguistically distinctive role; despite surface appearances each of these parameters is of the rigidly two-valued type, and the system of parameters forms a fixed hierarchy of precedence.[7] Furthermore, the details of the invariant system are not determined by mundane considerations such as vocal-tract anatomy or the need for easily perceived distinctions, but by much 'deeper' principles having to do with innate features of the human mind. Differences between the phonologies of languages are for Jakobson superficial variations on a fixed underlying theme. Jakobson thus attacks Saussurean/Boasian relativism for phonology, as we have seen Berlin and Kay attacking it for semantics.

The ideas just outlined are classically expressed in Jakobson, Fant and Halle's *Preliminaries to Speech Analysis* (1952). This short book lists a set of twelve pairs of terms which label the alternative values of what are claimed to be the twelve 'distinctive features' of all human speech. Notice that the word 'distinctive' here is used in a sense quite different from Bloomfield's. For Bloomfield, voicing (say) was distinctive in English and non-distinctive in Mandarin, but the question 'Is voicing distinctive in *language in general*?' would have been wholly meaningless, since *any* phonetic parameter could be and probably was used distinctively in at least a few languages. For Jakobson and his collaborators, on the other hand, 'distinctive' means 'able to be used distinctively in a human language': only twelve features are distinctive in this sense, and since there are so few the expectation is that almost all languages will actually make use of almost all the twelve features (although it is allowed that some languages may ignore one or two of the features).

Of course, if the Jakobsonian 'distinctive features' were equated directly with ordinary articulatory parameters, Jakobson's theory would be obviously false since many more than twelve articulatory parameters are exploited by the languages of the world. But nothing so crude is intended. An important part of the theory is that certain physically quite distinct articulatory parameters are 'psychologically equivalent', as one might say.[8] Thus, for example, the Jakobsonian feature 'Flat' (as in music – the use of impressionistic rather than technical phonetic terms is deliberate) represents interchangeably each of the following articulatory parameter-values: lip-rounding (as in rounded vowels or labialized consonants); pharyngalization (i.e. the secondary consonantal articulation which involves retracting the body of the tongue towards the [ɑ] position); and retroflex articulation (i.e., [ṭ] is 'Flat' where [t] is 'Plain' or non-Flat). In this fashion a wide range of articulatory parameters are reduced to a small set of 'distinctive features', and this reduction makes testable claims about what can and cannot happen in human languages. Thus the definition of 'Flat' implies that whereas some languages (e.g. Twi) distinguish labialized and plain stops, others (e.g. Arabic) distinguish pharyngalized and plain stops, and others again (e.g. many languages of India) distinguish retroflex from alveolar or dental stops, no language can contrast, for example, a labialized [tʷ] with a retroflex [ṭ] – even though they are made quite differently, and one can certainly learn to hear the difference – because the physical difference between the two sounds is psychologically non-existent (*Preliminaries*, p. 31).[9]

The notion that the universal distinctive features are organized into an innate hierarchy of relative importance or priority appears in a book which Jakobson published in the period between leaving Czechoslovakia and arriving in America (Jakobson 1941). He makes the point, to begin with, that a study of children's acquisition of language shows that the various distinctions are by no means mastered in a random order. Thus, among consonants, the distinction between labial and alveolar stops appears before the distinction between alveolars and velars: all children go through a stage at which, for example, *cat* is pronounced as something like 'tat'. Stops are acquired before fricatives. Back rounded vowels such as [u o] are distinguished from front spread vowels ([i e]) sooner than front rounded vowels (e.g. [y ø]) are distinguished from either: thus, in a language such as German which has vowels of all three kinds, [y ø] will be the last to appear in the child's speech. The opposition between [r] and [l] is normally one of the last contrasts learned among the consonants. And so on.

Jakobson then goes on to argue that this hierarchy of phonological features, which is established on the basis of data about children's acquisition of language, manifests itself also in comparative studies of adult languages and in the symptoms of aphasia. Thus, we find that the later distinctions acquired by the child are the distinctions which are absent in some adult languages: there are many languages which lack front rounded vowels [y ø] (e.g. English) or which have only a single liquid instead of a distinction between [r] and [l] (e.g. Japanese), but no languages fail to distinguish [p] from [t] (except for a few special cases of tribes which mutilate the lips for cosmetic purposes and are therefore *physically* incapable of producing labials). Furthermore, 'late' sounds are relatively uncommon sounds even in those languages which contain them: e.g. front rounded vowels are used less in French or German than vowels of the other two kinds. Thus there is after all good reason for the Englishman to regard French [a] as more straightforward than [y]; neither sound occurs in his own language, but the former is more basic in the universal hierarchy than the latter. (Jakobson adapts a term of Trubetzkoy's by calling [y] relatively 'marked' – meaning not that the opposition between [y] and [a] is 'privative' in Trubetzkoy's sense – it is not – but rather that [a] has a sort of universal psychological priority over [y].) In aphasics whose pronunciation decays gradually, the last distinctions acquired by the child are the first to go, and *vice versa*; and if, later, they regain their ability to pronounce, the order of reacquisition is the opposite of the order of loss, and is identical to the order in which children originally acquire the distinctions.

Jakobson uses observations of the latter categories as evidence against those who would suggest that his universals have relatively superficial physiological explanations. Thus, in his system the most basic contrast of all is between labial consonants [m b] and an open vowel such as [ɑ]. It is often suggested that the reason why labials are relatively early consonants is because they are made with an action similar to the sucking reflex which allows newborn children to feed at the breast; but not even 'the most extreme Freudian' will claim that this explains why labials are more resistant than other consonants to loss by diachronic sound-changes from adult languages (1941, p. 67), or – as Jakobson might have added – why labials are the last consonants to disappear from aphasic speech.[10]

In order to substantiate his belief that the phonological universals he discusses are determined by 'deep' psychological principles rather than by relatively uninteresting facts about oral anatomy or the like, Jakobson devotes considerable space to discussion of synaesthetic effects: that is, cases where perceptions in one sensory mode (in this case, speech-sound) correlate with perceptions in another mode (Jakobson considers mainly associations of sounds with colours). If he can show that, for people who make such associations, particular distinctive features as he analyses them are consistently linked with particular visual qualities, then clearly he has good evidence both for the validity of his system of distinctive features and for the claim that the reality to which the system corresponds is something in the mind rather than in, for example, the musculature of the mouth. Jakobson dismisses with some scorn, as 'completely untenable', such alternative explanations for synaesthetic associations as that of a German psychologist, K. Langenbeck, who suggested that he 'saw' the vowel *a* as red because the first toy *Wagen* (lorry) he was given was a red one: if this were the reason, the universality of these sound/colour correspondences would be inexplicable (Jakobson 1941, p. 83).

The difficulty with this aspect of Jakobson's work is that his evidence is highly anecdotal – he bases his 'universals' of synaesthesia on a tiny handful of reports about individuals; and one anecdote is always very vulnerable to a counter-anecdote. Thus, one of the claims that is important for Jakobson is that synaesthetic subjects tend to perceive vowels as coloured but consonants as colourless – black, white or grey (cf. Jakobson 1941, ch. 3; *Preliminaries*, p. 32). However, the present writer has since childhood perceived the letters of the alphabet as having certain fixed colours; and almost the only phonetic principle I can detect in my own synaesthesia is that while three of the five vowel letters (E, I, O) are colourless, all but two of the twenty-one consonant letters are coloured (the exceptions being the nasal letters M and N). The nature of Jakobson's evidence being what it is, this individual observation goes quite a long way towards refuting his claims about universals of sound-synaesthesia.

This anecdotal quality in Jakobson's argumentation applies not merely to his statements about synaesthesia but more generally to his claims about the distinctive features. Thus, there certainly have been sound-changes in some languages which resulted in the loss of labials; and Jakobson's statements about aphasia also seem to be based on very few cases. *Preliminaries to Speech Analysis* consists essentially of a series of *ex cathedra* pronouncements about the identity of Jakobson's twelve features, which may be correct or may be incorrect but which are backed up by reference only to scattered phenomena drawn, admittedly, from an impressively wide range of languages but each of which is described in isolation and, of necessity, at a fairly shallow level. In fact I see no reason whatsoever to believe in any universal set of binary phonological features, let alone in the particular set that Jakobson promulgates (cf. Sampson 1974a). Except for a ritual remark in the preface to *Preliminaries*, Jakobson's writings never, by their tone or by their content, encourage the reader to regard the statements contained in them as open to debate or testing, and this feature of Jakobson's work makes his failure all the more ignominious when counter-examples are in fact produced. To quote Martinet (in Parret 1974, p. 240):

Take for example a panchronic law, presented by Jakobson, according to which a language cannot combine a distinctive place of accent [i.e. contrastive stress] and phonological length .... Yet the two features happen to coexist in Franco-Provençal dialects: *bére* is opposed to *beré* and *bó:la* to *bóla*. And there goes your panchronic law ....

For further counter-examples to Jakobson's claims, see McCawley (1967). In view of considerations such as these, it becomes difficult to view Jakobson's approach to phonology as constituting a genuinely empirical theory; Jakobson might have been allotted fewer pages in this book were it not for the influence he has exerted over his juniors in America (an issue to which we shall return in later chapters).

Let us finish this chapter by considering another aspect of Prague thought, which has led to one of the most interesting and fruitful developments in the linguistics of the last decade or so.

One of the characteristics of the Prague approach to language was a readiness to acknowledge that a given language might include a range of alternative 'systems', 'registers', or 'styles', where American Descriptivists tended to insist on treating a language as a single unitary system. Consider, as a very crude example of the problem, the treatment of non-naturalized foreign loan-words. Many Englishmen, for instance, pronounce the word *restaurant* with a vowel, [ɔ̃], whose nasal quality is inherited from French (even if the timbre of the vowel differs in other respects from the French original). Nasal vowels are not usual in English; but this word is uttered by Englishmen, so a Descriptivist would find it difficult to justify the omission of / ɔ̃ / from a phonemic analysis of English. Yet once we admit / ɔ̃ /, where do we stop? I commonly refer to the Confucian concept of the *chün-tzŭ* or 'princely man' using the Mandarin pronunciation, since I know of no standard Anglicization of the term; almost all the sounds of *chün-tzŭ* are quite un-English – does my use of the term imply that they must be added to the inventory of English phonemes? A related problem arises when we compare the sounds of rapid speech with those heard in careful delivery of the same language. Many Englishmen, for instance, have a flap [ɾ] in very fast speech which does not occur in slow speech, and which represents both the phonemes / t / and / d / in intervocalic position: [pˈærɪ] is ambiguous as between *patty* and *paddy*. For the Descriptivist the choice seems to lie between treating [ɾ] as an allophone of one or the other of the phonemes / t / and / d / or setting it up as a further phoneme, but each of these three choices misses the point that [ɾ] is characteristic of a special style of speech. A Prague linguist would be ready, indeed eager, to say that English has a system of native phonemes which excludes / ɔ̃ / even though that sound may occur in a subsidiary stock of borrowed words, and that if the phonology of rapid English differs in various respects from that of English spoken slowly then their respective grammars should be kept distinct rather than merged together. The Descriptivists' reluctance to make such statements may have been because they often seemed methodologically unrespectable: if we agree that it is appropriate to exclude / ɔ̃ / from the phoneme-inventory of

English that is largely because we feel the sound to be foreign even though we may use it regularly, and it is not obvious what observable facts such feelings can be correlated with. We have seen that questions of scientific methodology did not concern the Prague linguists.

Because of their functional approach, it was natural that the Prague scholars were particularly interested in the way that a language provides a speaker with a range of speech-styles appropriate to different social settings. (As has already been mentioned, such differentiation of usage in terms of degree of formality or social milieu is particularly salient in Czech.) This aspect of their work has recently been developed into a rich and sophisticated theory by the American William Labov, formerly of Columbia University and since the early 1970s at the University of Pennsylvania.

Labov's work (see, for example, Labov 1966) is based on recorded interviews with sizable samples of speakers of various categories in some speech-community, the interviews being designed to elicit examples of some linguistic form – a *variable* – which is known to be realized in a variety of ways in that community. (Unlike the members of the Prague School proper, Labov is very much concerned with methodological issues, and indeed he is the outstanding exponent, both in theoretical writing and in practice, of empirical scientific method in contemporary American linguistics.) A typical variable is presence v. absence of postvocalic *r* in New York City: as in some towns in England, one can hear in New York pronunciations of, say, *farm* varying between [fɑ:m] and [fɑɾm] or the like (although the social implications of the respective pronunciations are very different in New York City from what they would be anywhere in England). In such a situation, a Bloomfieldian would acknowledge that various individual speakers may speak different 'idiolects', and would recognize the possibility of an idiolect in which pronunciations such as [fɑ:m] and [fɑɾm] were in 'free variation', as well as idiolects which consistently used one or the other form. But (apart from the fact that the difference between '*r*-less' and '*r*-ful' pronunciations of a word like *farm* is phonetically a gradient rather than a sharp two-way distinction, a complication we shall ignore here) in practice it turns out that almost everyone uses both *r*-less and *r*-ful pronunciations; and the term 'free variation' is quite misleading, because there is great regularity (although the speakers themselves are unconscious of the pattern) in the proportions of *r*-less and *r*-ful pronunciations uttered in various circumstances, but the regularities are statistical rather than absolute. Age and social standing of the speaker, degree of formality of the interview, and other factors all interact to determine in a highly systematic and predictable fashion the proportion of possible post-vocalic *r*s which are actually pronounced in any given utterance. (Cf. Trudgill 1974 for application of Labov's research techniques in an English context.)

What is particularly germane to issues discussed earlier in this book is the fact that while some determining factors, such as speaker's educational attainments, will be constant for a given speaker throughout his adult life, others, such as degree of formality of the speech-situation (which Labov controls in relatively objective ways), will vary for a given speaker from one occasion to another; and even in the case of factors which are constant for each individual speaker, it can be shown that hearers are acutely sensitive to the correlations between linguistic and social variables (although they cannot consciously identify the relevant linguistic variables). That is – to cite a hypothetical case resembling in principle some of the experiments conducted by Labov and his associates – if a young white linguist makes a tape-recording which deliberately includes the proportion of post-vocalic *r*s appropriate to an elderly uneducated New York negro, then another New Yorker hearing the tape will make the value-judgements about the recorded speech that he would normally make about elderly uneducated negroes, although he will have no idea that what he is reacting to is the pronunciation of the letter *r*. This implies that it is wrong to think of an individual as mastering a single idiolect, and understanding others' speech only insofar as it resembles his own. Rather, it seems that each speaker learns a structured range of alternative speech-patterns, together with the correlations between variation in his social environment and variation in that dialectal continuum. There is nothing particularly surprising in the finding that speakers are familar with a variety of speech-styles, of course, but many of us had supposed that such knowledge was patchy and largely inaccurate – as speakers' *conscious beliefs* about such facts certainly are.

What is staggering about Labov's work is the subtlety, consistency and mathematical regularity it reveals in speakers' use of statistical linguistic variables and hearers' reactions to them. Furthermore, when we examine the age factor it emerges that historical change is fuelled by social variation (cf. Weinreich *et al.* 1968). Often, what a given speaker perceives as a difference between more and less socially prestigious styles of speech will coincide historically with a difference between newer and older usage, as speakers in each generation unconsciously modify their speech slightly in order to raise their social prestige. Thus, in New York City, *r*-ful forms are used more by middle-class than by working-class speakers, more in formal than in informal situations, *and* more by younger speakers than by older speakers.

There is an irony here. Saussure stressed the social nature of language, and he insisted that linguistics as a social science must ignore historical data because, for the speaker, the history of his language does not exist – a point that seemed undeniable. The Prague School and, now, Labov, are among the linguists who have taken the social dimension of language most seriously; and they have ended by destroying Saussure's sharp separation between synchronic and diachronic study. For the individual, it turns out, a sizeable portion of the history of his language *is* psychologically real; only he perceives it not as history but as social stratification. To be a native speaker of a language is to have learned not just a momentary *état de langue* but a direction of movement – this is perhaps the explanation for long-term linguistic 'drift' in Sapir's sense (see page 82). It seems likely that the tradition which Labov is pioneering is destined to become one of the most fruitful avenues of future linguistic research. If so, we may expect the techniques of synchronic and diachronic linguistic description to resemble each other much more in future than they have done in the past.

6 Noam Chomsky and generative grammar

Any linguist today measures his intellectual position by reference to that of Noam Chomsky. Chomsky is commonly said to have brought about a 'revolution' in linguistics, and the political metaphor is apt. Just as books published in the Soviet Union on the most abstract academic topics once had to begin with a ritual obeisance to the guiding genius of Stalin, so nowadays even scholars researching aspects of language which have very little connection with Chomsky's work often feel obliged to claim publicly that their writings exemplify the Chomskyan paradigm of linguistic thought; and those scholars who acknowledge no such obligation are seen (and see themselves) as 'anti-Chomskyans' as much as proponents of their own views. Not just received beliefs about language but the whole atmosphere of linguistics as a discipline has changed as the movement initiated by Chomsky has triumphed. We must now turn to consider the nature of this 'revolution'.

Avram Noam Chomsky was born in Philadelphia in 1928, in a family of politically radical Jews of Russian descent. Chomsky's father was a Hebrew scholar of some standing, and Chomsky tells us that the childhood experience of helping to correct proofs of one his father's books on Hebrew was one hint which suggested to him that linguistics might suit his intellectual bent. As a student at the University of Pennsylvania Chomsky turned to linguistics partly through sharing the radical political views of Zellig Harris, who taught there; Chomsky's other subjects were mathematics and philosophy. In the early 1950s Chomsky pursued his research work as a Junior Fellow in Philosophy at Harvard, where Roman Jakobson was teaching; in 1955 Chomsky was given a teaching post at the neighbouring Massachusetts Institute of Technology, and he has remained there ever since.

The fact that he came to scholarly maturity within Jakobson's sphere of influence is one of the keys to Chomsky's thought. Jakobson, the reader will remember, was centrally concerned with the question of phonological universals: he believed that the different phonological structures found in the languages of the world were merely superficial variations on a common underlying system (a belief which conflicted both with the principled relativism of the Descriptivist school and, one might have supposed, with what an uncommitted observer would conclude from the weight of the *prima facie* evidence). Although Jakobson himself wrote mainly about phonological universals, he believed that the approach was applicable also to other levels of linguistic structure; he got his students the Aginskys to contribute an article on 'The importance of language universals' (dealing mainly with anthropological aspects of language) to an early volume of *Word*, the journal of European linguists exiled to America by the Second World War (B. Aginsky and E. Aginsky 1948). The essence of Chomsky's approach to language is the claim that there are linguistic universals in the domain of syntax; and Chomsky develops the hypothesis of syntactic universals into a theory of considerably more richness and depth than Jakobson's theory of phonological universals.

For Saussure, it will be recalled, syntax was not even part of *langue*, the structure of a given language: putting words together into sentences was something that individual speakers did on particular occasions, not something that a language does once for all – there is an endless variety of sentences possible in any language, even though the range of Saussurean 'signs' (roughly, words) available in any language is limited. Although later writers had not explicitly agreed with Saussure that syntax was a matter of *parole*, the fact remained that they had not on the whole succeeded in finding ways to incorporate syntactic analysis into the scientific study of language. Before he could show that the syntactic structures of different languages were similar, therefore, Chomsky had to show how it was possible to define the syntax of any given language.

Chomsky approached this question in a way that came very naturally to a mathematician, although it was much less natural to anyone whose education had been in the humanities (which is why earlier linguists had not seen the point clearly). To the mathematician it is a cliché that a class of entities may be *well-defined* while nevertheless having infinitely many members.

Think, for instance, of a circle on a sheet of graph-paper, with its centre at the origin (the point where x-axis and y-axis cross) and its radius equal to five of whatever units the graph-paper is marked off in – centimetres, say. (We are considering a geometer's 'ideal' circle, rather than a physical circle drawn by a pencil which makes a line having breadth.) Now we may treat the circle as a class of geometrical points – a subset of all the infinitely many points on the graph-paper. For instance, the point '$x = -5, y = 0$' belongs to the circle (it is the left-hand of the two points at which the circle crosses the x-axis), but the point '$x = 4, y = 4$' is not (it lies outside the circle to the upper right). Not only does the graph-paper as a whole contain an infinity of points, but the circle alone (and indeed any line or curve having extension in one or more dimensions) has infinitely many points. (Most of the points belonging to the circle will have co-ordinates which are not 'round numbers' like 4 or -5.) Although the set of points which we identify as a circle is infinitely numerous, it is perfectly well defined: it is defined by the equation '$x^2 + y^2 = 5^2$'. Of the infinitely many possible choices of x and y, the infinite subset for which this equation holds constitute the circle; all other choices correspond to points either inside or outside the circle.

Furthermore, not only can this particular circle be defined; we can just as rigorously define the *class of all possible circles* on the graph-paper, which is an infinitely numerous set of infinitely numerous sets of points. (If the reader finds the mathematics slipping out of his grasp here, I apologize; I am trying to keep things simple, but I realize that many people have a blind spot in this area. Normal service will be resumed in the next paragraph.) The class of all possible circles is defined by the equation '$(x - a)^2 + (y - b)^2 = c^2$': for any given a, b, c, the set of points corresponding to all choices of x and y which fit the equation will be a circle, and every circle corresponds to some choice for a, b, and c. (The choice of a and b determines the centre, and c determines the radius – in the case of the circle first described, a and b were both 0 and c was 5.) Thus the class of all possible circles is again a well-defined though infinitely numerous class.

An example of a *non*-well-defined class of linear figures would be the class of all beautiful figures. Some figures (probably figures whose equations would be highly complex) will be recognizably beautiful or at least attractive, others will be recognizably unattractive, and many (probably including most of the simple figures such as straight lines and circles) will be neither one nor the other. No doubt there will be an infinity of attractive figures, but is seems inconceivable that we could ever rigorously demarcate the membership of that class as we have demarcated the class of circles. The problem is not that attractiveness is a gradient (i.e. more-or-less) property whereas circularity is a sharp yes-or-no question – if *that* were the only difficulty, there are mathematical techniques which would solve it. Rather, the problem is that humans are constantly discovering (or perhaps 'creating' or 'inventing' would be better terms) categories of beauty that no one had previously recognized – we have to learn to see beauty, it is not a category given to mankind in advance; so that the notion of a fixed distinction between beautiful and unbeautiful entities (whether line drawings on a graph-paper or any other sort of thing) just does not apply. Any particular beautiful figure will be definable by a (probably highly complex) equation, but the class of all beautiful figures cannot be defined. It is significant that, in exemplifying the notion 'ill-defined class', I resorted to beauty, which is an aspect of humans' conscious reactions to things rather than a property that inheres in things independently of human-kind (as does the property of circularity). It seems to be exclusively Man, with his creative, unpredictable intelligence, who gives rise to ill-defined classes.

As a circle may be treated as a particular subset of the class of all possible points in a plane, so Chomsky proposed in his first book, *Syntactic Structures* (1957), that we should treat a language, from the syntactic point of view, as a particular sub-set of the class of all possible sequences of the items in its dictionary. (–5, O) belonged to the circle we discussed while (4, 4) fell outside it; similarly, the sequence *The cat is on the mat* belongs to English while the sequence *Mat the on is cat the* falls outside it. In Chomsky's terms, the former of these sequences is 'grammatical', or 'well-formed', the latter 'ungrammatical' or 'ill-formed'; the asterisk is used to mark ungrammaticality. (Note that these terms are used in a purely descriptive rather than evaluative sense. *I ain't never done nothing* is grammatical in a certain fairly widely spoken dialect of English, although not in the dialect in which this book is written; the fact that the former dialect is deprecated by our society does not make it any less worthy of study from the scientist's point of view. Since Chomsky is interested in discovering what kinds of language are 'natural' to humans, he might even think the former dialect *more* worthy of study than standard written English, since it has been less regimented by the artificial rules of purists.)

The class of grammatical sentences in any language will surely be infinitely large: after all, from any two declarative sentences in English one can construct a third by interposing the word *and*, and in principle there is no end to the applicability of sentence-forming devices of this kind. But at the same time Chomsky takes it for granted that the class of all grammatical sentences in a language will be well-defined. This is clearly not the truism that Chomsky takes it to be; grammaticality depends on human mental activity rather than being physically 'there' in the sound-sequence, and it might well be that grammaticality was a property akin rather to beauty than to circularity. However, the notion of grammaticality as a well-defined property has proved very fruitful, and I shall say here simply that although Chomsky did not give explicit arguments in favour of his assumption I believe that it has justified itself in practice. Chomsky's exposition of how in principle the syntax of a language can be brought within the purview of scientific linguistic description is a great positive contribution to the discipline.[1]

To call a class 'well-defined' does not imply that someone has already produced an explicit statement of the properties necessary and sufficient for membership in the class: it only means that in principle there is such a statement waiting to be discovered. The next problem for Chomsky was to find some formal means of generating the class of grammatical morpheme-sequences in a language, as the equation '$x^2 + y^2 = 25$' generates the set of points we call a circle. (This use of the term 'generate', normal in mathematics, was borrowed by Chomsky into linguistics, and his approach to syntax is accordingly known as 'generative grammar'.) At this point Chomsky looked to the work of his first teacher, Zellig Harris.

Harris (like his Descriptivist contemporaries, although Harris went rather further than most of them – see particularly Harris 1951) approached syntactic analysis by classifying morphemes into groups which resembled one another in their distribution with respect to other morphemes. Thus *cat, dog, boy, tail* and many other morphemes can each occur in the frame *The ___ is on the mat*; provided that we do not find a lot of other frames which differentiate between these morphemes, we will regard them as members of a single 'form-class'. Since this form-class is approximately that traditionally called the class of Nouns, we may as well symbolize the class by the letter *N*. It is important to realize, however, that Harris, like Fries (p. 65), by no means took it for granted that the traditional 'parts of speech' would appear in his analysis. Traditional grammatical terminology (which we inherit as the outcome of a several-centuries-long intellectual development culminating in the work of the Alexandrian Dionysius Thrax, *ca.* 100 BC) is based partly on logical analysis of the meanings of words, and partly on formal properties of the grammar of Classical Greek. Although pure distributional analysis applied to Modern English produces results which show considerably similarities with the traditional parts of speech (as well it might, English and Greek both being Indo-European languages) the results are only similar, by no means identical. When distributional analysis is applied to a non-Indo-European language, the classes obtained are often quite unlike those of our traditional grammatical theory (as Boas had stressed at the outset of the Descriptivist tradition); see Honey (1956) for a good example.

Having established that *cat, dog, boy, tail*, etc. belong to one class *N*, and that by parity of reasoning *good, bad, gigantic*, and so on belong to a single class, say *A*, we then find that sequences such as *good cat* or *gigantic dog* occur in the same frames that permit words such as *cat* and *dog* on their own – the two-word phrases are equally appropriate as replacements for the blank in *The ___ is on the mat*, for instance. We record this fact in an equation, '*A N = N*'. This is an example of an 'endocentric' construction, which as a whole has the same distributional privileges as one of its parts. We find also 'exocentric' constructions, which behave differently from any of their individual constituents. Thus, we can symbolize the class including *the, a, some*, etc. (each of which can fill the blank in *___ man is here*) as *R*; then we find that *R N* (e.g. *the cat, some bad boy*) behaves neither like *R* nor like *N*, but like a further class, the class of proper names – say *P*. (For instance, *the cat* or *some bad boy* can fill the blank _____ *is here*, and so can *John* or *Mary*, but neither *the* or *some*, nor again *cat* or *bad boy*, can appear in that slot in isolation.) Thus we have $R\ N = P$. In some cases it will even be convenient to symbolize a class of morpheme-sequences which substitute for one another although they never substitute for any individual morpheme. Thus, sequences such as *who snore -s, which whistle -s*, etc. (which might be symbolized $W\ V$ *-s* with W standing for relative pronouns and V for intransitive verbs) can replace one another in *The dog* _____ *is on the mat*, so we might recognize such sequences as exemplifying a category of their own by writing $W\ V$ *-s* $= L$ even though no single morpheme can act as an 'L'. We may then show that *the dog who whistles* is syntactically equivalent to *some gigantic boy* or to *John* by writing $P\ L = P$; and this is better than writing $P\ W\ V$ *-s* $= P$ directly, since the blank in *The dog* _____ *is on the mat* can be filled also by phrases not of the type $W\ V$ *-s*. For instance, *The dog with a gigantic tail is on the mat* is grammatical, so (given that *with* exemplifies a class E) we may write $E\ P = L$ as well as $W\ V$ *-s* $= L$.

The final step, taken explicitly by Chomsky, is to add a symbol S to stand for the class of complete sentences (so that we can write e.g. $P\ V$ *-s* $= S$, since *John snores* or *The boy whistles* are grammatical sentences). Chomsky prefers to turn the equations round and to replace the 'equals' sign by an arrow, so that equivalences such as those we have discussed would be recorded by Chomsky as follows:

Figure 3

$$S \rightarrow P\ V \ \text{-}s$$

$$P \rightarrow \left\{ \begin{array}{ll} P & L \\ R & N \\ John \\ Mary \end{array} \right\}$$

$$L \rightarrow \left\{ \begin{array}{ll} W & V \ \text{-}s \\ E & P \end{array} \right\}$$

$$N \rightarrow A\ N, cat, dog, boy, tail, \ldots$$

$$R \rightarrow the, a, some, \ldots$$

$$A \rightarrow good, bad, gigantic, \ldots$$

(A comprehensive grammar would of course need many more rules, e.g. to specify the membership of classes *V* and *E* and to introduce a large number of further form-classes and of further syntactic constructions not discussed above.) The point of replacing 'equals' sign by arrow is that it encourages us to think of the formulae as rules for constructing sentences.[2] We can produce a sentence by beginning with the symbol *S*, for 'sentence', and rewriting it as instructed by the arrows, making a choice at random whenever choices are provided by braces and commas, until we have replaced all capital-letter symbols with morphemes of the language under analysis. The language generated by such a system is the class of all sequences which can be reached from the symbol *S* by following the rules and making some particular choice whenever a choice is offered – just as the circle generated by the equation $x^2 + y^2 = 25$ is the class of all points defined by choices of *x* and *y* that satisfy the equation.

Although the geometrical equation involves only half a dozen symbols, there is an infinity of points which satisfy it. Similarly, although a grammar of the kind sketched in Figure 3 will be only finitely complex, it will generate an infinity of morpheme-sequences. A rule such as $P \rightarrow P\ L$, for instance, can be applied any number of times to its own output: e.g. *P* can be rewritten as *PL* which in turn is rewritten as *PLL*, and so on, thus allowing for complex constructions such as *the dog with a gigantic tail who snores*. The initial symbol *S* will itself appear on the right-hand side of a number of rules, in order to allow for sentences such as *John knows that the dog snores* (such a construction might be symbolized as '$S \rightarrow P\ C\ that\ S$', with *C* for the class of verbs that take part in such constructions), and clearly such a rule can again apply to its own output, thus permitting, for example, *John knows that the gigantic boy thinks that the dog snores*. Thus a finite (if complex) grammar of this type generates an infinitely large, though well-defined, language (class of sentences).

So far we have said nothing about universals. Chomsky's next point is his most original. He observes that the algebraic notation system which he has borrowed from Harris (and which is more or less similar to the schemes used by those others of the Descriptivist school who attempted to come to grips with syntax) embodies a strong empirical claim about the syntactic properties of human languages. The class of all possible grammars of the Harris/Chomsky type can itself be treated as a well-defined (though infinitely numerous) class: we may define it as containing any finite set of rules each of which is of the form '$A \rightarrow \varphi$', where A is some single symbol and φ is some sequence of symbols, morphemes, or both. (In Figure 3, groups of rules of this form were collapsed together by using braces and commas to indicate alternatives, but this makes no difference of principle: a rule such as '$L \rightarrow \{W\ V\ \text{-}s,\ E\ P\}$' is equivalent to the pair of rules '$L \rightarrow W\ V\ \text{-}s$' and '$L \rightarrow E\ P$', each of which is of the form '$A \rightarrow \varphi$'.) A set of rules which conforms to the definition just given is technically known as a 'context-free phrase-structure grammar'; since this term is rather cumbersome, I prefer to say 'constituency grammar'. Now, Chomsky (1959) has demonstrated mathematically that there exist well-defined classes of morpheme-sequences which cannot be generated by any constituency grammar, no matter how complex (just as there are linear figures which cannot be generated by any equation drawn from the class of equations defined by the formula '$(x - a)^2 + (y - b)^2 = c^2$'): the class of 'constituency languages' is a well-defined subset of the class of all possible languages, as the class of circles is a well-defined subset of the class of all possible linear figures in a plane. In other words, to assume that constituency grammar is the appropriate tool for describing the syntax of human languages is to assume that human languages all belong syntactically to a certain limited class – which is to say that there exist syntactic universals of human language. Chomsky felt (although this is highly contentious) that the Descriptivists did tacitly make this assumption about the appropriateness of constituency grammar (see Postal 1964, written under Chomsky's aegis), so that the Descriptivists' practice implied the existence of universals even though they claimed overtly to believe in unlimited linguistic diversity.

In order to make this alleged syntactic universal more comprehensible, we can express it pictorially. A constituency grammar associates, with each of the sentences in the language it generates, a 'constituency structure' or hierarchical tree-structure. For instance, the grammar of Figure 3 would associate the structure of Figure 4 with the sentence *The dog with a gigantic tail whistles*:

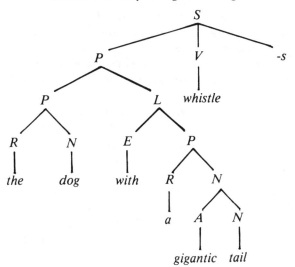

Figure 4

That sentence corresponds to the ordered sequence of 'leaves' of the tree in Figure 4, while the relationship between the rules of Figure 3 and the branching structure of Figure 4 should be clear. (Linguists conventionally draw their trees with the 'root', labelled *S* for 'sentence', at the top and the 'leaves', labelled with morphemes of the language under analysis, at the bottom; clearly linguists are even weaker than Hilary Putnam at nature study!) Constituency grammar could indeed be defined intuitively as the kind of grammatical notation appropriate for languages in which the criteria of grammaticality have to do with class-membership and hierarchical structure.

The fact that grammaticality in human languages has to do with the part-of-speech affiliation of words and with the way in which words are grouped hierarchically into phrases and clauses of various categories is of course by no means novel. Schoolboys were taught to parse their sentences by means of diagrams roughly equivalent to Figure 4 for centuries before Chomsky: the elements labelled *P* were traditionally called 'nominal phrases' (except when only one word long), that labelled *L* was traditionally a 'prepositional phrase', and so forth.[3] But Chomsky is himself arguing that constituency grammar corresponds to a tacitly familiar view of syntax: the novelty lies in the realization that, logically speaking, languages need not be of the constituency type – it is perfectly easy to define classes of morpheme-sequences to which our traditional grammatical notions would be inapplicable.[4]

Since Chomsky's aim is to establish the existence of syntactic universals, and since he has shown that some fairly standard views of grammar imply that human languages belong to a rather restricted class (in other words, imply the existence of strong syntactic universals), he might well have stopped at this point. In fact he developed his exposition in *Syntactic Structures*, along lines which considerably undermine the force of what had gone before. According to Chomsky, the belief that constituency grammar is adequate to generate human languages, though widely held in an inexplicit form, is actually wrong. He gives examples (which I shall not discuss in detail) of constructions found in English that cannot, he claims, be handled by means of constituency rules.

If this is so, one obvious conclusion might be that the class of languages usable by humans is not, after all, well defined. Chomsky was the first to imagine that there might be an empirical, falsifiable scientific theory of syntactic 'naturalness' (that is, a theory which defines a class of languages to which all extant human languages belong but which is smaller than the class of all conceivable languages); perhaps this enterprise is misconceived, as a Descriptivist who believed in unlimited linguistic diversity would suppose. Admitting that one can dream up classes of morpheme-sequences which look highly 'unnatural' as human languages, perhaps nevertheless the property of 'naturalness' for languages is akin to the property of beauty rather than circularity for linear figures.

This is not Chomsky's conclusion. Rather, Chomsky argues that the constituency theory of syntactic universals should be replaced with a modified theory, which he sketches out in *Syntactic Structures* and which he and many of his followers have developed at length since. The essence of the new theory of syntactic naturalness is that it expands the canonical notation system for grammars by allowing the constituency rules to be supplemented with a series of so-called 'transformational rules'. A transformational rule, briefly, is a rule which operates on the hierarchical structure assigned to a morpheme-sequence by a constituency grammar, and alters it into a new hierarchical structure in a way which modifies the string of morphemes acting as leaves of the tree. For instance, rather than producing a question such as *Whom did John meet last night?* by means of constituency rules different from the rules needed for a statement such as *John met Mary last night*, a transformational grammar can use just a single set of constituency rules to produce morpheme-strings exclusively in the declarative form; such strings will include *John met whom last night*, which is ungrammatical (unless given a special intonation to mark it as a request to repeat an imperfectly heard statement), but a transformation (or, in fact, a series of transformations) triggered off by the presence of the word *whom* will operate on this to give the correct form of the question.

Thus hierarchical structure still has the special role in Chomsky's new theory of syntax that it had in constituency grammar, however in the new theory a sentence will have not just one but a series of hierarchical structures. (As the theory has developed, the freedom to include transformational rules in grammars has been exploited to the point where all sentences in a language, including declaratives, are represented as having undergone numerous transformations in their 'derivational history'.) A morpheme-sequence belongs to the language generated by a transformational grammar if some tree produced by the constituency 'base' of the grammar, *after having been modified successively by such of the transformational rules as are applicable*, emerges as a tree containing the sequence in question as its leaves. That final tree is called the 'surface structure' of the sentence; the original tree as it emerged from the constituency base, before it was 'transformed', is the 'deep structure' of the sentence.

The 'transformational rule' aspect of Chomsky's work is much less persuasive than the material discussed earlier, For one thing, it is not clear of transformational grammar as it is of constituency grammar that it defines a class of languages smaller than the class of all logically-conceivable languages, i.e. that it makes a testable claim about syntactic universals – it appears possible that there may be a transformational grammar for *any* conceivable class of morpheme-sequences (Wall 1971). It may be possible to defend Chomsky's theory against that objection (Sampson 1973; *Form* [see p. 251, n.1], pp. 112–14); but the other problem is that Chomsky's arguments for the inadequacy of constituency grammar seem very shaky (*Form*, pp. 205–6), and, in the clearest cases of failure of constituency notation (such as co-ordinate constructions), transformational rules do not seem to help much either (Dik 1968). The theory of transformational rules strikes me, for one, as something of an unfortunate excrescence on the body of Chomsky's linguistic thought. The fact that it is this aspect of Chomsky's work that has attracted probably more attention than any other element, to the point where Chomsky's whole approach to language is often referred to as 'transformational linguistics', seems merely to exemplify the difficulty people sometimes have in distinguishing between the essential and the superficial in a novel body of doctrine.

Be that as it may, the fact is that since the early 1960s a company of scholars, by now very numerous indeed, have been engaged in developing Chomsky's modified theory of syntactic universals. A typical article in any of the many academic journals which are now largely devoted to Chomskyan linguistics will propose some novel candidate as a possible linguistic universal, or will cite evidence from some language to show that an earlier hypothesis about a possible universal must be rejected, or will argue that a deeper analysis of the syntax of the language in question shows it not after all to be a counter-example to the proposed universal, and so forth. In many cases the hypothetical universals have to do with aspects of syntax originally discussed by Chomsky. Typical examples of the kind of topics debated would be the following: What kinds of modifications to trees do and do not occur as transformations in human languages? To what extent do the constituency rules, as well as the transformations, differ from one language to another? (Some argue that there is a fixed constituency 'base' shared by all languages, with syntactic differences being referred exclusively to differences in the 'transformational component'; Emmon Bach (1971) has argued that even 'transformational components' differ only by including different choices from a universally fixed, finite menu of allowable transformations.) What principles determine the order of application of transformations? (It is widely agreed that the sequence of transformations in a language applies to complex tree-structures 'cyclically': that is, the rules are all applied in sequence to the smallest subordinate clauses – i.e. subtrees dominated by an S node – then re-applied in sequence to the next most inclusive clauses, and so on until they have been applied to the sentence as a whole; but writers disagree about whether any special transformations may apply before or after the cyclical application of the main sequence, and about what, if anything, determines the order of rules in that main sequence.) In other cases syntactic universals are proposed which have very little relationship with the matters treated by Chomsky. A survey of the range of universal hypotheses which have been put forward in the two decades since the publication of Chomsky's first book would be far beyond the scope of the present work.

One noteworthy characteristic of this search for universals is that hypotheses are standardly presented in the form of proposals to modify the canonical notation system for linguistic description, or to modify the interpretation of the previously accepted canonical notation. Consider e.g. Chomsky's discussion (1968, pp. 40 ff.) of the so-called 'A-over-A convention'. Briefly, this notion was proposed to account for the fact that, while it is normally possible to form a question from a statement in English by replacing one of the nominal phrases by an interrogative pronoun and moving it to the beginning of the sentence (making certain changes also to the verb and its auxiliaries) – thus sentence (1) below gives (2), if we choose to turn *the boy* into an interrogative – exceptionally, it is *not* possible from (3) to form a question (4).

1 The book interested the boy.
2 Whom did the book interest?
3 He read the book that interested the boy.
4 Whom did he read the book that interested?

Parallel facts can be observed in various other languages. The problem has to do with the fact that the phrase *the boy* in (3), which is the phrase to which the question-formation rules would have to apply in order to give (4), is a nominal phrase which is part of a larger nominal phrase (namely, *the book that interested the boy*), whereas *the boy* in (1) is not included in a larger nominal phrase. Chomsky's suggestion was that, universally, when constituents of the same syntactic type are nested one inside the other a transformation may apply only to the largest: thus, in (3), *the book that interested the boy* may be questioned to give *What did he read?*, but *the boy* alone may not be questioned in (3). In fact the situation has turned out to be rather more complicated than this, but that is beside the point here. What matters is this: Chomsky does not formulate his proposed universal as a prediction that, when we have adequate syntactic descriptions of the world's various languages, it will turn out that in each case rubrics have had to be appended to the transformational rules noting that they apply only to the largest of nested constituents of a given type. Rather, Chomsky argues that (if his hypothesis is correct) we should agree now to interpret the formulae in which transformational rules are expressed in such a way that they are understood automatically as applying only to the largest constituent in such cases, without this needing to be stated explicitly in the published grammars of individual languages.

Comparable theoretical discussions occur in connection with the conventional notation for abbreviating groups of constituency rules (see Chomsky 1965, pp. 42–5). Thus, it is usual to abbreviate a pair of alternative rules of the form '$A \rightarrow B\ C$, $A \rightarrow D\ E\ F$' by means of braces and/or commas: '$A \rightarrow \{B\ C, D\ E\ F\}$'; and rule-pairs such as '$A \rightarrow B\ C, A \rightarrow B\ C\ D$' are commonly abbreviated with brackets: '$A \rightarrow B\ C\ (D)$'. Chomskyan linguists do not discuss whether or not the languages of the world contain syntactic phenomena to which the conventions of abbreviating by means of braces or brackets respectively can usefully be applied; instead, they argue about whether or not the canonical notation system should permit braces and/or brackets.

Historically speaking it is understandable that Chomskyans have come to feel that their theory of universals must be embodied in their notation system. Chomsky began by showing that an accepted notation system (Harris's) presupposed a tacit theory of universals; so, once the theory was made explicit and was modified in certain respects, the natural response seemed to be to make corresponding modifications to the notation. However, from a wider point of view this proceeding is neither particularly natural nor at all desirable. To see its unnaturalness, consider an analogy. It is a universal of geology that all valleys belong to one of two types: flat-bottomed, 'U-shaped' (in cross-section) valleys formed by glacial action, and 'V-shaped' valleys eroded by water. If geologists acted like Chomskyan linguists, they would instruct map-makers to use just two different symbols to represent valley-types, instead of the current system of contour-lines which can indicate far more than two different cross-sectional configurations. Of course geologists do nothing of the sort, and there is no reason why they should: the fact that contour-lines can potentially indicate a wide range of valley-types in maps of particular territories does nothing to hinder the theoretical geologist in observing that only two out of this range actually occur in any territory, or in explaining why this is so.[5]

The reason why the equation of universal theory with notation-system is undesirable is that it tends to inhibit the process of testing and improving the theory. Just suppose that the accepted theory of geology is wrong and that there is in fact a third category of valleys, formed by some previously unsuspected process, which are W-shaped in cross-section, with a low hump in the valley floor. As things are, there is a good chance that geologists might discover this refutation of received theory about valley-formation by noticing that certain maps contain configurations which fit neither the U nor V categories. If, however, they had instructed cartographers to limit themselves to two notations for these two categories, then the theoretical geologists might never discover the inadequacy of their theory. The surveyors out in the field would do their best to fit the W-shaped valleys into the approved notation: they might map them as a pair of V-shaped valleys, and the theoreticians' own instructions would be to blame for the fact that the maps contained no information from which it could be discovered that the humps between these pairs of parallel valleys were less steep than the outer sides, unlike normal V-shaped valleys in which both sides rise at the same angle. If the rightness of a theory is felt to be no longer open to question in practice, then there might be some practical convenience in a description-system which allows for no more possibilities than those recognized by the theory (a map which indicated V-shaped valleys and U-shaped valleys by two discrete symbols might be less cluttered). While the theory is still being worked out and is open to challenge, though, it is desirable for the notation-system to be as flexible as possible so that counter-examples can be recognized and described for what they are.

Of course all systems of description make some assumptions about the things described. Even the cartographers' contour notation is not perfectly flexible – it does not allow for the representation of hypothetical valleys whose sides overhang massively so that the valley floor is wider than the airspace at the top. There are obvious engineering reasons why such valleys are impossible, so this limitation in standard map-notation does no harm. Linguistics is in a different case: the search for the limits of syntactic diversity is a new enterprise, many of the worlds's languages have not been researched in this connection, and there is much disagreement about the interpretation of the evidence already examined. If the search is to succeed, our reaction to inflexibilities in the standard descriptive notation should be to encourage field-workers to be ready to change the notation without ceremony whenever it seems convenient to do so, and we should certainly not strive to confine ourselves to a descriptive technique even more formally regimented than the one we inherited.

The ill effects which I suggested might follow from adoption by geologists of the 'theory equals notation' principle are certainly very noticeable in Chomskyan linguistics. Since the Chomskyan 'revolution' it has become usual for a training in linguistics to focus heavily from the start on mastery of the approved grammatical notation system, and this has become highly elaborate as the theory of linguistic universals has evolved. Such a training obviously encourages the student to see examples, in the languages he examines, of the features he is taught to describe, and to overlook features for which no descriptive means are provided. In other words, it trains him to see confirming instances of the theory of universals and to ignore counter-evidence.

This drawback in Chomskyan linguistics has often been aggravated by an intolerant attitude, on the part of members of this school, towards purely descriptive work. One might suppose that a group concerned to discover universal features of language would be delighted about the existence of other linguists who aim to describe various individual languages for their own sake, and that the 'universalists' would warmly encourage such people to continue their work: such a division of labour means that instead of having to do their own donkey-work out in the field, the 'universalists' get much of the data they need handed them on a plate. But the Chomskyans have not always seen the matter in this light; members of this school have on occasion gone so far as to claim explicitly that purely descriptive lingusitic work simply has no right to exist (see, for example, Schreiber 1974). By contrast with the situation in America before the rise to prominence of the Chomskyan school, during much of the 1960s and 1970s field-work on exotic languages has tended to become a dying art – with obvious adverse consequences for the search for universals. That search, in its relationship to purely descriptive linguistics, may be compared to the work of the theoreticians *vis-à-vis* that of the experimentalists in subjects like physics or chemistry. People who pursue those subjects are well aware that progress in them comes only from a healthy symbiosis between scholars of both categories.

There is an additional reason for the 'theory equals notation' principle, which may excuse the Chomskyans for adopting that principle although it does not reduce the harm caused by it. This has to do with the implications Chomsky believes to flow from the existence of linguistic universals, and we shall now examine those implications before explaining how they connect with the 'theory equals notation' principle.

The reason why Chomsky believes it is important to study universals of human language is the reason why Chomsky's work has attracted great attention in recent years from scholars working in disciplines such as philosophy and psychology, and has made linguistics a subject of much wider public interest than it had ever been before. Chomsky argues that the explanation for the fact that all languages of the world are cut to a common pattern (assuming that they are) is that the inherited structure of Man's mind forces him to use languages of that particular type. Chomsky's Descriptivist predecessors were empiricists, who believed that men are capable of learning as much as they do because the human mind is a thing of great flexibility, capable of accommodating to and finding pattern in the most diverse experiences which may impinge on it. Chomsky, conversely, is a rationalist in the tradition of Plato and Descartes, who believes that the mind is a thing of highly complex fixed structure which largely determines the form of human mental activity: what we can learn depends less on the stimuli that happen to impinge on us than on whether those stimuli are of the appropriate form to trigger off our pre-existing mental potentialities. For an empiricist, there is no general reason to expect any one kind of language to be more natural than another. Chomsky, on the other hand, sees the child's acquisition of language as the filling-in of relatively trivial details in a pre-ordained structural plan; if one tried to teach a child a language not conforming to that plan, Chomsky suggests, then, no matter how 'simple' the language might otherwise be, the child would be innately incapable of mastering it. It is true that hypothetical non-hierarchically-structured 'languages' invariably seem so artificial that one cannot imagine how they could possibly be used as communication-systems in real life, but to make this point does nothing to remove the force of Chomsky's argument; it merely re-states the question which Chomsky claims to answer. We know that non-hierarchical languages are unnatural for humans, and we want to know why: Chomsky claims that the reason is because we are born with minds geared to hierarchical languages.

I have discussed and criticized these general philosophical aspects of Chomsky's work fairly exhaustively elsewhere (*Form of Language, Liberty and Language, Making Sense*); of Chomsky's various statements of his position the most accessible to the general reader are perhaps (1972a) and (1976). Language is for Chomsky only one source of evidence (though it is a particularly clear case) in favour of rationalism as a general view of human nature. (Incidentally, Chomsky's rationalist approach to language very clearly shows the influence of Roman Jakobson, and runs directly counter to the assumptions of all Chomsky's American predecessors without, I believe, a single exception.)

I shall argue at the end of this chapter that Chomsky is correct in holding that there exist certain logically unnecessary (i.e. contingent) universals of linguistic structure, and he may well be right to claim that this is evidence for a rationalist account of mind. But it should be said also that the existence of linguistic universals is, for Chomsky and his followers, not so much a finding which has emerged from their research despite their expectations, but rather a guiding assumption which determines the nature of the hypotheses they propose in order to account for data. The Chomskyans are always eager to suggest an explanation in 'universalist' terms for data which might well have some 'non-universalist' explanation if one were willing to look for it. When such explanations are false they can, of course, be refuted by counter-evidence from other languages, but to find and to publish such counter-evidence takes time. For this reason (and for other reasons to be discussed later), at any given time the Chomskyan school tends to believe in a much richer system of universalist hypotheses than are really warranted.

I shall give one example of this 'rush to universals', which happens to concern phonology rather than syntax but has the advantage of being an especially clear (although not unusual) case. Paul Kiparsky (1971) notes a difference between Biblical Hebrew and Modern Israeli Hebrew. In Biblical Hebrew, the stops [p t k b d g] all alternated with fricative counterparts [f θ x v ð ɣ]; of the latter, only [f x v] survive in modern Hebrew, and Kiparsky proposes a rather subtle universal principle of sound-change to account for that fact. One might of course attack Kiparsky for basing a hypothesis about linguistic universals on a single phenomenon in one language, but in the context of his article this is not wholly unreasonable (he suggests a tenuous similarity with certain phenomena in other languages). The point I want to make here is that there is another explanation, in terms specific to Hebrew rather than in terms of linguistic universals, which Kiparsky does not even consider. For some two millennia between the extinction of Biblical Hebrew and the rise of the modern Zionist movement, Hebrew was a dead language learned by Jews as Englishmen learn Latin. We pronounce Latin not with the alien sounds that Romans no doubt used, but with sounds drawn from our own native tongue. For many centuries past the native language of most of the Ashkenazic (East European) Jews from whom the Zionists drew their membership was German, and German happens to contain the sounds [f x v] but not [θ ð ɣ]. All this is quite well-known, but it is characteristic of the Chomskyan approach to linguistics to ignore the possibility of explaining data by reference to particular concrete external facts in favour of postulating universal, abstract linguistic theories.

Let us return to the principle that the theory of linguistic universals is to be encapsulated in an approved set of notational conventions for describing individual languages. Given Chomsky's rationalist explanation for the existence of linguistic universals, the point of this principle is that it enables us to distinguish clearly between the aspects of linguistic structure which a child 'knows before it starts' and the information which it has to learn through exposure to the speech of its parents and others. The general theory, which prescribes the notation and the proper interpretation of the notation, corresponds to the inherited linguistic faculty; the grammar of an individual language will contain only elements that the individual has to learn. The A-over-A principle for applying transformations is universal, therefore innate, therefore the child does not need to learn it and thus the grammar of English, for example, should not state it explicitly. The convention about use of brackets (say) is appropriately included in the canonical notation scheme if children are pre-programmed to abstract out of experience the particular type of patterning which brackets represent. If children are pre-programmed in that way, then a syntactic structure part of which is describable by a pair of rules such as '$A \rightarrow B\ C, A \rightarrow B\ C\ D$' will be simpler for a child to master than an otherwise similar structure which instead contains, say, '$A \rightarrow B\ C, A \rightarrow E\ F\ G$'. Use of brackets will reflect that relative simplicity by allowing the former pair of rules to be shortened to '$A \rightarrow B\ C\ (D)$' while the latter pair cannot be written so compactly. Thus, once the correct theory of linguistic universals has been discovered and has been embodied in a corresponding notation system, the relative 'naturalness' for humans of a given hypothetical or real language should correlate directly with the length of the shortest possible description of that language allowed by the canonical notation. (Cf. Sampson 1976 and Hurford 1977 for discussion.) This constitutes a motive for the 'theory equals notation' principle which has no analogue in the geological case, although, as already said, that motive does nothing to mitigate the harmful effects of the principle.

Many scholars do linguistic research without necessarily being greatly interested in the general philosophies of human nature presupposed respectively by Chomsky and by his empiricist predecessors. Perhaps the most salient and pervasive difference between Chomskyan linguistics and the linguistics of the Descriptivist school is an issue, separate from the matters already discussed (although related to them), of research method. According to Chomsky, the appropriate source of data for the linguistic analysis of a language is the introspective judgement of speakers of the language. (For references to various statements of this point of view by Chomsky and his followers, see, for example, Botha 1968, p. 70; Labov 1971; Derwing 1973, pp. 40–2; my *Form*, p. 202.) When a Descriptivist said that some sequence of words was a sentence of English and should therefore be handled by a grammar of English, ·he meant, roughly speaking, 'I believe that I have encountered cases of this kind uttered by speakers of English, and if anyone disputes this I am prepared to look for documentary evidence to back up my claim.' When a Chomskyan says that some sequence is grammatical in English, on the other hand, he means, roughly speaking, 'This sentence feels right to me as a speaker of the language; and the possibility of disagreement does not really arise, because my introspections are authoritative at least for my own "dialect" [i.e. idiolect] of English, which is what I am describing.' To use data from introspection rather than fieldwork takes much of the effort out of linguistic research, and at the same time reduces the chances of having one's analysis proved wrong (at least by one's own standards); for both these reasons, Chomsky's methodology has attracted many linguists who care relatively little about his claims concerning inherited mental structure.

The saving of effort is greatest if one uses one's own introspections about one's native language. It is much less noticeable if one works on an 'exotic' language, because the effort of training a member of another culture to recognize his grammatical introspections and to report on them coherently is comparable with the effort of fieldwork in the old style, in which one was supposed to 'accept everything the native speaker says in his language and nothing he says about it'. Therefore the Chomskyan school has tended to concentrate on English and a few closely related European languages at the cost of spending much less time than the Descriptivists on exotic languages. Again, it is obvious that this policy would considerably reduce the chances of successfully developing a theory of linguistic *universals*, even if introspection were acceptable as a basis for the analysis of any particular language.

It is perhaps understandable that Chomsky believes introspection to be an acceptable source of evidence: this is a corollary of his rationalism. The essence of philosophical rationalism is the idea that knowledge is in us from the beginning, and 'learning' means merely learning to recognize and articulate what was in our minds already – observation of the outside world is more or less irrelevant. (Chomsky is quite explicit about the relationship between his approach to linguistics and the philosophical rationalism of Plato and Descartes; see, for example, Chomsky 1966; 1976, pp. 6–8.) But although it may be understandable that Chomsky makes the mistake he does, one cannot take very seriously the extension of philosophical rationalism to the question of linguistic methodology. Even extreme rationalist philosophers recognize that one knows many factual matters only from experience – Descartes would not have suggested that I had inborn knowledge of what colour dress my wife would wear today, for instance. Clearly any speaker knows a fair number of truths about his language – even an empiricist would be surprised if he did not, considering the opportunities he has had to observe it. But if we ask in a spirit of honest enquiry whether speakers have access to an interior source of authoritative truths about either their personal idiolects or the larger languages spoken by their community, then by all the tests one can think of the answer is a clear 'no'; in the case of syntax, speakers' knowledge in the 'know-that' sense comes nowhere near to matching their 'know-how'. Speakers are often straightforwardly, and startlingly, wrong in their sincere convictions about even the most elementary facts of their own languages. (As mentioned earlier, this has been established most convincingly by William Labov, e.g. 1971, 1975; cf. Snow and Meijer 1977.) And the syntactic introspections of linguists themselves are likely to be the least reliable of all, since (unlike the average speaker of a language) the linguist has a vested interest in the correctness of particular syntactic judgements. A linguist half-sees that it would be convenient for him if some particular, fairly unusual sequence of words were grammatical, perhaps because it enables him to make some part of his grammar of English especially elegant, or because it constitutes a counter-example to some well-entrenched theory of universals and thus leads to fame for him as the David who overturns the theory; he mulls the word-sequence over in his mind for a while and pretty soon, lo and behold! he perceives (quite sincerely) a clear intuitive conviction that the string is indeed grammatical (in 'his dialect'). This sort of thing occurs over and over again in the linguistics of the Chomskyan school, and obviously the results of such 'research' are valueless. Thus, ironically, while Chomsky showed how syntactic analysis could be a scientific discipline by propounding the notion of grammaticality in a language as a property whose extension is well-defined though infinite, by advocating introspective methodology he simultaneously ensured that syntactic analysis ceased to *be* scientific in practice. Fortunately the solution to this problem is simple, if linguists can be persuaded to adopt it: they should stop writing grammars to generate the strings they feel to be grammatical and instead base their grammars on what they observe to be uttered in speech and/or writing. (Some Chomskyans have suggested that there are reasons of principle why 'objective' grammars of this kind cannot be produced, but those suggestions are naïve: cf. *Form*, ch. 4.)

It is important to realize that, for Chomsky, introspection is not just a supplementary source of linguistic data but actually has an authority which is denied to observation; where the two conflict, according to Chomsky it is introspection which should determine the nature of the linguist's grammar. Even a Descriptivist uses introspection as a 'short cut', rather than attempting to document every single remark he makes about a language with which he is familiar; but if any particular remark is challenged, the Descriptivist will look for objective evidence to back up his claim (rather than waste time discussing the strength of his introspective feeling), and this is all we demand of an empirical science. For Chomsky, an appeal to objective evidence in such a situation would be inappropriate. We have seen Chomsky using the terms 'competence' and 'performance' to distinguish a language as a system from individual exemplifications of the system; but he uses these terms also in another way. (Equivocation on 'competence' and 'performance' is a major source of problems in Chomsky's thought, and it is unfortunate that such confused concepts have been taken up as widely as they have; cf. Fodor and Garrett 1966; Moravcsik 1969.) There are many cases where a grammar will generate some 'sentence' that nobody would actually utter, e.g. because it is too long to be used in practice; in such cases. Chomsky argues that the sentence is 'in our competence' – it is grammatical in the sense that we allegedly 'feel' it to be grammatical – even though it is not observed in our 'performance'. That is, 'competence' is here the class of strings corresponding to the 'ideal' language, in an almost Platonic sense, while 'performance' is the class of strings occurring in the imperfect language actually spoken in this sublunary world.

In many cases Chomsky is correct in saying that there will be a discrepancy between the predictions of a linguist's grammar, taken in isolation, and observed speech; however, these discrepancies argue not for the use of introspective data, but for the principle that (since our various beliefs and theories affect one another's predictions) they should not be considered in isolation from one another, which is a standard principle of empirical science (*Form*, p. 66). Thus, it is an empirically confirmed fact that the duration of human beings' attention-span is limited, and this leads to predictions about maximum length of utterable sentences which will often override the linguist's prediction that some long sequence conforms to the grammatical patterns found in observed shorter sentences and is therefore itself utterable. In other cases (cf. page 180) there is no empirical justification for the discrepancies between the 'ideal language' generated by Chomsky's grammar and the real, observable language, i.e. the Chomskyan grammar is simply wrong.

Chomsky's error about method is in fact precisely the same as the behaviourist fallacy discussed in Chapter 3, except that Chomsky commits the fallacy in reverse. The 'bad behaviourists' reasoned that, because it was forbidden to the scientist to use introspective evidence, therefore there was nothing to introspect. Chomsky holds (rightly, although his rationalism perhaps leads him to lay special emphasis on the point) that we have complex minds with a life of their own to which introspection gives us access, and he infers that it is acceptable to use introspection as evidence in scientific theorizing. Each of these arguments is as bad as the other. The objection to introspective evidence in science is not that there are no such things as introspections, but rather that introspection, while just as fallible as observation, cannot be constructively criticized as reports of observations can. Where a dispute between rival theorists turns on conflicting introspections, there is no method of resolving the dispute short of a shouting-match; the virtue of the scientific method is that, in those intellectual areas to which it is applicable (which include the study of syntax), it gives mankind a means of rising above shouting-matches.

'Shouting-matches' in the literal sense are happily rare even among Chomskyan linguists, but what is noticeable in that school is that a smallish group of scholars who have succeeded in attracting public attention (whether by force of personality, known intimacy with the founder of the school, or in other ways) are invested with an exaggerated aura of authority, so that their lightest speculations are taken as significant contributions to scholarship while the work of others is largely ignored. (This phenomenon is discussed, for example, by Anttila, 1975; Householder 1978, p. 170; Newman 1978, p. 927.) When correspondence with observation is systematically ruled out as a criterion for choice between theories, it is inevitable that it will be replaced by the criterion of relative charisma of the respective theorists – will be replaced, in fact, by a resurrection of the medieval system of arguments from authority.

One practical difficulty for anyone who believes, with Chomsky, that the data for a grammar should be drawn from introspection is to decide just what categories of fact about his native language a speaker is supposed to be able to introspect. All Chomskyans agree that one can 'intuit' the grammatical status of particular strings of words, but most go much further than this. Chomsky, for instance, has never given syntactic evidence (as Harris did) for the range of form-classes which appear in his grammars: he simply intuits that the terms we inherit from the Alexandrians (Noun, Verb, etc.) are the correct ones.[6] Some writers seem to suggest that we can introspect the 'surface-structure' trees associated with our sentences but not their 'deep structures' (of course, the ordinary speaker untrained in linguistics needs careful prompting to help him articulate his syntactic introspections, but this is not taken as refuting the idea that he 'knew' the facts all along – cf. Langendoen 1969, ch. 2; linguists' classrooms differ from courts of law in having no rule against leading questions). Understandably, the question is very rarely discussed explicitly.[7] I believe that one reason for Chomskyan impatience with purely descriptive work is that the logical conclusion of Chomsky's views on method would be that speakers can ultimately introspect everything about the grammar of their language, so that description of an individual language consists merely of rehashing 'what every speaker knows' and only the theory of linguistic universals involves genuine addition to the total of human knowledge. (However, one Chomskyan has even suggested that we have authoritative intuitions about linguistic universals – Bach 1974, pp. 165–6; and indeed this might seem to follow from Chomsky's doctrine of linguistic universals as corresponding to innate knowledge of language.)

One special consequence of Chomsky's introspectionist methodology has to do with semantics.

As we saw in Chapter 3, Bloomfield quite rightly felt that the semantic structure of a language was not open, at least in practice, to scientific investigation. Syntax is about the membership of word-sequences in a language, and we can check this objectively by listening to the sequences speakers utter. Semantics is about the chains of inference which allow us to pass from one set of beliefs or hypotheses to others. Here the only observables are the end-points of the chains: a belief will often be induced in a man's mind by his observation of the outside world (which we can observe at the same time), and conversely a man will often reason his way to a conclusion which causes him to act in some observable way. But individual 'inputs' and 'outputs' are commonly linked by such long chains of reasoning that there is no practical possibility of reconstructing the intermediate steps on the basis of objective data about the end-points – each particular intermediate step is wholly unobservable (we cannot observe a man inferring *Mary's neighbour is male* from *Mary's neighbour is a bachelor*).[8]

One point not understood by Bloomfield was that the problem is more than just a practical difficulty about the indirectness of 'input/output' relationships. Philosophers such as Karl Popper (1945), Willard Quine (1951), Ludwig Wittgenstein (1953), Russell Hanson (1958) and Jonathan Cohen (1962) have shown us that, *even if individual inferences could be observed*, the semantic structure of a language still could not be treated scientifically because it is not fixed. An Englishman constructs sentences according to syntactic rules which remain (to a close approximation) constant over time and as between speakers; but in choosing how to move inferentially from one sentence to another we regularly make up and continually modify the rules as we go along. The question 'Does *Mary's neighbour is a bachelor* entail *Mary's neighbour is male*?' is more like the question 'Is this figure beautiful?' than like the question 'Is this figure circular?' – the class of valid inferences in any real language (as opposed to artifical 'languages' constructed by logicians) is not a well-defined class, it is constantly modified unpredictably by men's creative intelligence. Therefore the semantic structure of a language can be discussed only in the anecdotal, non-predictive fashion proper to arts subjects, rather than analysed scientifically – not just because the data are unavailable but because, if objective evidence were available, it would immediately refute *any* analysis that might be proposed.

This point has never been grasped by Chomskyan linguists, even though they cannot plead, as a defender of Bloomfield can, that the philosophical point was made after their time. One reason for this is that Chomsky himself (together with many of his followers) subscribes to what has been called the fallacy of 'scientism' (Hayek 1955) – he imagines that any subject which can be discussed at all can be treated by the scientific method (cf. Mehta 1971, p. 212).[9] But Chomsky's introspectionist methodology is also a contributory factor in his misunderstanding of the nature of semantics. When a native speaker introspects about the syntax of his language, he produces more-or-less sketchy, vague approximations to the truth; Chomsky argues that there is a complex, precise, fully articulated syntactic structure to which these hints approximate, and he is right, although we have no reason to suppose that the speaker tacitly 'knows' that structure. If one asks a speaker to introspect about the meanings of his words he again produces sketchy, vague, rough statements, and it is natural that Chomskyans again imagine there to be a precise, complete statement waiting to be articulated; but in the semantic case there is not. A linguist with a well-trained introspective faculty can of course set about *creating* a 'scientific theory' which purports to describe the semantics of his language, and many Chomskyan linguists from J. J. Katz and J. A. Fodor (1963) onwards have done so. But the writers just quoted, and many other members of the Chomskyan school (including its founder), have failed to take the first step of realizing that the aim of semantic description is to state the relationships of inference which hold between sentences. They have supposed instead that the aim is to *translate* sentences into an artificial language which is somehow semantically more transparent than the ordinary languages people actually speak, and they 'intuit' that simple words in everyday languages correspond to complexes of 'components' or 'semantic markers' in this 'conceptual language'. This approach seems so fundamentally misguided that it is difficult to find any virtues at all in the theories produced in accordance with it; these theories cannot be *disproved*, because they make no testable claims – they are just empty. To my mind there is no aspect of the Chomskyans' treatment of semantics, including the long debates about the so-called 'generative v. interpretative semantics' controversy, in which the positions adopted by the scholars in question are clear enough to merit examination in a book of this kind. (I criticize the Chomskyan approach to semantics at length in my *Making Sense*.)

Given what I have said so far about the general characteristics of the Chomskyan school, the reader may be surprised to hear that it has gained such a complete ascendancy, and especially to hear that it has been accepted as authoritative by the many scholars who are more interested in description of particular languages than in the search for universals. (Many even of these people feel obliged nowadays to apologize for their imperfect Chomskyanization, like practitioners of art for art's sake behind the Iron Curtain; cf. Hagège 1976, pp. 10 ff.) Here again the answer lies largely in the contrast between rationalist and empiricist methodology. Empiricism tells us to regard our opinions as fallible, and continually to seek counter-evidence to them; rationalism tells us that we are born with true knowledge already in us. This difference of approach operates at all levels: not just in the analysis of English syntax, say, but equally in debates about the theoretical and methodological foundations of the discipline. In general, empiricist philosophy encourages one always to think 'I may be wrong, and the other man may well be right'; rationalism encourages one to think 'I know the truth, so the only point in talking to the other man is in order to show him the light.' When scholars of these contrasting frames of mind encounter one another, it is clear which man is likely to win the debate.[10]

It is no accident that many linguists of the Chomskyan school have enthusiastically embraced Thomas Kuhn's doctrine of the history of science as a series of 'Gestalt switches' or 'conversion experiences', in each of which no reasoned grounds can be assigned for the adoption of the new intellectual 'paradigm' and the old 'paradigm' has disappeared ultimately only because its remaining adherents died out (Percival 1976). Kuhn's claim resembles the claim that social change has often occurred through political revolution. The constitutionalist's reply is, 'Yes, since people are not political saints that has often happened, but such changes have been for the worse as often as for the better; how much greater genuine progress would have occurred if reformers had always worked within the legal framework of a liberal constitution' (the latter being the political equivalent of an agreed method for selecting between rival theories on their merits by reference to interpersonally-sharable considerations). The thoroughgoing rationalist, however, is obliged to prefer revolution to constitutional reform (in science and in politics): if the correctness of a theory, or the desirability of a form of society, is knowable by the pure light of reason rather than by practical experiment, then no means of peaceful persuasion are available when an opponent obstinately persists in claiming to see things differently. Naturally, those Chomskyan linguists who follow Kuhn, like political revolutionaries, lay much more stress on the notion that it is legitimate for them to come to power through an irrational Kuhnian 'paradigm-shift' than on the corollary that an irrational paradigm-shift which unseated them would have to be accepted as equally legitimate.

Another consequence of the contrast between rationalist and empiricist intellectual styles is a tendency for Chomskyan linguists to abandon the principle that science is cumulative. An empiricist scholar takes it for granted that, although his predecessors in any given field may well have been wrong in many ways, he is able to progress as far as he can only because of the work they have already done. We advance in knowledge by criticizing and replacing elements of the framework of ideas we inherit from previous generations, and a person who was taught nothing by his elders and was thus forced to work out his structure of ideas completely from scratch would never get beyond the cave-man stage. The rationalist does not see matters that way; he thinks of the individual as 'inheriting' true knowledge in the genetic sense, the main problem being to draw out into the open knowledge which is already there inside one – the thought of previous generations is redundant insofar as it is correct, and merely misleading where it is wrong. Accordingly, we find that the leading scholars of the Chomskyan school display unusual reluctance to acknowledge any virtue in studying the works of predecessors (or, for that matter, contemporaries) of other schools – an attitude which differentiates the Chomskyans as a group from all other schools of linguistics. (See the references to Householder 1978, and Newman 1978, already cited above.) Since humans do not in fact have innate knowledge about linguistic theory, the consequence of this is that much research by members of the Chomskyan school, even when it is not vitiated by reliance on fallacious introspective judgements, consists of time-wasting rediscovery of facts or principles that had long been common knowledge outside the Chomskyan camp. (It should be said in fairness that this tendency is less noticeable in Chomsky's own work than in that of many of his associates.)

I shall quote just one example of this: Morris Halle's 'Prolegomena to a theory of word formation' (Halle 1973). Halle's article is on the theory of morphology (i.e. the organization of morphemes into words, as contrasted with syntax which strictly speaking deals with the arrangement of complete words in sentences);[11] and Halle begins by claiming that the subject 'has been studied only to a very limited extent'. Now Halle is no half-trained neophyte; he is the Chairman of Chomsky's department at MIT, and was elected President of the Linguistic Society of America (the highest honour which the American linguistic community can bestow on one of its number) for the year after his article appeared. But the fact is that there is a vast published literature on morphology (written by scholars who do not belong to the Chomskyan school), although Halle ignores it completely. In a critique of Halle's article, Leonhard Lipka (1975) concludes:

has Halle brought up any problems which have not already been treated, or proposed any solution for such problems which [has] not been offered elsewhere? It seems that the answer . . . is no.[12]

When I say that rationalism encourages scholars to ignore the work of their predecessors, I mean only that the general frame of mind induced by rationalist assumptions promotes this attitude – certainly I do not suggest that, if René Descartes were alive today, he would explicitly argue that it is desirable for linguists of the Chomskyan school to cut themselves off from others' researches. Chomskyan linguists may object that my account of them is unfair because they know better than to confuse rationalism as a specific thesis about the nature of mind with rationalism as a very general attitude to scholarship. To this there are two answers. To my mind, the methodological matters discussed in the last paragraphs are much more closely related to Descartes's rationalism than are points (such as the 'A-over-A principle') which Chomsky explicitly claims to be known independently of experience as Cartesian 'innate ideas'. But in any case, if the Chomskyans were to defend themselves as I have just suggested, they would need to give their own explanation of why they are so unusually turned in on themselves intellectually, because about that fact there can scarcely be any dispute.

Whether because the rationalist frame of mind induces in scholars an impatience with the usual disciplines of academic publication, or merely because new technology has made the development possible, one further salient phenomenon associated with the rise of the Chomskyan school has been the spread of what is sometimes called 'underground' or 'samizdat' publication in linguistics, whereby individuals who have failed to get their work accepted (or failed to get it published quickly enough) by standard scholarly journals arrange for the material to be distributed, in mimeographed or photocopied form, through various more or less informal channels. Scholars have always sent their colleagues copies of forthcoming articles for comment, of course, but previously such informal dissemination of ideas did not 'count'; it was merely a preparation for the fully public advancement of knowledge by way of properly printed journal-articles and books. Within the Chomskyan school of linguistics, however, 'underground publication' counts for a great deal, and much has been felt to hang on whether or not one was on the mailing-list of the scholars whose reputation stands highest (cf. McCawley 1976, p. 2). There have been cases of linguists who are accepted as having established a secure scholarly reputation almost entirely on the basis of articles distributed in this informal fashion.[13] The problem about this style of scholarship is that 'underground' work does not normally attempt to meet the standards expected by responsible academic publishing houses or editors of reputable journals; it is regarded as quite permissible in a 'Working Paper' or 'Report of Research in Progress' to omit the hard grind of checking details of data, verifying the references, dealing exhaustively with recalcitrant counter-examples, and the like. As Hagège points out (1976, p. 35), when the ideas of these scholars are successful they take the credit, but when their work turns out to be thoroughly bad they shrug if off as never having been meant very seriously anyway.

For all the reasons discussed in the preceding paragraphs, members of the Chomskyan school (together with onlookers who take them at their own self-evaluation) usually have an exaggerated impression of how much this school has actually discovered about language. A not untypical view is expressed by Paul Postal (1972, pp. 161–2), who says (referring to Otto Jespersen's monumental seven-volume *Modern English Grammar*, published over the forty-year period 1909–49): 'of course we [Chomskyans] have probably uncovered since the early sixties [i.e. in less than a decade – Postal's paper was originally given as a talk in 1969] more new facts than could be put in a dozen works like Jespersen's biggest'. If Postal is referring purely to the physical quantity of documents circulated by members of his school, then certainly he is right. It is so much easier to do research in the Chomskyan style that far more has been done by Chomskyans than by other schools in a comparable length of time. But the overwhelming majority of the 'facts' Postal has in mind simply are not facts at all.

In many (perhaps most) cases they concern sentences which are claimed to be 'ungrammatical' where what is really meant is that the writer has not succeeded in thinking of a situation in which the sentence would make sense. In his first book, *Syntactic Structures* (1957), Chomsky was careful to draw the distinction between ungrammatical word-sequences and sentences which are nonsensical but syntactically well formed – his famous example of the latter category was *Colourless green ideas sleep furiously*. To call a word-sequence ungrammatical is to say that it simply does not conform to the structural norms of the language, which seems to be a yes-or-no matter; to say that a sequence is nonsensical is to say that it *does* conform to those norms, but that one cannot see any use for that individual example – which is a comment about one's own powers of imagination rather than about the language. (Not surprisingly, the implied challenge was soon taken up in the *Colourless green ideas* case: Harman 1974, p. 1.) But Chomsky soon reversed himself on this issue in practice (*Form*, pp. 80 ff.), and few if any of his followers have ever taken much account of the ungrammaticality/nonsensicality distinction (probably because, although the distinction is of great importance methodologically, our introspective faculty seems rather insensitive to it).

In many other cases, Chomskyans' new 'facts' are genuinely beliefs about the syntactic rather than semantic status of a sentence, but the beliefs are based purely on introspection and are as likely to be false as true. When the 'facts' are statements about linguistic universals rather than about an individual language, in most cases they are hypotheses which were once put forward tentatively but have long since been abandoned even by their author (the informal style of publication common among the Chomskyans makes it difficult to discover which proposals have been retracted). And even 'facts' about linguistic universals which have stood the test of criticism of the kind practised by the Chomskyan community usually turn out never to have been tested against observational evidence, so that they can hardly be regarded as facts in any ordinary sense.

It is true that there are a number of linguists working today who regard themselves as belonging to the Chomskyan rather than to any other school, but who either base their linguistic analyses on documentary evidence, or, if they do not go as far as that (since nowadays it does not do to give people a chance to call one an empiricist), at least use intuitions exclusively about categories of fact which in principle could be checked against observation and which seem very likely correct. (No one denies that we have many true intutions about our native language; the empiricist insists only that such intuitions must not be treated as authoritative.) But the more 'respectable' (by empiricist standards) these scholars are, the less specifically Chomskyan their work is – particularly since those who are most empiricist in their method tend to make relatively few claims about universals. The best of these scholars are to all intents and purposes continuing the Bloomfieldian, Descriptivist tradition without acknowledging the fact; and there would probably be many more like them, if Descriptivist linguistics had not been given such a bad name.

Clearly, the ascendancy of the Chomskyan school has been a very unfortunate development for the discipline of linguistics. It has occupied many men's attention and has produced a very large corpus of doctrine, and people naturally feel that this work cannot, surely, all have been in vain; but people no doubt felt similarly about astrology or alchemy when these were flourishing activities, yet we know they were wrong. Is there nothing, then, to be saved from the wreck?

In fact I believe there is; but it has very little to do with the mass of activity by a plethora of scholars over the last twenty years, because it was already stated, about as adequately as it ever has been since, in Chomsky's first book. What I have in mind is the special role of hierarchical structure in the syntax of all human languages. The significant point in Chomsky's *Syntactic Structures* is not the claim that human languages are generated by transformational grammars, which is very possibly a vacuous claim and is in any case not very well confirmed even if empirical; what matters is the statement that, at least to a very close approximation, all human languages can be generated by constituency grammars, and that there is no reason in logic why that should have to be so. It is mathematically proven that many 'languages', in the sense of well-defined classes of morpheme-sequences, cannot be generated by constituency grammars; and I would be prepared to argue that constituency notation is not just very nearly but completely adequate to generate any human language (*Form*, pp. 205–6). If that is so, then Chomsky is right to claim that human languages are all 'cut to a common pattern'; and he *may* be right to infer from this that our species inherits complex, non-plastic psychological machinery which largely determines the structure of our mental life.[14]

The hypothesis that all human languages have constituency grammars can be tested against purely observational evidence, by attempting to construct such grammars to generate the ranges of utterances which we hear or read produced by speakers of different languages in their unstudied moments. As I say, confirmation of the hypothesis might justify Chomsky in adopting a rationalist rather than empiricist theory of the human mind. But nothing about such a discovery could conceivably justify us in abandoning empiricism as a *scientific methodology*; to confuse empiricism as a theory with empiricism as a method is a naïve fallacy.

And certainly nothing in Chomsky's argument for rationalist theory justifies the way in which, for a decade or more, the energies not just of a few enthusiasts but of almost an entire discipline have been diverted away from the task of recording and describing the various facets of the diverse languages of the world, each in its own terms, towards that of fitting every language into a single, sterile formal framework, which often distorts those aspects of a language to which it is at all relevant, and which encourages the practitioner to overlook completely the many aspects of language with which it is not concerned. This has been simply a wrong track taken by linguistics. Happily, in the late 1970s there are many signs that the discipline is returning to a more healthy, pluralist mood. 'Some welcome breezes are blowing now across the formal desolation', to quote one scholar who never succumbed to the orthodoxy (Bolinger 1977, p. 519).

7 Relational grammar: Hjelmslev, Lamb, Reich

Language, Saussure said (1916, p. 113) is 'a form, not a substance'. The only 'things' that have any concrete existence in connection with language are, on the one hand, speech-sound – which is not part of a given language, but a physical phenomenon exploited in different ways by the various languages of the world; and on the other hand, perhaps, meaning: the ideas, concepts, and/or outside-world objects and properties which languages are used to express and to denote, and which may be claimed also to exist independently of individual languages (we shall not pursue this latter, highly controversial point here). The realms of speech-sound and of meaning are inherently formless, unstructured; a given language imposes a particular structure on each, but the structural elements of a language are not independent 'things' so much as labels for relationships between bits of sound and/or bits of meaning. No English-speaker ever utters the phoneme / l /. He sometimes utters the sound [l], sometimes the sound [lʷ], and sometimes other sounds; to speak of the English phoneme / l / is an abbreviated way of referring to the fact that the sounds [l] and [lʷ] are in complementary distribution in English, and that the two sounds between them contrast with the other sounds uttered by English-speakers. And the question of what particular extra-linguistic meanings or sounds occur as terminals of the system of relationships which make up a language is irrelevant to the identity of that language: English is still English whether spoken, written, or transmitted in Morse, just as chess played with marked pieces of paper instead of wooden men is still the same game. 'Initially the concept is nothing, that is only a value determined by its relations with other similar values, and . . . without them the signification would not exist'; 'phonemes are characterized not . . . by their own positive quality but simply by the fact that they are distinct . . . [they are] opposing, relative, and negative entities' (Saussure 1916, pp. 117, 119).

Yet linguistics as it developed in practice in the decades after Saussure did hypostatize large numbers of theoretical entities of diverse categories which languages were said to contain. Indeed, traditional approaches to language had always done so: the idea that a language contained phonemes, morphemes, and perhaps some other 'emes' was new, but the idea that it contained words, for instance, was very old. Was there not a contradiction between the claim that a language consisted purely of relationships between 'things' that themselves lay outside the language, and the notion that languages were to be described as systems of thousands of 'things' of various sorts?

One scholar who felt that there was a contradiction here was the Dane, Louis Hjelmslev (1899–1965). I turn to his ideas at this point in the book because they have led in recent years to what is perhaps the most interesting radical alternative on the contemporary linguistic scene to Chomsky's theory of language.[1]

According to Hjelmslev, language manifests two distinctions, form v. substance and content v. expression (the latter pair of terms refers to the opposition between meaning and speech-sound-or-writing-or-Morse . . .); and these distinctions intersect one another to produce four 'strata', namely content-substance, content-form, expression-form, and expression-substance, of which the middle two belong to language proper and the first and last are the external realities which it is the task of a language to link with one another. A language consists purely of relationships: 'external' relationships between elements in different strata, and 'internal' relationships between the elements in one stratum, but, except for the sounds and meanings in the two outer strata, the 'elements' between which these relationships obtain *are themselves relationships* – there is nothing else. A truly general, pure theory of language will discuss only the various possible categories of relationship which may obtain in language, ignoring the properties of extralinguistic 'substance'.

All this is highly abstruse, not to say airy-fairy, in a way that seems characteristic of a certain style of Continental scholarship; the empirical-minded English-speaking reader will feel that the proof of the pudding lies in the eating, and will wait to see what Hjelmslev's ideas imply in practice for the analysis of actual languages. It must be said at once that, as far as Hjelmslev's own work is concerned, his wait will be in vain. Hjelmslev did not develop his theory by applying it to any serious extent to the description of concrete linguistic facts, but rather by elaborating a highly complex, sparsely illustrated terminology for describing hypothetical relationships of various kinds (see e.g. Hjelmslev 1943), while his collaborator Uldall worked out an equally or more abstruse system of algebraic symbolism for the same purpose (Uldall 1957). There does exist one book-length linguistic description whose author see himself as working within the Hjelmslevian framework, namely Knud Togeby's *Structure immanente de la langue française* (1951), but apart from a few pieces of jargon there is little in Togeby's account that could not have been written by a linguist of another school. Hjelmslev himself seems to have felt about the real world rather as some people feel about alcohol, that while it might be all right in its place he personally had little time for it; consider, for instance, the claim he makes at one point – with no suggestion of deliberate paradox – that there may well in the past have existed languages which never had any speakers (1963, p. 84). All in all, it is difficult not to read a heavy irony into Hjelmslev's criticism of his predecessors' work in linguistics as 'dilettantish and aprioristic theorizing' (1943, p. 7).

Much more interesting than Hjelmslev's own work is the development it received at the hands of the American Sydney Lamb (b. 1929), formerly of the University of California at Berkeley and since 1964 at Yale, and of Lamb's follower Peter Reich, of the University of Toronto.

Lamb (see Lamb 1966; Lockwood 1972) begins by listing a few simple, common types of relationship that obtain between units in a language. One relation is that of *alternation*, where a given unit at a 'higher' (nearer meaning) level is realized (either indifferently, or depending on circumstances) as one of several alternative elements at a 'lower' (nearer sound) level; if we accept that *go* and *move* are close synonyms, then we may say that a single 'meaning-unit' LOCOMOTE is realized alternately as the lexical item *go* or the lexical item *move*. (The notion of 'meaning-unit' or, in Lamb's terminology, 'sememe', symbolized here by small capitals, is of course philosophically speaking very naïve and crude; and indeed the whole notion of a stratum of 'content-substance' is highly questionable – cf. Uldall 1957, pp. 26–7; Lyons 1962. I prefer to pass over this point here, however, since Lamb's treatment of meaning is no worse, though it is no better, than Chomsky's or almost any other linguist's, and I wish to concentrate on the more positive, worthwhile aspects of Lamb's work.) Similarly, the units *under* and *beneath* might be viewed as alternative realizations of a semantic unit LOWER THAN. The opposite of alternation is *neutralization*, in which a single lower-level unit represents either of two or more higher-level units. Thus the lexical item *move* may represent the meaning-unit LOCOMOTE, but it may alternatively stand for the specialized meaning which it has in *I move that these minutes be accepted* – say, PUT A MOTION. Alternation and neutralization are both what Lamb calls 'or-relations': element A at one level corresponds to element B *or* element C *or* element D at another level. 'Or-relations' contrast with 'and-relations'. Thus, in *composite realization*, one higher-level unit is realized as a sequence or set of lower-level units. For instance, the simple meaning-unit UNDERGO is realized in English as the morpheme *under* followed by the morpheme *go*, although the meanings which these units have as independent lexical items have little or nothing to do with the meaning of the combination; one can tell that *undergo* consists of two morphemes, rather than constituting a single morpheme parts of which happen to resemble other morphemes, from the fact that it conjugates irregularly: *undergo/underwent* parallel to *go/went*. The morpheme *under*, in its turn, is realized compositely as a sequence of phonemes / ʌ /, / n /, / d /, / ə /; and the phoneme / d / is realized as the set of phonetic features Alveolar, Stop, and Voiced. The converse of composite realization is *portmanteau realization*, where two higher-level units are jointly realized as a single lower-level unit; thus when the root morpheme *go*, normally / gəu /, is followed by the past-tense morpheme which otherwise appears as / d /, the two are represented by the single morph / went /.

Lamb diagrams these relations, using a triangle for 'and', a square bracket for 'or': thus, the examples just given might in the first instance be diagrammed as in Figure 5 (page 170).

Once we have the diagrams, however, we no longer need the labels for units such as phonemes, morphemes, lexical items, and the like. The 'morpheme' *under* is simply the element which occurs as one of the two unordered lower terminals of relation

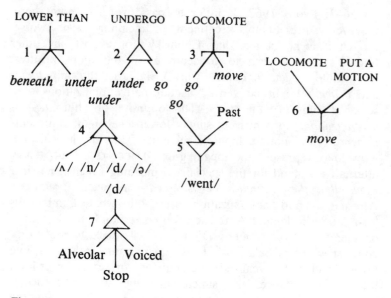

Figure 5

1, as the first lower terminal of relation 2, and as the upper terminal of relation 4; to say which relations this element enters into is to define it completely, and to call it 'the morpheme *under*' adds nothing to our knowledge. Similarly, the 'phoneme / d /' is simply the element which occurs as upper terminal of relation 7 and as third lower terminal of relation 4 (and as a lower terminal of thousands of other and-relations, in a complete description of English). Therefore we may as well drop the labels for elements internal to the language, and show its structure more directly by linking the relation-terminals as appropriate (see Figure 6).

Here the and-nodes and or-nodes numbered 1 to 7 are identical to those with the same numbers in the previous diagram, but five further nodes have been added to represent facts left inexplicit in that diagram. Node 8 shows that the morpheme *under* neutralizes (stands for each of) the semantic unit LOWER THAN and the first portion of the lexical item *undergo*; node 9 shows that the morpheme *go* plays a similar dual role; node 10 shows that the morpheme *go* has alternative allomorphs – it has

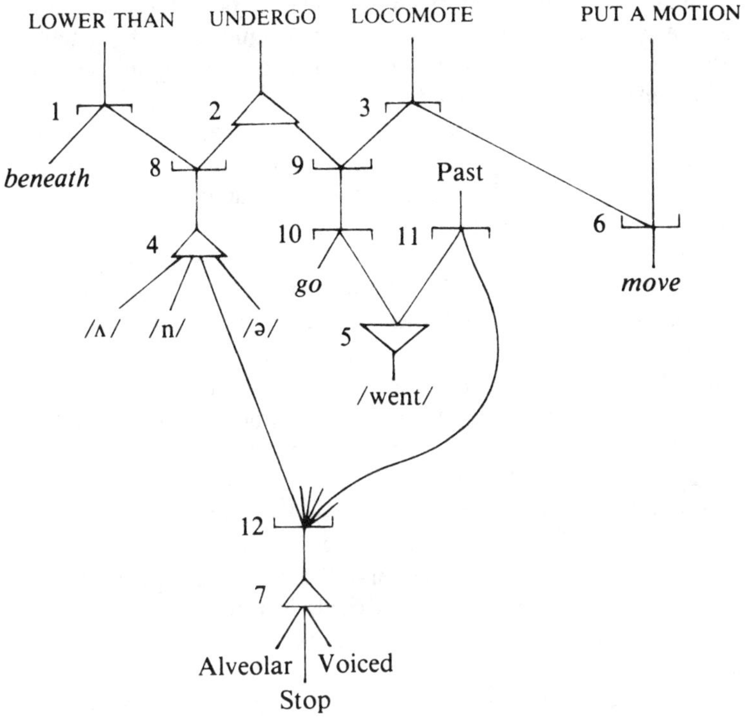

Figure 6

a portmanteau representation with the past-tense suffix, but is represented by a morph of its own (pronounced / gəu /, although this is not shown) in other environments; node 11 shows that the past-tense suffix likewise has alternative representations, and node 12 shows that the non-portmanteau alternative for the past-tense suffix (in a complete description of English this would be just one of the non-portmanteau alternatives) is identical to the third element in the realization of the morpheme *under*. (Node 12 has further lines sprouting from the top to suggest that, in a more complete description of the language, there will be many other morphs realized partly by the phoneme / d /.)

The numbers in the diagram serve only for ease of reference in discussing the diagram, and they can be eliminated without changing what the diagram tells us about the English language. Similarly, the remaining labels for linguistic units, such as *beneath*, / ʌ /, etc., can be eliminated by adding further lines and nodes showing how those elements are realized. Thus it ought ultimately to be possible to represent all the realizational relations in a language as a whole in terms of a (very complex) network having labels for semantic units at the top, labels for phonetic features at the bottom, and nothing in between but nodes representing relationships and lines linking those relationships. In this context, 'entities' such as phonemes and morphemes really are nothing more than convenient but inessential mnemonic devices for talking about the relationships: thus the 'morpheme *under*' is just a name for the line linking nodes 8 and 4, 'phoneme / d /' is a name for the line linking nodes 12 and 7, and the lines and nodes are what they are irrespective of whether one gives them names or not.[2]

What virtues are there in charting languages as networks of pure relationships in this way? Quite a number.[3]

In the first place, as a general theory of language Lambian grammar scores heavily over its rivals in terms of simplicity. All sciences aim to reduce complex observed phenomena to simple, elegant theories. To say that Lamb's theory is 'simple' in this sense does not mean that a Lambian grammar is easy for a newcomer to understand, or anything of that sort; in fact the tangled skeins of lines and nodes that Lamb uses to represent the structures of a language are at least as baffling, to the non-initiate, as the sequences of quasi-mathematical formulae which occur in a Chomskyan grammar, but Lamb, like Chomsky, quite rightly regards this as irrelevant to the scientific status of his theory. Rather, the simplicity we look for in a scientific theory is something like fewness of elementary concepts employed; and in this respect Lamb beats Chomsky hands down. Chomskyan linguistic theory uses many diverse theoretical concepts at different points: 'constituency rule', 'transformational rule', ·'phonological rule', 'constituency-marker', 'phonetic feature matrix', 'lexical entry' are only a few of the more obvious, and most of these – 'trans-formational rule' being a particularly clear case in point – are themselves complex ideas which have ultimately to be spelled out in terms of numerous more basic concepts. Lamb, on the other hand, defines only a few very elementary kinds of relationship which occur at all linguistic levels, as represented by the differently shaped nodes (there are more types of node than mentioned above, but not many more – perhaps half a dozen or so in all) together with the simple notion of linking relationship-terminals with one another and with extra-linguistic features of sound and meaning: and this is *all* the theoretical apparatus Lamb uses to define the entire structure of a language, including semantics, syntax, and phonology.

Moreover, this simplicity in his general theory gives Lamb a large advantage in connection with another aspect of simplicity: that of defining a formal criterion for choosing between alternative analyses of particular linguistic data. Chomsky has stressed that 'simplicity' in this sense is not an intuitive concept but rather a property which must be investigated empirically (Chomsky 1965, pp. 37 ff.). The limited data about his parents' language available to an infant will always be compatible with many different grammars, so children must have some built-in 'evaluation measure' for selecting among the alternatives, and part of the job of linguistics is to discover just what evaluation measure would lead children to acquire the particular grammars they do acquire. (What Chomsky says on this subject is in fact rather muddled – see Sampson 1976; but let us leave that point aside here.) Although Chomsky stresses the need for a formal measure of simplicity of grammars, ironically enough Chomskyan grammars do not lend themselves at all naturally to the definition of such a measure (and Chomsky makes no concrete suggestions about what the measure might look like). For instance, within the Chomskyan framework one often has the option of reducing the number of constituency rules at the cost of introducing an extra transformation; one can only decide whether the option should be taken in any given case by weighing the relative 'cost' of the transformation against that of the constituency rules, but these two categories of rule are formally so different that one does not see how to define any 'rate of exchange' between them. Lamb grammars, by contrast, are highly homogeneous, having elements of the same type at all levels. In a Lamb grammar, a quantity such as the number of lines (i.e. links between nodes) is both easy to count and very plausible as a measure of the overall complexity of the grammar. With such a well defined simplicity criterion, old chestnuts such as the question whether English *ch* is one phoneme or two can be answered straightforwardly; one draws networks corresponding to the alternative analyses, counts lines, and the analysis with the lowest score wins. (See Lamb 1966, pp. 52–4, for a worked-out example.)

Lamb's theory also captures in a neat way a property of language which has proved resistant to explanation within Chomsky's system: namely, the existence of independent principles of patterning at different linguistic levels.

A Chomskyan grammar contains a set of rules which define a range of allowable structures at one level of the grammar – the constituency 'base' component; and all the other rules in the grammar are rules for *altering* the structures defined by the base component in order to turn them into surface syntactic structures and, ultimately, phonetic representations on the one hand, or into 'semantic representations' on the other. The theory gives us no reason to expect to find any patterning in, say, the range of surface structures of a language, other than patterning which is imposed on deep structures by the base component and which happens not to be destroyed by the operation of transformations. But such independent patterning commonly is found; to take a simple example, English does not tolerate sequences of two present participles (e.g. *It is continuing raining*), and this is a rule about surface rather than deep syntactic patterning, since present participles have various syntactic sources in a Chomskyan grammar and it would be impossible to state the rule in a general form in terms of deep structure (cf. Ross 1972). Both in syntax and in phonology, Chomskyan linguists have been forced to recognize the existence of what have been called 'conspiracies', in the sense that the outputs of a given bloc of rules manifest patterning which is present neither in the inputs to that bloc of rules nor in the rules themselves (Perlmutter 1970; Kisseberth 1970); given Chomsky's theory, the occurrence of conspiracies is quite arbitrary and unexpected.

Lamb's theory, on the other hand, predicts it. So far, we have discussed only how Lamb grammars represent the relationships between units at different linguistic levels – the 'external relationships', in Hjelmslev's terms. In cases of alternation, however, unless the alternants are in free variation (which, as we have seen, is uncommon), the grammar must somehow tell us which alternant is used in given circumstances: thus the

morpheme *good* must be realized as the morph / bet / before
-*er* but as / gʊd / in most other circumstances; the phoneme
/ l / is a plain lateral before a vowel but velarized otherwise,
and so forth. This sort of information is included in a Lamb
grammar in the shape of a *tactic pattern*, which is a statement of
the possible combinations of units at a given linguistic level – a
statement of the 'internal relations' of a stratum. (Lamb uses
Hjelmslev's term 'stratum', although he does not limit himself to
just four strata, and the identity of Lamb's strata is determined
empirically rather than by *a priori* conceptual analysis.) Lamb's
diagrammatic notation is readily adapted to the representation
of internal relations; thus the Chomskyan constituency rules of
Figure 3 (page 136) would translate into Lamb's notation as shown
in Figure 7 (page 176).

A tactic pattern of this kind, when complete, is 'hooked up' to
the realization network discussed earlier by linking the lowest
lines of the tactic pattern to corresponding lines at the
appropriate level of the realization pattern; the tactic pattern
just illustrated deals with 'internal relations' among words
(Lamb's 'lexemes'), so for example the line labelled *boy* will be
joined to a line at the word level in the realization pattern (a
line which will perhaps be in an and-relation with semantic units
YOUNG, MALE, HUMAN at a higher level, and with the phonemes
/ b /, / o /, / i / at a lower level). Again, once the connections
are made in the diagram, the labels of the tactic pattern become
redundant. But it is essential to Lamb's theory that the grammar
contain not just one tactic pattern but several, at different
levels: choices are continually introduced by or-nodes as one
moves upwards or downwards in the realization pattern, and
these choices are decided by looking to see which alternatives
are compatible with the next tactic pattern. The tactic pattern
which organizes words into sentences will rule out sequences of
present participles; the tactic pattern which combines
morphemes into words will select / bet / rather than / gʊd /
before -*er*; the tactic pattern which combines phonetic features
into well-formed syllables will decide whether a given lateral
should be velarized. On Lamb's theory, a language not only may
but *must* display independent patterning at various levels.

One aspect of linguistic structure in which this concept of
'independent patterning' is relatively obvious is that of
derivational morphology. ('Derivational morphology' refers to

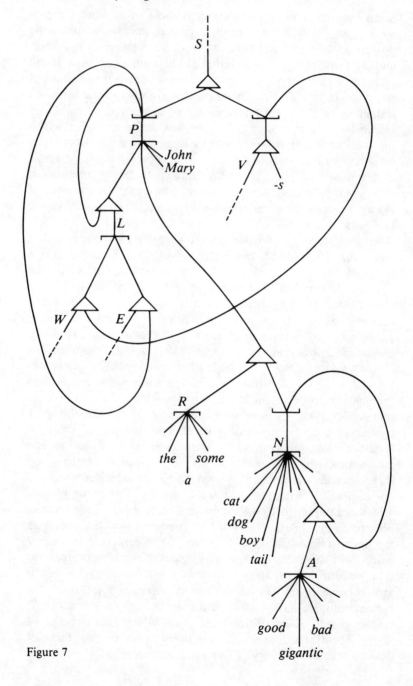

Figure 7

the construction of complex vocabulary items from simple roots
– e.g. *king-ly, reg-al* – as against 'inflexional morphology' which
concerns the varying grammatical forms of words – *smoke,*
smoke-s, smok-ing.) We have seen that Morris Halle was right
to say that morphology had not been much studied *within the*
Chomskyan school, and there is a good reason for that. The
Chomskyan principle that relative length of grammar reflects
relative naturalness of a language for human users implies that,
if the Chomskyan canonical notation permits alternative
grammars of different length for the same language, the shortest
is the only one with any scientific status. (Any grammar can
easily be made gratuitously complex, so that it would be
nonsense to suggest that a language was 'unnatural' just because
it was *possible* to construct an inordinately long grammar for it.)
Now, in a Chomskyan grammar, statements about derivational
patterns (e.g. that the adjective-forming suffix *-ly* normally
occurs on Germanic noun roots while *-al* applies to Latin roots)
are redundant, in the sense that they do not affect the identity
of the language generated by the rest of the grammar. Such
regularities are not 'productive' – one cannot affix *-ly* to *any*
Germanic noun-root, e.g. the adjective from *book* is *bookish*
rather than **bookly*, and *tree* gives neither **treely* nor **treeish*;
that means that those compound words which do occur in
the language must be listed individually in the 'lexicon' of a
Chomskyan grammar, and if that is so then statements of
morphological regularities have no job left to do in generating
the class of grammatical sentences. Halle's morphological rules
ought to be eliminated by the methodological criteria to which
Halle himself subscribes. On the other hand, these
morphological regularities do exist and a linguistic description
which fails to record them seems to be missing something about
the language; in a Lamb grammar they find a natural place in
the tactic pattern of the morphemic stratum.

All these somewhat technical considerations do not yet touch
on the real reason for the appeal of Lambian grammar,
however. The chief attraction of the system is that it is much
more plausible than its rivals as a model of how speakers and
hearers actually operate. Lamb and Chomsky agree in seeing a
language as linking 'semantic representations' – messages – with
'phonetic representations' – pronunciations. If that is an
appropriate way of thinking about language, then presumably

someone who speaks converts a semantic structure constituting the message he wishes to convey into a corresponding phonetic structure or pronunciation, and a hearer performs the opposite conversion process. Yet Chomskyan theory does not show how this two-way conversion process is carried out, but rather aims merely to enumerate the semantic/phonetic pairings without suggesting machinery whereby one can be recovered from the other. Chomsky *asserts* that a successful speaker/hearer model will incorporate a generative grammar in his sense (1965, p. 9), but he gives us no reason to believe this assertion, and it seems rather implausible. For one thing, it is a characteristic of Chomskyan grammar-rules that they go only in one direction. Thus, we might perhaps suppose that a speaker 'thinks in deep structures' which he then converts into pronounceable sequences by applying transformational and phonological rules; but there is no way of 'throwing transformational rules into reverse' and using them to recover deep structures from surface structures, so, if we tried in this way to interpret a Chomskyan grammar as a model of the speaker, it would appear to predict that the hearer's task in dealing with syntax is either much more difficult than the speaker's or else uses some quite separate machinery – both of which may seem unreasonable conclusions.

A Lamb grammar, on the other hand, is perfectly symmetrical as between speaker's and hearer's viewpoints, and the processes of conversion between sound and meaning and *vice versa* are central to Lamb grammars, with tactic patterns functioning merely as adjuncts to the realization pattern in facilitating conversion in either direction – unlike Chomskyan grammars, in which the 'unnatural' task of enumerating all-and-only the well formed sentences is central, and semantic and phonetic rules are seen as merely 'interpreting' the products of the base component. A Lamb grammar permits one to 'feed in' semantic units at the top and get the corresponding pronunciation out at the bottom, or *vice versa*, and in either case the same network is being used in the same general way. These processes of 'encoding' and 'decoding' in a Lamb grammar can be simulated on a computer (Reich 1970b), The diagrammatic notation is reminiscent of microphotographs of neurons and their synaptic interconnections; Lamb (who is not a timid man) firmly believes that when the neurophysiologists eventually succeed, in their plodding fashion, in discovering the details of how the brain works, they will come up with 'circuit diagrams' identical to those he draws.

That may sound unrealistically optimistic. However, there is a measure of support for it. When Peter Reich uses simulation techniques to explore the behaviour of Lamb grammars interpreted as networks of pathways along which impulses are propagated and nodes at which the impulses interact, he discovers effects that had not been foreseen by Lamb, but which accurately reflect aspects of human language behaviour that Chomsky does not attempt to cope with. The most striking of these has to do with the syntactic phenomenon of 'self-embedding'. It is well known that speakers of any language find it markedly difficult to deal with (to utter or to understand) sentences in which a constituent of a given category is part of a larger constituent of the same category which is in turn part of a yet larger constituent of the same category, provided that in each case the included element occurs in the middle rather than at the beginning or end of the constituent which includes it. Thus the sentence:

$_{NP}[_{NP}[_{NP}[_{NP}[John]$'s wife]'s aunt]'s house] is listed Grade II.

presents no special problems, because although nominal phrases ('NPs') are embedded within nominal phrases to a depth of four the lower nominal phrase is in each case at the beginning of the containing nominal phrase; and likewise, in:

This is $_{NP}[$the dog that chased $_{NP}[$the cat that killed

$_{NP}[$the rat that ate $_{NP}[$the malt]]]]

the contained nominal phrase is always at the end of the nominal phrase which includes it. On the other hand, a sentence like:

$_{NP}[$The man that $_{NP}[$the girl that $_{NP}[$my wife] taught]

married] writes thrillers.

is in practice virtually unusable, although its degree of embedding is only three: each nominal phrase is in the middle of the next-larger nominal phrase. Chomsky is well aware of the phenomenon, and dismisses it as a 'performance' effect. But while it is legitimate for Chomsky to ignore, under the rubric of 'performance', the fact that (for example) million-word sentences are never uttered (because we know independently of linguistics that humans cannot successfully execute such lengthy behaviour-patterns, and we do not need linguistics to repeat facts which we know without its help), the case of self-embedding is rather different: this phenomenon seems to concern language specifically, lacking any analogue in other categories of behaviour, so that the linguist rather than anyone else owes us an explanation of it. The real reason why Chomsky ignores the phenomenon of self-embedding is that he is unable to explain it: within his theoretical framework constituency rules rewrite symbols such as '*NP*' without regard to the larger structure in which they occur, and, although Chomsky could certainly modify his theory so as to forbid self-embedding, this would be a purely *ad hoc* manoeuvre which would explain nothing. Reich shows, however, that within a relational-network grammar exactly the phenomena observed in connection with self-embedding in human languages (which are in fact even more complex than reported here) can be *predicted* to occur: Reich's theory would have to be modified in an *ad hoc* way if these phenomena were *not* observed (Reich 1969). Reich's development of Lamb's relational-network theory was not designed in order to achieve this result; the prohibition of self-embedding is an unexpected bonus of a theory which was worked out with quite different considerations in mind. That prohibition is therefore a very notable success for relational as against transformational grammar. Another respect in which relational grammar offers potential as a model of the speaker/hearer is that, it has been claimed, various known symptoms of aphasic speech can be simulated by excising specific portions of a Lamb grammar (Fleming 1967).

All this is very promising. However, Lamb's theory lays itself open to serious criticisms: it is simply not clear that relational networks are capable of representing some of the commonest phenomena that occur in human language. One of the *prima facie* attractions of Lamb's system as against Chomsky's is that the former is an 'item-and-arrangement' rather than 'item-and-process' system (cf. Chapter 3). A Chomskyan grammar is full of rules which *change* underlying representations of sentences into other representations: the deep structure of a sentence contains certain morphemes grouped into a certain hierarchical structure, but the transformational rules eliminate or modify some morphemes, introduce others, and remodel the structure; words are stored in the lexicon in a given phonetic shape, but this may be very different from the pronunciation they possess on emerging from the phonological rules (on this latter point see Chapter 8 below). The picture is of sentences being processed into their finished form like products on a factory conveyor-belt; and this picture has seemed hopelessly unrealistic as an account of how speakers actually operate even to linguists who acknowledge that 'process' statements about language are convenient as descriptive fictions. Bloomfield, for instance, discussing the alternation in the shape of the English plural suffix between [z] after voiced and [s] after voiceless sounds, points out that it is handy to treat irregular plurals such as *knives* [naivz] by saying that the root [naif] 'first' becomes [naiv] and 'then' takes what is now the expected form [z] of the suffix; but he adds (1933, p. 213):

the descriptive order . . . is a fiction and results simply from our method of describing the forms; it goes without saying . . . that the speaker who says *knives,* does not 'first' replace [f] by [v] and 'then' add [-z], but merely utters a form *(knives)* which in certain features resembles and in certain features differs from a certain other form (namely, *knife*).

To someone who shares the assumptions revealed in this quotation, Lamb grammars are very reassuring: nothing ever *changes* into anything else, and the network of relationships merely states the complex *arrangements* in which semantic and phonetic units actually occur in sentences as we know them in practice. However, Chomsky uses process rules not because he happens to enjoy thinking in conveyor-belt terms, but because, when one investigates syntax more deeply than Bloomfield did, one finds the data to be such that, arguably, only process rules can handle them. Process rules are so indispensable that it becomes difficult to dismiss them as convenient descriptive tricks: they seem to correspond to some genuine property of natural language. The syntactic phenomena that most clearly demand to be treated in process terms are phenomena which appear highly resistant to handling in terms of Lambian networks.

Consider, for instance, the relative clause in English. A relative clause is a constituent which resembles an independent sentence, differing principally in that a relative clause is short of one nominal phrase as compared to a full sentence. The missing phrase may (and in some cases must) be represented by a relative pronoun, which will appear at the beginning of the clause. Thus

The man [John left the book by an old cupboard] is bent

is not a possible sentence, because the constituent which ought to be a relative clause has all the nominal phrases of a full sentence; and

The man [(who) left the book by] is bent

is equally bad (with or without the relative pronoun *who*) because *two* nominal phrases are missing; but each of the following are well formed in English:

The man [who left the book by an old cupboard] is bent
The man [(whom) John left by an old cupboard] is bent
The man [John left the book by] is bent.

The obvious way of stating the facts is to say that relative clauses are formed from normal sentences by deleting one of their nominal phrases, or by replacing it with a relative pronoun; relative pronouns are subsequently moved to the front of their clause. These are just the kinds of process which transformational notation is designed to handle: such rules operate on the elements of a sentence in ways which *depend on the underlying structure of the sentence as a whole*. The realization pattern of a Lamb grammar, on the other hand, which states what different material at other linguistic levels may stand for a given unit at any one level, treats each elementary form separately and in isolation from the structure in which the form occurs. Thus it would be easy enough for a realization pattern to state that the individual unit *John* may be realized as zero, but there is no obvious way in which the realization pattern could allow *the book* or *an old cupboard* to be deleted *en bloc*. Furthermore, while a tactic pattern might be designed so as to allow zero as an option at each nominal-phrase position in a relative clause, it seems impossible within Lamb's notation to prevent the zero option being chosen more (or less) than once in a single clause. This is not merely a question of failure by the present writer to see how to achieve the desired result within the system; the small sample grammar of English presented in Lamb's own published outline of his theory treats relative clauses as if they were identical to independent sentences (Lamb 1966, p. 80).

Lamb has clarified his disagreement with Chomsky on this issue by drawing an analogy with eating in a cafeteria (see Parret 1974, p. 195). One walks along a cafeteria counter and chooses the elements of a meal in the order in which they happen to be arranged on the counter: perhaps dessert first, then the main course, then soup and then coffee. One goes to a table and proceeds to eat and drink these items in a quite different order. Now, Lamb suggests, the Chomskyan approach to this phenomenon, in terms of transformational rules, would be to say that one derived the sequence for eating by applying an operation to the sequence in which one had collected the items – say, '1 2 3 4 ⇒ 3 2 1 4' to get the correct order 'soup – main-course – dessert – coffee'. This would seem to imply that if, say, a woman let her escort collect the meal (so that she did not know the collection-sequence) she would have no way of working out the proper eating-sequence, and that if the cafeteria re-arranged the sequence of items on its counter the customers would automatically rearrange their eating-sequence. But of course that does not happen. The sequence for eating is governed by its own pattern, which is entirely independent of the pattern of food on the counter (or, for that matter, of the pattern of food-preparation in the cafeteria kitchen, and so on).

This analogy succeeds admirably in making Lamb's position clear. However, one of the points which the analogy highlights is that there is an important structural difference between arranging words into a sentence and eating lunch. Given a plate of sausages and chips, a helping of treacle tart, and a bowl of Brown Windsor, there is only one way to arrange them into a 'well-formed' meal; but out of the words *John, Mary*, and *loves* we can construct two different sentences. Meals normally contain only one example of any given 'category' of food, but sentences regularly contain multiple nominal phrases, multiple adjectival phrases, and so on. True, a greedy person might take two puddings, but then it would presumably not matter which order they were eaten in. It makes all the difference in the world, on the other hand, whether we say *John loves Mary* or *Mary loves John*. In order to get the sequencing right at the syntactic lunch-table, we need to know the positions occupied by the elements on the semantic cafeteria-counter; Lamb appears to be deliberately ruling this out.

That example has nothing to do with the phenomena for which Chomsky uses transformations, but when we introduce these the situation becomes even worse. The point I made about relative clauses resembling main clauses from which any one nominal phrase has been dropped was designed to show that what counts as a well-formed relative clause is not a question that can be answered by reference purely to the surface grammar of the language (or at least, an answer in such terms will be perversely complex) – rather, the simple way to answer is in terms of an underlying 'logical form', identical to a main clause, to which an operation is applied to derive the surface form. Returning to the gastronomic analogy, what counts as a well formed meal here is a function of what is on offer at the counter (unlike in real cafeterias, where these two questions are quite independent and mismatches are entirely possible).

Certainly, it may be that Chomskyan transformations are the wrong way to handle such phenomena; I would be prepared to argue that myself. But Lamb has done little to show that he has a better way (indeed, *any* way) of dealing with such cases. Lamb's inability to handle structure-dependent syntactic processes is a particularly grave shortcoming in his theory because these phenomena play a central role in Chomsky's theorizing, and Chomsky's theory was first in the field. When a novel theory is brought forward to challenge established belief it is good to hear that it solves problems that were shelved by the proponents of the older doctrine, but it is surely at least equally important to know that the new theory can match its rival on the terrain where the latter has been particularly successful. Lamb addresses himself to the task of winning over a scholarly community which has been almost wholly converted to Chomsky's views, but he shows no sign that he is aware of the need to meet Chomsky on Chomsky's ground. Peter Reich has been more responsible in this respect (see Reich 1970a); but, although the cited work makes a promising start at the job of demonstrating that relational networks can cope with the sort of syntactic phenomena discussed by Chomsky, they do not go very far, and in the last few years Reich appears to have given up publishing on this subject. That might be because Reich's interests have changed rather than because the job cannot be done; but a theory is judged by its concrete achievements rather than by the gleam in its inventor's eye, and as things stand the verdict on relational grammar must surely be that it was a good idea which has turned out not to work.

The foregoing perhaps suffices as a criticism of relational grammar. There is one further point, however, that deserves making because of its general interest. We have seen that the Danish relational grammarians set great store by the notion that a theory of language – of *langue* rather than *parole*, in Saussure's terms – should concern itself purely with formal structure, and not allow itself to be contaminated by considerations of the substance which realizes that structure. The trouble about this elegant logical principle is that, if we abstract too far away from the concrete realities of speech, we risk ending up with a theory that tells us little about even the formal aspects of language; and it seems that the 'glossematicians' fell into this trap. Thus, Eli Fischer-Jørgensen (1967, p. x) says that 'For Uldall glossematics [i.e. what I am calling "relational grammar"] is a formal theory, which is not defined by any specific material, but designed explicitly to be used for *all* human activity' (my italics). Lamb, similarly, regards it as a strong point of his system that it can represent the 'grammars' of phenomena such as baseball and Indian dancing as readily as those of languages in the ordinary sense (cf. Lockwood 1972, pp. 283 ff.). But, while flexibility in a notation system is an excellent thing, the concept of an infinitely adaptable formal notation system is a contradiction in terms. The only kind of description system which can be adapted to describe *anything whatsoever* is a natural language itself, the semantics of which is extended creatively by its speakers rather than regimented by formal rules. Any formal notation system must make assumptions about the subject-matter to which it is applied: the system of contour-lines used by map-makers is adaptable to a great diversity of terrain, but it could hardly be used to represent the structures of organic molecules or the distribution of incomes in a society, for instance. If one's notation system is invented in deliberate disregard of the contingent properties of the material to be described, then (since it must make *some* theoretical assumptions) it will just embody some false theory about that material, and hence will be both unhelpful to the descriptive worker and misleading to the theoretician.

The lesson we should draw, surely, is that the aprioristic decision to consider language as pure form, divorced from the substance that realizes it, is mistaken; linguistic substance largely determines linguistic form. Our languages are the way they are in large part because they are spoken; any attempt to ignore the medium of speech and to analyse the nature of language in the light of pure logic alone is doomed to sterility.

8 Generative phonology

For the Descriptivists of the middle decades of this century, phonology was pre-eminent among the various branches of linguistics. To study linguistics within that tradition meant first and foremost to master the technique of reducing a welter of phonetic data to an elegant system of phonemes. If we take Martin Joos's *Readings in Linguistics* (1957) as a representative sample of the most influential articles produced by the Descriptivist school, we find many more items in it dealing with the theory and practice of phonemic analysis than with any one other topic – certainly more than deal with syntax. Moreover, when the Descriptivists did deal with other linguistic levels their treatment was heavily influenced by notions which had proved useful in phonology: their use of the terms *morph/allomorph/morpheme* parallel to *phone/allophone/phoneme* is just one example of this.

For Chomsky, on the other hand, it might well be claimed that syntax is the heart of linguistic science. Chomsky's first published book was *Syntactic Structures*; his reputation both within and, even more clearly, outside the discipline of linguistics owes far more to his ideas about syntax than to his phonological work. Now that the 'Chomskyan paradigm' has attained a position of hegemony in the linguistic world, it is not unusual for published proceedings of academic conferences and the like to be divided into sections headed 'Syntax' (or 'Syntax and Semantics') and 'Other Topics' – a division of the field that would have seemed remarkable twenty years ago.

It is by no means clear that Chomsky himself would agree with this claim that he has shifted the emphasis of linguistics away from phonology. Although his first book was on syntax, his first piece of research was a thesis on the phonology of Hebrew, and his published writings on phonology are at least comparable in bulk to what he has written on syntax. Indeed, Chomsky has said

more than once that he regards phonology as a more interesting
area of research than syntax on the grounds that, in the present
state of our knowledge, it is easier to reach firm conclusions in
the former than in the latter field. However, the fact that most
scholars, rightly or wrongly, see phonology as occupying a
subordinate status under the new dispensation is reflected in the
name, 'generative phonology', given to the phonological theory
espoused by Chomsky and his disciples. Chomsky's syntactic
theory is called 'generative' for the good reason that it deals with
grammars which define, or in mathematical parlance 'generate',
all-and-only the syntactically well-formed sentences of a
language. A 'generative phonology' is not so called because it
defines all-and-only the phonologically well-formed sequences of
a language – that is one thing that it does *not* do;[1] rather, current
phonological theorizing is called 'generative' purely because it is
related to, and is practised by the same people as, 'generative'
syntax.

Apart from the personalities involved, the common feature
linking 'generative phonology' with Chomskyan syntax is not that
both are 'generative' in any clear sense but that both are
concerned with universals. Generative phonologists, like
'transformational' grammarians, are primarily concerned to work
out general theories about limits to the diversity of natural
language (and they believe that there are quite narrow limits to
be discovered); generative phonologists are concerned only
secondarily, if at all, with producing detailed and useful
descriptions of the phonological phenomena of individual
languages for their own sake. Generative phonology in fact began
as a development of Roman Jakobson's work on phonological
universals, but as this tradition became 'naturalized' in America
in the 1950s it shifted its attention to universals of another kind.

'Generative phonology' in the modern sense is essentially the
creation of Morris Halle of MIT (b. 1923), whom we have
encountered in the early stages of his career as a collaborator of
Jakobson's. Under Halle, the empirical basis of the theory of
phonological universals expanded to take in a new and rich
category of data. Halle used Jakobsonian distinctive-feature
theory to explain the phenomena of morphophonemic alternation,
something which Jakobson scarcely mentioned.

The term 'morphophonemic alternation' is used for cases,
common in most languages, where a given morpheme exhibits

distinct but related pronunciations in different circumstances. We met an example in Chapter 5: the German root *Bad* 'bath' is pronounced with a consonant [d] when followed in the same word by an inflexional suffix, so that the verbal infinitive *baden* 'to bathe' is ['ba:dən], the genitive *Bades* is ['ba:dəs], and so on; but in the nominative, which takes no suffix, the [d] is replaced by a [t] – *Bad* is said [ba : t]. That is not a fact peculiar to this one root – every German [d] becomes [t] in word-final position, so that similar alternations are observed e.g. with *Band* 'volume', *Leid* 'hurt', and so on.[2]

How is the notion of 'distinctive feature' relevant to morphophonemics? In this way. Bloomfield, and many of his followers, had tended to write as if the elementary phonological building-blocks of a language were its phonemes. It is not in fact at all clear that Bloomfield himself intended 'phonemes' to be more than convenient ways of talking about simultaneous bundles of distinctive parameter-values – convenient because phonemes can be symbolized by alphabetic letters and utterances can be transcribed phonemically in a linear fashion similar to ordinary orthography, whereas if we wish to represent the various parameter-values separately we have to resort to a cumbersome system of transcription in which utterances are represented as two-dimensional matrices in which rows correspond to parameters, columns to successive temporal segments, and cells are filled by symbols representing the various values possible for the parameter in whose row the cell occurs. Certainly some of the phonemicists were quite clear that phonemes were no more than handy abbreviations (see, for example, Hockett 1942); but it does appear that others thought of phonemes as themselves being the primitive theoretical units. However, that view is not only implausible in itself: it leads to testable predictions about patterns of morphophonemic alternation, and those predictions can be refuted.

If phonemes are the primitive units of our theory, then processes affecting individual phonemes will be simpler to state within the theory than processes affecting groups of phonemes, which would have to be listed one by one. If, on the other hand, parameter-values are basic, then it will be simpler to state a process which affects a 'natural class' of sounds – say, all voiced consonants – than one which affects just, say, the consonant [d], since the latter would have to be identified by listing the

parameter-value 'voiced' *together with* all the parameter-values
that distinguish [d] from other voiced sounds. A process which is
theoretically simple is presumably a process which has a relatively
high probability of occurring in practice, other things being equal:
and we do indeed find many instances of morphophonemic
alternations which affect 'natural classes' of sounds, and relatively
few which affect individual sounds. Consider again the [d] ~ [t]
alternation in German. In fact not just [d] but all voiced stops
lose their voice in word-final position: thus with *grob* 'coarse' we
find ['gro:bə], ['gro:bən] etc. but [gro:p]; with *Tag* 'day' we
find ['ta:gə] v. [ta:k]. Since voiced stops act as a class with
respect to this morphophonemic alternation, they should be
treated by the theory as a class – i.e. they should be specified in
terms of their common phonetic features rather than in terms of a
list of phoneme-symbols.[3]

Not only can morphophonemic data be used to show that
phonology must deal in phonetic features rather than in unitary
segments, a point which is only marginally controversial; they
also provide evidence for or against alternative hypotheses about
the nature of the set of universal distinctive features, which is
much more interesting. Consider for example the proposal that
the set of features should contain the pair Obstruent/Sonorant,
where 'Obstruents' are defined as sounds made by interrupting
the smooth flow of air through the vocal tract (i.e. stops,
fricatives) while 'Sonorants' are sounds which permit the smooth
flow of air (vowels, approximants, nasal and liquid consonants).
The terms are not necessary for purposes of pure definition – any
sound which is 'obstruent' can equally well be called 'stop' or
'fricative'; the question is whether 'obstruents' in fact function as
a natural class. Continuing with our German example, we find
that, indeed, they do. The true German rule is not that *stops*
alone lose their voice word-finally but that all and only *obstruents*
do so, so that with, for example, the adjectives *brav* 'gallant' and
mies 'weedy' we find forms such as ['bra:və] v. [bra:f], ['mi:zə]
v. [mi:s] (whereas roots ending in sonorants, such as *steil* 'steep'
or *schlau* 'sly', exhibit no such alternations). The fact that both
stops and fricatives lose their voice word-finally would be a
surprising coincidence, if stops and fricatives were treated by the
theory as unrelated classes of sounds having nothing in common
as against the other sound-types; but it is predicted, if stops and
fricatives are merely sub-varieties of the basic class of obstruents.

Therefore (given that the German data are not an isolated phenomenon that might indeed be treated as coincidental, but are reinforced by evidence tending in the same direction from various other languages) we conclude that Obstruent/Sonorant should be added to the list of universal distinctive features.

The trouble is that, once we take morphophonemic evidence into account, Jakobson's theory of twelve universal distinctive features soon looks very shaky. The pair Obstruent/Sonorant was in fact not among the original twelve; but let us consider an even worse case, where the evidence seems not merely to call for an additional feature but to argue against the features already in the list. Place of articulation in stops is a parameter with three main values, as in the sounds [p t k]. Three-valued parameters are awkward for a theory dealing in binary features: it is easy enough to treat a single articulatory parameter as corresponding to *two* binary distinctive features which interact to produce the articulatory values, but the combinations of values of two binary features amount to four rather than three possibilities. Accordingly, Jakobson dealt with place of articulation in a way suggested by the Slavonic languages, which include palatal stops such as [c] alongside [p t k]. For Jakobson, [k c] are Compact as against [p t] which are Diffuse, while [k p] are Grave and [c t] Acute (Jakobson *et al.* 1952, p. 33). Languages such as English, which lack palatals, happen to be defective in that Compact consonants are not divided into Grave and Acute. Jakobson did not present this analysis as making testable claims about morphophonemic alternations – indeed, it is not clear in what sense his analysis constitutes an empirical hypothesis at all. As soon as it *is* tested by reference to morphophonemic data, the analysis fails. Thus, one of the characteristics of the Slavonic languages is widespread alternation between alveolars and palatals. If, as Jakobson claims, [t] is to [c] as [p] is to [k], then we must predict that, in environments where [t] is replaced by [c], [p] ought always or usually to be replaced by [k]; but this never happens.

Despite problems of this kind, for many years Jakobson's successors in the development of generative phonology maintained their belief in the correctness of the original set of twelve features. In 1966, Noam Chomsky was still claiming that the features of *Preliminaries to Speech Analysis* were the correct ones. However, by the time of the publication in 1968 of

Chomsky and Halle's *Sound Pattern of English*, the 'bible' of more recent work in generative phonology, this position was quietly abandoned. Not only does *SPE* (as the latter book is commonly called) use different features from those of *Preliminaries*; it gives up entirely (indeed, it ignores as if it had never been voiced) the notion that certain articulatorily-distinct parameters are psychologically equivalent, and instead takes the common-sense line that any independently controllable articulatory parameter ought to be represented by a distinctive feature of its own (*SPE*, p. 297; cf. McCawley 1967).

Two of the anti-Descriptivist aspects of Jakobsonian phonology were retained – the notion of 'markedness' (the idea that speech-sounds form a natural hierarchy rather than being equal in potential usefulness) and the notion that all distinctive features are psychologically binary, even if continuous in articulatory terms.

Markedness can be dealt with quickly, since what is being claimed is perfectly true but by no means has the implications which the generative phonologists suppose. If we return to the case of front rounded vowels such as [y], we find the generative phonologists arguing essentially along the following lines. To combine front tongue position with rounded lip position is no more difficult, physically, than to combine lip-rounding with back tongue-position or front tongue-position with spread lips. Yet we find that vowels such as [y] are much less common in the languages of the world than [u] or [i]; so we must characterize 'Front + Rounded' as a 'marked' combination in our phonological theory, and this concept of 'marking' must correspond to some interesting innate property of human mental organization, since it is constant across languages and does not correspond to anything physical. The answer to those who argue in this way is that they have not looked hard enough for a physical explanation. The articulatory gestures involved in producing [i y u] respectively are all on a par; but acoustically speaking the pattern of airwaves corresponding to the vowel [y] is intermediate between the patterns of the other two vowels. In other words, to the hearer [i] and [u] are more different from one another than either is from [y], so naturally a language which uses only two close vowels will choose the former two. This no more suggests the existence of some previously unsuspected innate psychological principle than does the fact that a system of two coloured signal flags will use the colours red and green in preference to, say, red and orange.

Binarity is more interesting. I suggested just now that generative phonologists misunderstood the facts about front rounded vowels through thinking exclusively in articulatory terms; but there is no doubt that the binary principle entered generative phonology because of an emphasis in the early days of the theory on the hearer's as opposed to the speaker's role in oral communication. In the years after the Second World War when generative phonology was being developed, two other novel developments very much 'in the air' in Cambridge, Massachusetts, were speech spectrography (whereby for the first time it began to be possible to make statements about sounds in terms of airwave patterns rather than in terms of the articulatory gestures which produce the airwaves) and information theory, the quantitative study of efficiency of communication. (On the intellectual atmosphere of this academic milieu at the period in question, see for example Bar-Hillel 1970, ch. 25.) From the information-theorist's point of view, a particularly obvious question to ask about an utterance is: what decisions does the hearer have to make about the properties of the utterance in order to know what message it contains? Information theory tells us that the 'code' in which the utterance is expressed will be maximally efficient if each of those decisions is a binary, yes-or-no choice and is independent of all the other decisions: hence it seemed *a priori* likely that the distinctive features of phonology would be binary (Jakobson and Halle 1956, pp. 47–9), and it was supposed that these binary features would turn out to have relatively clear-cut meaning in acoustic terms, even though a given acoustic property might be produced by a variety of alternative articulatory gestures. Articulatory phonetics was merely the 'plumbing' by which acoustic effects were achieved (ibid., p. 35), and accordingly it held less appeal for the theoretically-minded linguist – the fact that articulation was the only aspect of phonetics about which anything was known in detail was an unfortunate accident.

Linguists soon changed their mind about the relevance of information theory to their discipline, and the notion that the Jakobsonian distinctive features might have a more direct meaning in acoustic than in articulatory terms did not survive subsequent advances in acoustic research. In any case, even if the acoustic or perceptual effect of labialization were similar or even identical to that of pharyngalization, say, nevertheless a complete description of Arabic would have to state that speakers use the latter rather than the former articulation, and *vice versa* in a description of Twi; so ultimately a theoretical apparatus which ignored the difference between distinct articulatory parameters could not but be unsatisfactory, and, as we have seen, generative phonologists eventually abandoned this aspect of the theory. But they did not abandon the binarity notion which had originally gone with it: indeed, in later work this notion was applied even more rigidly. Originally, the fact that English and many other languages distinguish three degrees of vowel aperture was handled by saying that the Compact/Diffuse feature (which covered aperture in vowels as well as place of articulation in consonants) was simply exceptional: this feature was 'binary' in the somewhat Pickwickian sense that a sound could be located at either of its two poles or at neither, i.e. sounds could be intermediate between Compact and Diffuse (*Preliminaries*, pp. 9–10, 28). Once such an uncompromising thinker as Chomsky became associated with the theory, however, this sort of exception was quite rightly ruled out. In *SPE* aperture is handled by two binary features, '+/− High' and '+/− Low' (the convention of giving names to the two poles of a distinctive feature was dropped in favour of using one name for the feature and pre-fixing it with a plus or minus sign to indicate the two values). These two binary features permit just three possible combinations: [ɪ] is +High and −Low, [e] is −High and −Low, and [æ] is −High and +Low (the combination +High and +Low is inadmissible on logical grounds). It is appreciated that these feature-combinations will not have identical realizations in different languages or even in different dialects of one language (the [æ] of RP *pat* is somewhat less open – 'higher' – than the [a] of French *patte* or of a Northern English pronunciation of *pat*, for instance, though all these sounds will equally be described as −High, +Low); but the universal features determine the number of possible contrasting sounds and the kind of morphophonemic relationships they may enter into – the precise phonetic realization in a given language or dialect of a combination such as −High, +Low will be specified by so-called 'Detail Rules' which do not interact in an interesting way with other components of the phonological system (and which, somewhat ironically, are never discussed in detail).

To say that speech-sounds are properly described in terms of a universal set of distinctive features all of which are binary in this sense seems to be to make a surprising claim about natural language. After all, we know that languages other than English distinguish more than three values on the parameter of aperture, for instance. Remarkably, Chomsky treats binarity as an uncontroversial matter of logic. He argues that every linguist has always presupposed a fixed, standard set of phonetic features (1964, p. 77):

> No procedure has been offered to show why, for example, initial [pʰ] should be identified with final [p] rather than final [t], in English, that does not rely essentially on the assumption that the familiar phonetic properties (Stop, Labial, etc.) are the 'natural' ones. ... With freedom of choice of features, any arbitrary grouping may be made simpler.

and he and Halle argue that binarity is non-controversial for the features simply because 'yes' and 'no' are the two possible answers to the question whether some segment belongs to a given category (*SPE*, p. 297):

> In view of the fact that phonological features are classificatory devices, they are binary, as are all other classificatory features in the lexicon, for the natural way of indicating whether or not an item belongs to a particular category is by means of binary features.

But this is a clear equivocation. The former quotation makes the point that everyone agrees on the existence of a fixed set of features, where 'features' means 'phonetic parameters' in our sense; the latter quotation suggests that there are just two answers to the question whether a segment possesses a given feature, when 'feature' means 'parameter-*value*'. Certainly no one disputes that the parameter 'aperture' is a universal category relevant to the description of vowels in all languages; and, equally, no one suggests that there are more than two possible answers to the question 'Is the vowel X half-open?', to cite one particular value of the parameter. One cannot go on to infer that every continuous phonetic parameter must of necessity be resolvable into the same fixed number of discrete steps in every language; *a priori* it is equally reasonable to suppose, with Bloomfield, that languages make independent decisions (as it

196 Schools of Linguistics

were) about how many steps to distinguish on a given physically continuous parameter. If the theory of universal binary features is correct, it can only be because it leads to testable predictions which can be confirmed by observation – it cannot be treated as a truth of logic.

Once it is recognized that the binarity theory is an empirical claim if it is anything at all, facts such as the differing number of distinctive degrees of vowel aperture in French as against English become *prima facie* refutations of the theory: if the correct features are + / − High and + / − Low, allowing the three levels of English, then a four-level language like French should be impossible. *Prima facie* refutations can always be countered by modifications to the theory: according to Jakobson, the difference between French [e] and [ɛ] is not a matter of aperture, but rather of Tenseness v. Laxness – French [e] is to [ɛ] as English [i:] is to [ɪ]. This may or may not be phonetically defensible; the obvious risk is that the more of these apparently *ad hoc* modifications are made, the less testable the theory becomes until it ends up entirely vacuous.

I have tried to ascertain whether the binarity theory can be regarded as a true empirical statement about the nature of language by examining what has been said about the analysis in terms of universal binary features of one continuous articulatory parameter, namely pitch, as used in tone languages (Sampson 1974a). I chose pitch partly because it is much more easily and accurately measurable than vowel aperture, and also because generative phonologists have made relatively clear-cut statements about it, whereas their treatment of aperture remains somewhat inconclusive.

Pitch is ignored in the original list of distinctive features, perhaps because Roman Jakobson (like myself) happens to belong to the minority of the world's population whose native languages are non-tonal. It is mentioned by Jakobson and Halle (1956, pp. 22–3), but their analysis is supported by very limited evidence.[4] The most influential generative-phonological treatment of tone is by William Wang (1967b), whose analysis is cited with approval by Chomsky and Halle (*SPE*, p. 329) and by other scholars. Wang presents a set of binary features which can be used to represent not only level pitches but the relatively complex 'contour tones' (e.g. Falling, Falling-Rising) found in many Far Eastern languages. Since pitch can be measured accurately, it is easy to show that Wang's binary features fail to make true predictions about the actual physical nature of the tone-contours in such languages (Sampson 1974a, pp. 248 ff.); if Wang's analysis has any substance at all, it can only be in terms of morphophonemics rather than 'surface phonetics', and this is how Wang seeks to justify his treatment. He argues for the correctness of his feature-set by showing that it permits a unified, relatively simple statement of a superficially highly complex pattern of morphophonemic alternation among the tones of Amoy Hokkien, a dialect of Chinese. This language contains five tones which, in a given environment the nature of which is irrelevant here, alternate with one another as indicated by the arrows in Figure 8 (thus the high level tone becomes mid level, and so on). Within Wang's binary-feature analysis, these five tones

Figure 8

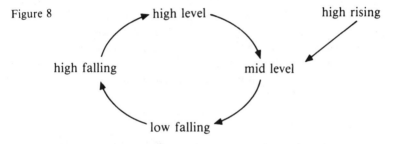

will be described in terms of the three features +/− High, +/− Falling, and +/− Rising: level tones are '−Falling, −Rising', and mid and low pitches are adequately described as '−High' since the value of the feature Falling will be enough to distinguish the mid level tone from the low falling tone in Amoy. Now Wang points out that if his binary features are accepted, then all five alternations can be reduced to a single rule:

$$\begin{bmatrix} \alpha\text{High} \\ \beta\text{Falling} \end{bmatrix} \rightarrow \begin{bmatrix} \beta\text{High} \\ -\alpha\text{Falling} \end{bmatrix}$$

(where α and β stand for either '+' or '−': thus a +High tone becomes '−(+Falling)', i.e. −Falling, and so on).

It is clear that many scholars have felt that Wang's success in reducing the complex alternations of Amoy to a single general rule in this way constitutes strong evidence in favour of the correctness of his universal tone-feature hypothesis. How much weight should be given to the Amoy example in evaluating

Wang's claims about the binary treatment of tone depends entirely on how restrictive his notation is, however. The fact that the Amoy data can be described by the rule Wang gives might be good evidence for the correctness of Wang's theory, provided that the pattern of tone-alternation actually found in Amoy is unusual among the various possible hypothetical patterns of alternation between a comparable range of units in permitting a rule of such relative simplicity. But calculation shows (Sampson 1974a, pp. 245–6) that rather more than half of the conceivable alternation-patterns can be stated in Wang's notation by rules at least as simple as his rule for Amoy. Consider a man who tosses a coin just once, finds that it comes down heads, and concludes that it must be weighted so as to come down heads regularly; would we think him judicious? His evidence for his theory about bias in the coin is actually rather stronger than Wang's evidence for his theory about universal features of tone (Wang submits his theory to no serious test other than the one already discussed).

As an example of the kind of argumentation used to support the notion of binary distinctive features, Wang's article is untypical only in being relatively clear and therefore easily pinned down. I infer that this strand of generative-phonological thought is wholly bankrupt, and that, where a phonetic parameter is physically capable of taking a large range of values, the number and identity of the parameter-values which are used distinctively is quite likely to differ unpredictably from one language to another. There is no 'universal phonetic alphabet' innate in men's minds; the only phonological constraints on human language are those set by the physical facts of vocal-tract anatomy.

The notion of a universal phonetic alphabet, however, is only one way, and in recent years not the most important, in which generative phonologists have claimed to offer evidence for the Chomskyan view that languages are organized in our minds according to principles very different from anything that could be immediately inferred from the superficial forms of our utterances. The other central strand in current generative phonology has to do with the pattern of morphophonemic rules, as opposed to the features in terms of which the rules are stated.

On the whole the Descriptivists had not discussed in depth the formal properties of the rules governing alternations between sounds in a language. The reason was that most Descriptivists (there were exceptions) tended to concentrate on giving explicit statements of the relationships between phonemes and their allophones; and, as these relationships tended to be fairly simple, subtleties of formalization were irrelevant. (Furthermore, since the Descriptivists did not believe in linguistic universals they obviously had no idea of encapsulating a theory of universals in a canonical formal notation.) Many Descriptivists, including Bloomfield himself, alluded to the notion of *morphophonemes* (though most of them did not use that term) which have phonemes as their members as phonemes in turn have allophones: thus the word *loaf* might be spelled morphophonemically as |ləuF|, with a morphophoneme |F| realized as the phoneme / v / before the plural suffix and as phoneme / f / elsewhere. But the Descriptivists tended not to carry out detailed analyses at the morphophonemic level, because they were primarily interested in the problem of how hearers abstract out of the wealth of phonetic detail in an utterance just those features which carry communicative value in the language in question. Knowing that one need pay no attention to the question whether a lateral is velarized or not, because in English both 'clear *l*' and 'dark *l*' are allophones of one phoneme / l /, is a matter of knowing the phonological system of English; deciding whether a given phoneme / f / represents the special morphophoneme |F| which is sometimes realized as / v /, or the ordinary morphophoneme |f| which is always phonemic / f / (as in *oaf*, *oafs*) has nothing to do with the system of English phonology but is merely a matter of acquaintance with the vocabulary.

One of Morris Halle's earliest arguments was to the effect that, if our aim is the purely scientific rather than practical one of stating as economically as possible the relationships between sounds and meanings which constitute a language, then this distinction in phonology between morphophonemics and 'subphonemic' processes is artificial and leads to undesirable results. Halle's example (1959; cf. Chomsky 1964, pp. 88 ff.) was from Russian, which has a rule by which voiceless obstruents become voiced before a following voiced obstruent: thus a verb ending in, say, [t] would replace the [t] with [d] before the conditional suffix [bʷi], though the [t] would remain [t] before the interrogative suffix [li] (since [l], although voiced, is not an obstruent). Voice is normally distinctive in Russian obstruents; thus / t / and / d / are different phonemes, and the process is a morphophonemic one (though it differs from the *loaf* example in being fully regular: *any* [t] will be replaced by [d] in the appropriate environment). However, there are a few cases of voiced obstruent sounds which occur *only* as replacements for their voiceless counterparts in accordance with this rule: for instance, the voiced velar fricative [ɣ] occurs only as a replacement for the voiceless [x]. Therefore a phonemicist would group [ɣ] with [x] as allophones of a single phoneme, say/ x /. But now this means that the single simple Russian rule must be torn apart into two separate and more complex rules: at the morphophonemic level we need a rule saying 'obstruent morphophonemes *other than* |x|, etc., are represented by voiced counterparts at the phonemic level before voiced obstruents', while subphonemically we must say 'phoneme / x / (etc.) is realized as its voiced allophone before a voiced obstruent but as its voiceless allophone elsewhere'. But this is absurd; and, since the absurdity is created by the decision to retain a distinct level of phonemes between the level of morphophonemes and the phonetic level, Halle concludes that the phoneme level must go.

In the light of our earlier comments on the notion of a 'universal phonetic alphabet', we can see that what Halle has shown here is rather different from what he thinks he has shown. If phonemes were credited with an existence of their own over and above the distinctive parameter-values that make them up, then Russian [x] and [ɣ] (but not [t] and [d], etc.) would have to be united into one phoneme and the absurd results would ensue. We have already accepted Halle's by no means original point that phonemes are only convenient abbreviations for bundles of simultaneous parameter-values. Halle has *not* shown that the phonemicists believed in a redundant third level of representation between the abstract level of morphophonemes and the concrete level of physical phonetics, since he too assumes an intermediate level: namely, the level of universal binary distinctive features, or what he and Chomsky call 'systematic' (as opposed to 'physical') phonetics. At the level of systematic phonetics there is said to be only a universally fixed finite set of possible phonetic parameter-values (as against the infinitely numerous parameter-values available at the level of physical phonetics, where many parameters are continuous rather than discrete). If one believes in systematic phonetics, then certainly it will be redundant to posit also a *fourth* level which recognizes only the

smaller finite set of parameter-values relevant for the particular
language under discussion. But Bloomfield did not dream of the
notion of a universal systematic phonetics, so he was bound to
use a level of language-specific 'systematic phonetics'. Halle
makes his argument superficially stronger by using an example
involving one of the parameters (Voiced/Voiceless) which
arguably is binary even in physical terms. But, although the
parameter-values Voiced and Voiceless may recur from language
to language, in general, as I have indicated, Halle's notion of a
fixed set of distinctive parameter-values is without foundation; so
that a level much like that of the classical phoneme is inevitable
(even if Russian [x] and [ɣ] would have different representations
at that level, since voice is *in general* distinctive in Russian).

Leaving aside the question of the status of the phonemic level,
once one begins to analyse in detail the kind of
sound-alternations traditionally called 'morphophonemic' in
addition to the subphonemic alternations, it rapidly emerges that
the data, for most languages, are rich enough to necessitate a
formal apparatus of considerable complexity.

Most morphophonemic alternations in a language like English
occur not in productive constructions such as pluralization of
nouns, but in non-productive derivational processes whereby
affixation and compounding are used to form complex vocabulary
items. Thus we find a regular alternation between [k] and
[s] in words like *opaque ~ opacity* [ə'peik ə'pæsɪtɪ],
decagon ~ decennial ['dekəgɔn des'enjəl]. Consideration of
several such cases suggests that the rule is that |k| becomes [s]
before front vowels in the close-to-mid aperture region (contrast
decathlon in which |k| remains [k] before an open front [æ]),
although this statement must be qualified so as not to apply in
words of the native Germanic stock – thus *kiss* is pronounced
[kɪs] not [sɪs]. Again, we find a regular alternation between the
checked vowel [ɪ] and the diphthong [ai], as in *suffice ~ sufficient*
[sə'fais sə'fɪʃnt], *decide ~ decision* [də'said də'sɪȝn̩]. Here the
simplest solution is arguably to posit a not-quite-
English-sounding (since it is tense but short) underlying
morphophoneme |i| which is laxed to [ɪ] in non-final syllables
(ignoring considerable complications) and is diphthongized to [ai]
in final syllables. It turns out that the rule which converts |i| to
[ai], when written in terms of features rather than segmental
units, will predict several other vowel alternations found in

English, e.g. the [æ] ~ [ei] alternation occurring in *opacity* ~ *opaque* already encountered, or in *insanity* ~ *insane* [ɪnˈsænɪtɪ ɪnˈsein]. But now consider words like *decade* and, conversely, *elasticize*. In *decade* the |k| of *decagon* remains a [k] even though it is followed by the front mid [e] of [ei], which ought to turn it into [s]; while the |k| which shows up as such in *elastic* has become [s] in *elasticize* before the *open* vowel of the suffix [aiz]. In fact these words are not at all exceptional with respect to the rules we have sketched, provided we specify that the rule converting |k| to [s] applies *before* the rule converting pure vowels to diphthongs. In that case, at the stage when the '*k*-to-*s*' rule applies, *decade* still has |æ| where it later has [ei], so that |k| is unaffected, whereas the suffix *-ize* has the pure vowel |i| rather than [ai], so that the preceding element *-ic* is converted to [ɪs]. In other words, morphophonemic alternations must be stated in terms of rules operating on underlying phonological forms to produce the observed pronunciation, and these rules must be stated in a definite linear sequence.

The Sound Pattern of English gives a series of forty-three such rules for English, many of which are extremely complex in themselves, and it posits underlying phonological representations for English words which are often very far removed from their actual pronunciations. (Thus, in one of Chomsky and Halle's *tours de force*, they demonstrate to their own satisfaction that the word *righteous* must contain an 'underlying' velar fricative |x|, corresponding to the *gh* of the standard orthography, despite the fact that such a sound *never* occurs in 'surface' English – indeed, many Englishmen find it unpronounceable when they attempt to speak foreign languages containing the sound; without an underlying |x|, rules which Chomsky and Halle set up to account for the alternations found in other words would predict the pronunciation *[ˈrɪʃəs] for *righteous*.)

The obvious objection is that what the generative phonologists are doing here is using the clues left behind by past events to reconstruct the history of the language, not (as they claim) showing how it is organized in the mind of a modern speaker. The rule converting |k| to [s] is essentially a reconstruction of a process which occurred in Late Latin, before the words were borrowed into English in the Middle Ages, whereas the diphthongization rule corresponds to the Great Vowel Shift which occurred in English between the fifteenth and eighteenth centuries: naturally the latter rule must follow the '*k*-to-*s*' rule in the reconstructed sequence. The reason why the spelling of *righteous*, and indeed English orthography in general, reflects the *SPE* 'underlying forms' rather accurately is not because (as Chomsky and Halle believe: *SPE*, p. 49) our spelling is a near-perfect encoding of the pronunciation of our words as they are stored in our (subconscious) minds, but because the underlying forms correspond phonetically to the distant ancestors of our modern words, and English spelling is highly conservative. Chomsky (1970) has actually gone on record as predicting that spelling mistakes by mature native speakers of English should be restricted to the few cases where the *SPE* rules are ambiguous as to the underlying representation of a given word; but the evidence I have seen suggests that he is quite wrong – bad spellers commonly make mistakes which would be quite inexplicable on Chomsky's assumptions, although they are fully predicted if we suppose that learning to spell consists of learning correspondences between letters of the alphabet and phonemes of the Descriptivist variety (Sampson 1970, pp. 621 ff.). Chomsky seems to be making the same mistake here that we have seen him making in the case of syntax – that of overestimating the ordinary man's knowledge of his language. Those of us who become professional linguists tend to have the kind of abilities which make one a good speller in childhood, so that it is possible for us to delude ourselves into thinking that traditional English orthography is in some sense 'psychologically natural'; but one must surely lead a sheltered life not to realize, by witnessing the struggles of intelligent but less 'language-minded' people with the system, that this idea is a delusion?

Those who attack generative phonology along these lines are commonly met by the counter-argument that, whether or not the morphophonemic alternations of (say) modern English were brought into being by historical events of the distant past, nevertheless they are facts of the modern language and must be accounted for as economically as possible in a synchronic description of modern English. If the most economical account turns out to be one in which surface forms are derived by an ordered sequence of rules from underlying forms that mirror a past state of the language, then we have made the interesting empirical discovery that languages tend to change less in their underlying, psychologically real structures than they do in terms of superficial appearance. To deny the psychological reality of the rules because of the parallel with history constitutes a know-nothing refusal to play the game of scientific discovery.

But this is a misunderstanding of the nature of science (cf. Sampson 1975b). Scientific research does not – or, at least, should not – proceed in compartments rigidly sealed off one from another, so that a datum of synchronic linguistics needs an explanation in terms of synchronic linguistics, and no other explanation will do. If facts noticed by a worker in one discipline turn out to be explainable from principles established by another discipline, then it is folly *also* to seek an explanation in terms familiar to the first discipline. If morphophonemic alternations can be explained as the residue of historical sound-changes, then we have no right to posit a second explanation in terms of psychological rules used by modern speakers unless we have *independent* evidence for these. The generative-phonological type of statement is 'economical', in one sense: it allows the great majority of roots to be stored in a single phonetic form, but at the cost of considerable 'processing' (i.e. rule-application) when a given root has to be uttered in a particular context. It is equally reasonable to suppose that we may simply store mentally the alternative surface pronunciations of our roots, or indeed of our words as wholes not analysed into their constituent elements, with statements of the circumstances in which each alternative is appropriate. This would mean relatively lavish use of mental 'storage space', but little or no 'processing' when we actually speak; from the little we know about how the brain works, this latter possibility seems at least as plausible as the former.

Indeed, if we are talking in terms of scientific methodology, the 'common-sense' view of phonology is preferable because it is stronger – that is, it generates more testable predictions. From the generative phonologist's point of view, in which phonological systems exist in people's minds as sequences of rules, one obvious way in which a language might *change* phonologically would be by the addition of a new rule to the sequence; but the generative phonologist has no reason to expect such new rules to appear at any particular place in the sequence – they might pop up at the beginning, middle, or end. If on the other hand one thinks of the rule-sequence as an account of past history, then a new sound-change must by definition correspond to a rule at the *end* of the sequence. It does indeed emerge that, in generative-phonological terms, new rules are always added at the end of the sequence (King 1973), which argues strongly for the interpretation of the rules as history rather than psychology.[5]

If the generative phonologists are to defend their position, they must use not philosophical principles but concrete evidence for their beliefs. I know of two relatively promising lines of argument available to them.

The first of these has to do with the notion that some phonological rules, like syntactic transformations, apply cyclically (see page 142 above). It seems at least *prima facie* difficult to see how a cyclical rule could be interpreted diachronically, since it would be somewhat absurd to think of processes of this kind occurring in regular cycles through history (particularly as complex forms need more cycles than simple ones). However, the phenomena for which cyclical rules have been posited in phonology are very restricted. Cyclical rules seem fairly clearly applicable to the distribution of different levels of stress over the words of a sentence (cf. Bresnan 1971), but that is more a matter of syntax than of phonology proper; it is common ground that, if transformations are needed in syntax, they must apply cyclically. *SPE* also uses cyclical rules for the assignment of stress within words. But, whereas this might be persuasive if the cyclical principle permitted the complex stress-patterns of English words to be predicted by relatively simple rules, in fact the *SPE* stress rules are both highly complex and depend on an *ad hoc* assignment of constituency boundaries within words (on the latter point see Brame 1971); many writers who are otherwise true believers in generative phonology have argued that non-cyclical rules are equally adequate for word-stress (Ross 1972c; papers by Lee and Schane in Goyvaerts and Pullum 1975). Scarcely anyone has suggested the need for cyclical rules in segmental (i.e. vowel-and-consonant) phonology (see Truitner and Dunnigan 1975, against Kaye and Piggott 1973). And, finally, it is less clear to me now than it originally seemed that cyclical rules cannot be interpreted diachronically (Sampson 1978); so, for all these reasons, I shall not consider this defence of generative phonology further.

The second, more genuinely worrying point has to do with the child's acquisition of phonology. Neilson Smith, of University College, London, has published a detailed account (Smith 1973), much more complete than anything we have had before, of the acquisition of English phonology by a child (his son). The obvious explanation of why young children systematically mispronounce adult words is that they begin with a relatively limited range of sounds and 'hear' adults' words in terms of the system of sounds they have so far mastered; but Smith argues that this account simply will not fit the facts. Instead, he suggests, the data he presents can be explained only on the hypothesis that the child stores adult words mentally in their correct adult pronunciation, and applies a long ordered series of rules, formally similar to the rules which generative phonologists attribute to adults, to these underlying pronunciations in order to derive his own mispronunciations. The child's phonological development consists not of acquiring *new* abilities but rather of gradually *eliminating* these 'incompetence rules', to use Smith's memorable term. One reason for holding this view is that when a new phonetic distinction appears in the child's speech (say the [s ~ ʃ] distinction – at an early stage Smith's son pronounced both of these adult sounds as [s]) the new sound is immediately used correctly in all the words containing it, even though the child has not heard an adult model for many of those words since long before he began to make the distinction: this suggests that *sh*-words 'really' had a |ʃ| for the child all along, even though he *said* [s]. Again, two of Smith's son's incompetence rules had the effect of turning *puddle* into [pʌgl̩] but *puzzle* into [pʌdl̩], which are the pronunciations he would give if asked to repeat the respective adult words. That is, the child could say *puddle* perfectly well if asked to say *puzzle*, but he could *not* say *puddle* if asked to say *puddle*! – a finding wholly inexplicable, not to say bizarre, if one supposes that the child approximates to adult speech as best he can within his restricted sound-system, but which fits the pattern of the incompetence rules quite satisfactorily.

An obvious question about Smith's theory is: why on earth should children do anything so perverse as to distort their speech by means of incompetence rules?; but Smith has an answer to this. The infant hearing his parents' speech for the first time is confronted with an anarchic welter of slightly differing sounds, in which he must discover some system. If there is a 'simplest' or most 'unmarked' type of phonology for human language, then it may be quite a sensible strategy for the child to begin by assuming that the speech he is hearing exemplifies that simplest system and that all the apparent complexity is due to irrelevant subphonemic variation which he may safely ignore – a position from which the child then retreats step by step as the evidence shows that some phonetic distinction is after all contrastive in the adult language.[6] A maximally simple phonological system will presumably be one without consonant clusters or diphthongs, with only 'unmarked' sounds and with much vowel and consonant harmony;[7] and the incompetence rules posited by Smith, when fully in effect, did regiment English in just that direction.

What matters for present purposes is that, if we are forced to accept Smith's theory of how children operate with phonology, then the generative-phonological account of adult phonology loses much of its implausibility. One is reluctant to take Chomsky and Halle's *Sound Pattern of English* at face value because the apparatus of exotic underlying forms and ordered rules corresponds to nothing of which one is aware when introspecting into one's own speech processes. Yet Smith posits underlying forms connected with very different surface forms by means of ordered rules in the child, and if the child's rules have any reality it can, surely, only be a psychological reality (there can be no question of the child's incompetence rules being a reconstruction of history). The child's rules are not identical to the adult's (our surface forms are the child's underlying forms); but the general shape of the system is the same, so perhaps we should recognize that our introspections about how we speak are misleading and admit that the adult rules of *SPE* are psychologically real.

There is, I believe, some force in this argument. We should note, however, that the linguistic world has not yet had very long to work out counter-arguments to Smith's hypothesis (see, now, Braine 1976), and that, whereas one can see a certain motive for children to impose complex processing on their words, there seems much less motive for adults to do anything similar. Furthermore, as evidence for generative phonology what Smith has produced seems rather thin and indirect (which is no criticism of Smith, since his aim was not to defend Chomsky and Halle but to study child language for its own sake): it is surely a remarkable thing if the enterprise of generative phonology, which has led to the teaching of course after course and the publication of book after book all over the world, depends for its validation ultimately on the speech of one young inhabitant of Hertfordshire. Even if there were no positive evidence against the psychological reality of Chomsky-Hallean phonological analysis, the odds against it would surely be very long.

In the last few years, furthermore, a good deal of positive evidence of various kinds has been brought forward to show that adults do *not* operate with rules of the Chomsky-Hallean kind (see, for example, articles by Hsieh, Skousen, Steinberg and Krohn in Koerner 1975), and that the only phonological universals are consequences of physical facts of anatomy or acoustics (see, for example, Liljencrants and Lindblom 1972; Ohala 1974). It now seems likely that, even when speakers do construct for themselves generalizations linking, for instance, the [s] of *decennial* with the [k] of *decagon* because they realize that both words incorporate the same root meaning 'ten', these generalizations will be *ad hoc* and not couched in terms of a phonetic analysis of the alternating segments. (We might also notice against Chomsky and Halle that it is often very implausible to think of the average native speaker as making these connexions even in an *ad hoc* fashion. Thus, one of their rules for English is posited partly to account for the alternation between the [pʌgn] of *pugnacious* and the [pjuːn] of *impugn*; but the present writer is one native speaker of English who did not appreciate that these words contained a common root before he read the relevant passage of *SPE* – despite the clue given by the spelling, which for Chomsky and Halle ought not to be necessary.) At least one leading theoretician (Vennemann 1974) has come to the view that we store our vocabulary, not in terms of underlying phonetic forms of roots, but simply in terms of the surface pronunciations of words, with separate entries for each of their various derivational and inflexional forms. This new trend is sometimes called 'Natural Generative Phonology', making it sound as if it incorporated some novel theoretical insight. A better name might be 'Commonsense Phonology'; it boils down to the view that the true theory of phonology is that there is virtually no 'theory of phonology'.

If this is the position to which we must ultimately come, and I believe that it is (although the generative phonologists continue to fight a lively rearguard action, and it is clearly not possible in a work of this nature to deal with every separate point which they raise in their defence), we might lastly ask why it is that theories so *prima facie* implausible and backed, it seems, by such meagre evidence have retained their influence as long as they have.

One factor which enabled the theory of binary phonetic features to survive is that, to put it bluntly, American linguists tend not to be very good at phonetics. In Britain, phonetics was an established subject long before linguistics as such came into being, and it is normally taken for granted today that a degree in linguistics will incorporate a strong component of phonetics. In the USA this is much less true. At MIT itself, indeed, I am told that doctoral students in linguistics not only are not obliged to study, but are not even *offered*, any course in phonetics. The system of phonetic transcription of the International Phonetic Association, which provides for very accurate recording of the minutiae of pronunciation, is not used in America. Until it shifted its custom to British printers in 1974, *Language*, for fifty years the premier linguistic journal of the USA, could not print IPA symbols – which is almost as if a science journal were unable to print the standard abbreviations for physical units or the normal notations for chemical formulae. And this is not simply a question of 'separate but equal' conventions of transcription: the conventions commonly used by Americans are cruder and less codified, and it has been established by experiment that linguists who have undergone the training associated with mastery of the IPA system can consistently draw finer phonetic distinctions than otherwise well qualified linguists who have not (Ladefoged 1967). It is understandable that a theory which claims that only a few crude distinctions between sounds matter will appeal to scholars who can hear only a few crude distinctions and are deaf to the finer details.

There is little doubt in my mind, though, that a main reason why people have been unwilling to give up their belief in generative phonology is that it is too much fun.

This aspect of the theory may well not emerge from my account; in any case, the kind of enjoyment to be derived from generative-phonological analysis is no doubt a minority taste. But for that minority (to which I confess that I belong) the enjoyment is intense. The data for such an analysis are the morphophonemic alternations of the language under study: facts which may well be completely known to someone with a reasonable proficiency in the language, or which at worst can be checked by consulting one or two reference books. Given that neatly delimited data-base, one juggles with alternative formulations of rules like a Sherlock Holmes in his armchair ravelling out the elegant solution over a pipe of tobacco; and, when the solution is found, one has not solved a mere Sunday-paper puzzle but has actually discovered novel facts about the hidden thought-processes of some race or nation.

Once generative phonology is reinterpreted as reconstruction of history, the situation becomes very different. There is no scientific value in reconstructing just those parts of the history of a language which can be inferred from morphophonemic alternations that happen to have survived to the present. Historical reconstruction is a worthy enterprise, but those who undertake it are bound to use whatever sources of data are available, and these will never be confined to a few reference books. One must spend long hours and weeks studying old and inaccessible manuscripts; one must learn, and learn thoroughly, other related languages for the light they shed on the past of the language in question; one must master the intricacies of scribal conventions and consider hypotheses about word-borrowings from and into distant languages in which one has no interest; and, since the data-base is now open-ended, there is every probability that one's fondest theories will be rendered untenable by some piece of evidence that emerges after publication. The historical linguist's work is less like that of Sherlock Holmes than like that of a real-life detective, patiently and unglamorously amassing facts with only a limited chance of reaching worthwhile conclusions. If generative phonologists dimly sense this consequence of reinterpreting the theory, no wonder they dig in their heels and resist the pressure to abandon their faith. There is no suggestion of conscious dishonesty here; only of the wishful thinking universal among humankind.

Some readers may feel that considerations such as those discussed in these last paragraphs have no place in a serious academic treatise. To anyone who thinks thus I would suggest that he is a victim of the common illusion that scholarship, and science in particular, is an activity practised by superior beings sharing none of the failings of the ordinary man in the street. (Cf. Lakatos 1976, p. 142 n. 2, on the vices of the de-personalized 'inductivist style' in science.) The truth is, of course, that scientists are fully as fallible and often irrational as other men. The glory of the scientific method lies not in the perfect rationality of those who practise it, but rather in the fact that it enables a community of thoroughly fallible individuals progressively to weed out the errors which they severally commit. To purge an account of any branch of scholarship of references to the human sources of error, as is often done, is to make it unnecessarily difficult for the new crop of scholars to grasp where the errors lie, and hence to avoid them.

9 The London School

England is a country in which certain aspects of linguistics have
an unusually long history. Linguistic description becomes a
matter of practical importance to a nation when it evolves a
standard or 'official' language for itself out of the welter of
diverse and conflicting local usages normally found in any
territory that has been settled for a considerable time, and it
happens that in this respect England was, briefly, far in advance
of Europe. Elsewhere, the cultural dominance of Latin together
with the supranational medieval world-view made contemporary
languages seem to be mere vulgar local vernaculars unworthy of
serious study; but England was already developing a recognized
standard language by the eleventh century. The Conquest
obviously destroyed this incipient advance; and, when Latin lost
its role and cultures began to fission along national lines in the
Renascence, other countries turned to the task of standardizing
their languages sooner than we. But, from the sixteenth century
onwards, England was remarkable for the extent to which various
aspects of 'practical linguistics' flourished here, by which term I
refer to such activities as orthoepy (the codification and teaching
of correct pronunciation), lexicography, invention of shorthand
systems, spelling reform, and the creation of artificial
'philosophical languages' such as those of George Dalgarno and
John Wilkins. All these pursuits require or induce in their
practitioners a considerable degree of sophistication about
matters linguistic.

One consequence of this tradition for the pure academic
discipline of linguistics which emerged in Britain in our own time
was an emphasis (as mentioned in the previous chapter) on
phonetics. Phonetic study in the modern sense was pioneered by
Henry Sweet (1845–1912). Sweet was the greatest of the few
historical linguists whom Britain produced in the nineteenth
century to rival the burgeoning of historical linguistics in

Germany, but, unlike the German scholars, Sweet based his historical studies on a detailed understanding of the workings of the vocal organs. (Such phonetic research as took place in Germany was carried out mainly by physiologists with little interest in linguistic questions.) According to C. T. Onions in the *Dictionary of National Biography*, Sweet's *Handbook of Phonetics* of 1877 'taught phonetics to Europe and made England the birthplace of the modern science'. (Sweet was the original of 'Professor Higgins' in Shaw's *Pygmalion*, turned into a musical under the title *My Fair Lady*. He worked as a private scholar throughout his life; largely because of personal animosities, and to the amazement of foreign linguists, he was never appointed to any of the academic positions to which his work and publications entitled him.) Sweet's phonetics was practical as well as academic; he was actively concerned with systematizing phonetic transcription in connection with problems of language-teaching and of spelling reform – the full title of the *Handbook* just cited continues with the words *Including a popular exposition of the Principles of Spelling Reform*. Sweet was among the early advocates of the notion of the phoneme, which for him was a matter of practical importance as the unit which should be symbolized in an ideal system of orthography.[1]

Sweet's general approach to phonetics was continued by Daniel Jones (1881–1967), who took the subject up as a hobby, suggested to the authorities of University College, London, that they ought to consider teaching the phonetics of French, was taken on as a lecturer there in 1907 and built up what became the first university department of phonetics in Britain. Daniel Jones stressed the importance for language study of thorough training in the practical skills of perceiving, transcribing, and reproducing minute distinctions of speech-sound; he invented the system of cardinal reference-points which made precise and consistent transcription possible in the case of vowels. Thanks to the traditions established by Sweet and Jones, the 'ear-training' aspect of phonetics plays a large part in university courses in linguistics in Britain, and British linguistic research tends to be informed by meticulous attention to phonetic detail. American linguistics, like many other aspects of American scholarship, was more influenced by German than by British practice. As a result, even the Descriptivists in America were startlingly cavalier by comparison with their British counterparts about the phonetic facts of the languages they described (while, for the Chomskyans, it is a point of principle to ignore 'mere phonetic detail').[2]

The man who turned linguistics proper into a recognized, distinct academic subject in Britain was J. R. Firth (1890–1960). Firth, a Yorkshireman, read history as an undergraduate, before soldiering in various parts of the Empire during the First World War. He was Professor of English at the University of the Punjab from 1919 to 1928, and returned in the latter year to a post in the phonetics department of University College, London. In 1938 Firth moved to the linguistics department of the School of Oriental and African Studies, where in 1944 he became the first Professor of General Linguistics in Great Britain (his department, itself the first of its kind in the country, had been established only in 1932). Until quite recently, the majority of university teachers of linguistics in Britain were people who had trained under Firth's aegis and whose work reflected his ideas, so that, although linguistics eventually began to flourish in a number of other locations, the name 'London School' is quite appropriate for the distinctively British approach to the subject.

It is significant that British linguistics began at the School of Oriental and African Studies. SOAS, a constituent college of the University of London, was founded in 1916 as a very belated response by Government to the need for an institute to study the languages and cultures of the Empire.[3] SOAS was (and is) full of people who had spent much of their careers in first-hand contact with various exotic languages and cultures, so that London linguistics was a brand of linguistics in which theorizing was controlled by healthy familiarity with the realities of alien tongues. (Firth himself taught and wrote a good deal about several Indian and some other languages.) The British Empire was to the London School what the American Indian was to American Descriptivists, in the sense that both groups were inoculated by quantities of unfamiliar data against the arid apriorism that disfigures some Continental and most Chomskyan linguistics. There was a difference, though: the Americans were dealing largely with languages on the verge of extinction, which needed to be recorded for their scientific interest as a matter of urgency, while London linguists were typically dealing with languages that had plenty of speakers and which faced the task of evolving into efficient vehicles of communication for modern civilizations. This meant, on the one hand, that the practical aspect of the British linguistic tradition was reinforced: issues such as the creation of writing systems and national-language planning loomed large, and Firth taught courses on the sociology of language in the 1930s, long before that subject appeared on the American linguistic agenda. Paradoxically, it also meant that London linguists were prepared to spend their time on relatively abstruse theorizing based on limited areas of data; they did not feel the same pressure as the Americans to get the raw facts down before it was too late. Hindustani with its eighty million or more speakers was not going to be lost to science because one spent a year or two polishing and re-polishing one's elegant abstract analysis of six of its irregular verbs (to cite an imaginary example). Supporters and critics alike agree that Firth's own work suffers by being too fragmentary and programmatic; few attempts at complete descriptions of languages emerged from the London School.

Firth's own theorizing concerned mainly phonology and semantics, which we shall consider in that order.

One of the principal features of Firth's treatment of phonology (and we shall see this feature recurring in London School linguistic analysis at other levels) is that it is *polysystemic*, to use Firth's term. To see what is meant by this, let us return again to the discussion (pages 70–3 above) of Chao's problem in Mandarin Chinese phonology. The alveolopalatal fricative [ɕ] occurs before high front vowels, in complementary distribution with three fricatives [s ş x] which contrast with one another before other vowels. This poses a difficulty for phonemic analysis, since one does not know which of the latter fricatives to equate with [ɕ]. For Firth, this would be a pseudoproblem: the phonology of a language consists of a number of systems of alternative possibilities which come into play at different points in a phonological unit such as a syllable, and there is no reason to identify the alternants in one system with those in another. (This is very different from Trubetzkoy's idea that 'neutralized' oppositions are realized by an 'archiphoneme' – see Chapter 5; Trubetzkoy assumes that the range of sounds found in the special neutralizing environment will be related in a regular way to the range found in other environments, but Firth sees no reason to make any such assumption.)

Even an American Descriptivist, after all, would not normally think of identifying the elements which occur as syllabic nuclei with those that occur as syllabic margins. That is, suppose we encounter a language in which all syllables are of a simple consonant + vowel + consonant shape, with five vowels [i e a o u] and eleven consonants [p t k b d g m n l s ?]: a Descriptivist would not pair off vowels with consonants as allophones of single phonemes, and certainly would not see any difficulty in the fact that there are more contrasting consonants than contrasting vowels. In Firth's terms, the syllable-nucleus system is simply different from the syllable-margin system; and, he would add, in Chinese the system of consonants operating before close front vowels is different from that operating before other vowels. One can easily multiply examples of phenomena which are problematic for phonemic analysis but dissolve when thought of in polysystemic terms. For instance, again in Mandarin Chinese, the only consonants which can occur at the end of a syllable are [n ŋ], of which the latter is not among the many consonants which can occur syllable-initially. A phonemicist would presumably want to treat [ŋ] as an allophone of one of the initial consonants, but which? – [k]? [m]? – while Firth simply recognizes a two-member syllable-final system which is very different from the multi-member syllable-initial system.

Firth argues, correctly in my view, that phonemicists are led into error by the nature of European writing systems. A phonemic transcription, after all, represents a fully consistent application of the particular principles of orthography on which European alphabetic scripts happen to be more or less accurately based. It is natural that scholars working with Oriental cultures, many of which had scripts based on other principles and whose traditions of philological discourse were independent of European thought, should be sceptical about elevating their own tribal speech-notation system into an axiom of science. Certainly the Chinese, who had a very old-established vocabulary for discussing the pro-nunciations of words, would never have described, say, the syllable that we would transcribe [nán] as consisting of a sequence of three segments in which the first and third were identical.

On the other hand, it might be argued that the polysystemic principle ignores a generalization about human language which is valid as a statistical tendency even if not as an absolute rule. As we noticed on page 73, languages do not display too great a variety of phonological 'systems': thus we do not on the whole find languages with quite different kinds and numbers of consonants before each distinct vowel, and in Chinese there is a considerable overlap between the consonants other than [ɕ s ʂ x] which occur before close front and other vowels, respectively. However, although this is not an issue that would have interested Firth, it is not clear that his polysystemic phonology does fail in this respect. Although the theory *allows* for an unlimited variety of systems, the more distinct systems (and, presumably, the more different phonetic parameter-values) a given description recognizes the more complex that description will be, so that Firthian theory could be said to meet Chomsky's goal of providing simple descriptions for relatively 'natural' languages and complex descriptions for less natural languages.

Another respect in which Firth felt that phonemic analysis was unduly influenced by alphabetic writing was with respect to the segmental principle. A phonemic transcription, like a sentence in ordinary European orthography, consisted of a linear sequence of units like beads on a string. Americans were forced to recognize certain 'suprasegmental' units, such as phonemes of stress and, in tone languages, phonemes of tone, which co-occur with whole syllables rather than forming part of particular vowels and consonants; intonation patterns might stretch over sequences of many syllables. But 'suprasegmental phonemes' were felt to be an awkward inelegance in phonemic theory, and they were allowed only in connection with certain special phonetic parameters such as loudness and pitch. To Firth this was irrational. Consider, for instance, the English word *limp* [lɪmp]. Both elements of the terminal consonant–cluster are bilabial, and we know that this is no coincidence – such clusters may not differ in place of articulation in English, so that we find *lint* [lɪnt] and *link* [lɪŋk] but no *[lɪŋp], *[lɪmt], or the like.[4] Therefore the fact that the cluster in *limp* is bilabial ought to be represented once, not twice, in the phonological analysis: we should write not / limp / but, say, / liν̅τ /, where ν and τ are 'phonematic units' representing respectively nasal and voiceless stop of unspecified place of articulation, and the horizontal line is a 'prosody' of bilabiality which contrasts with other place-of-articulation prosodies at the level of the consonant-cluster rather than that of the individual phonematic unit.[5] If the 'reality' to which a phonological analysis is meant to correspond has to do with the nature of the neural instructions passed by a speaker's brain to his vocal organs, as the generative phonologists would have it, then it is surely more plausible to suppose that we tell our mouths once-for-all to make the final cluster of *limp* bilabial than that we give separate instructions for the two elements of the cluster? And the hearer likewise needs, and presumably does, listen for bilabiality only once.

A Firthian phonological analysis recognizes a number of 'systems' of prosodies operating at various points in structure (e.g. at the levels of consonant clusters, of syllables, of words, etc.) which determine the pronunciation of a given form in interaction with segment-sized phonematic units that represent whatever information is left when all the co-occurrence restrictions between adjacent segments have been abstracted out as prosodies. (The terminological distinction between 'prosodies' and 'phonematic units' is not essential – 'phonematic units' could as well be thought of as 'prosodies' that happen to be only one segment long, as far as I can see.) One result of this is that utterances are represented as having a phonological hierarchical structure, in addition to the syntactic hierarchical structure which they are widely recognized as possessing. Prosodic theory thus finds room naturally for such multi-segment units as the syllable, which has been a long-standing puzzle for both Descriptivists and generative phonologists: intuitively, and to the layman, the syllable seems an important entity (consider its role in poetic metre, for instance), yet in terms of phonemic or generative-phonological analysis syllables are purely arbitrary groupings of an intrinsically unstructured sequence of segments. In Firthian terms, on the other hand, the syllable plays an essential role as the domain of a large number of prosodies. In other writing (Sampson 1970) I have argued that there are facts about what is commonly regarded as segmental phonology in certain languages which cannot be stated in general terms unless we recognize the kind of hierarchical phonological structure that prosodic analysis implies.

Like the polysystemic principle, prosodic analysis is a good dissolvent of pseudoquestions, in this case questions about the direction of dependencies which are in fact mutual. A particularly clear illustration is provided by vowel-harmony languages such as Turkish (though the point could be exemplified several times over in virtually any language). In a typical vowel-harmony language, vowels will be divided into groups, say front vowels [i e æ] versus back vowels [u o ɑ], and any given word will contain only vowels from one group – thus [kilæ] or [puno] would be possible words but *[loni] would not. A generative phonologist could capture the generalization about the similarity of vowels found in the same word by marking frontness or backness, in the underlying form of any word, for only one of its vowels, say the first, and by writing a phonological rule saying in effect 'Make each vowel agree in frontness or backness with the first vowel of the word.' But this treatment implies that the nature of the first vowel is basic while that of later vowels depends on the first. The generativist could equally choose to make the last vowel, or even an intermediate vowel in a polysyllabic word, the 'determining' vowel: but the point is that, given a segmental phonological system, he must choose – and there is (in many cases) no basis for such a choice. In reality the units determine each other – 'frontness' is essentially, not just superficially, a property of a word as a whole, which is how prosodic analysis represents it. (For a clear prosodic treatment of Turkish vowel-harmony, which is in fact more complex than is suggested here, see Hill 1966.) A good example of the theoretical blinkers worn by many Chomskyans occurs in D. T. Langendoen's critique of the London School, where the author presents this characteristic of Firthian phonology as an objectionable point on the ground that in a prosodic description 'It is . . . left up to the ingenuity of the interpreter' to determine which element determines which (Langendoen 1968, p. 53); in other words, because generative phonology forces one to make such a decision, Langendoen does not see that it may be an unreal one.

The concept of the prosodic unit in phonology seems so attractive and natural that it is surprising to find that it is not more widespread. In fact just one American Descriptivist, Zellig Harris, did use a similar notion; but Harris's 'long components' (1951, ch. 10), though similar to Firth's prosodies, are distinct and theoretically less attractive (for one thing Harris's 'long component' analysis rests on a prior analysis into phonemes, so that none of the pseudo-problems created by phonemic analysis are avoided – cf. Robins 1969, pp. 112–13). The generative phonologists seem to have been so intent on arguing for the 'horizontal' division of a stretch of speech-sound into distinctive features (as against those Descriptivists who thought of phonemes as indivisible atoms) that they have never thought to call into question the 'vertical' division into segments.

Again, however, it is possible to argue that prosodic analysis ignores a tendency which is present in human language, which phonemic analysis and generative phonology are wrong to treat as an absolute rule but which should at least be recognized as a statistical tendency. Let me explain by referring to a lecture I once heard on prosodic analysis applied to Russian. Russian has a contrast between palatalized and nonpalatalized (plain or velarized) consonants (I shall indicate palatalization by a superscript [j]); and palatalization goes with relatively forward articulation of vowels, so that we have for example:

[mɑt] 'checkmate, mat'
[mʲæt] genitive plural of 'mint'
[mætʲ] 'mother'
[mʲɛtʲ] 'to knead'

– the more consonants are palatalized, the further forward the vowel, and *vice versa*. There is a temptation here (to which the lecturer succumbed) to postulate a 'prosody of yodization', say, which makes vowels front and consonants palatal, and to say that the above words contain the same phonematic units but differ in yodization. However, if yodization is a syllable-level prosody, then there should be only two rather than four syllables – one with yodization, the other without; while, if yodization were a segment-sized feature applicable equally to vowels and consonants, we should expect eight possibilities since the two-way choice would be made independently for each segment. The only explanation for the occurrence of just four distinct syllables is that 'yodization', or rather palatalization, is essentially a feature of consonants only, and that the frontness of vowels is determined by the nature of the adjacent consonants. (This is the standard treatment of Russian by non-Firthian phonologists.) In other words, in this case of relationship between adjacent segments we *can* point to a reason for choosing one of the segments as determiner and the other as determinee; and there does seem to be a general tendency for phonetic features other than pitch and loudness to inhere in specifiable individual segments, or at least in small multi-segment units such as consonant clusters and diphthongs – vowel harmony languages are the exception rather than the rule.[6]

The Russian example introduces a further weakness in prosodic analysis. The prosodies I mentioned earlier were realized in a simple, phonetically-unambiguous way – bilabial closure, frontness of vowels. In the case of 'yodization', although palatalization of consonants is similar in articulatory terms to the move from [ɑ] through [æ] to [ɛ], there is more to the matter than that – if one wished to use a prosody of yodization one would need, in a complete description of Russian, to explain just how that prosody was manifested in consonants and in vowels respectively. But prosodies are often realized much more diversely than this. For instance, Eugénie Henderson's analysis of Vietnamese (1966) posits a prosody 'dark' which corresponds in various circumstances to at least the following phonetic features: bilabial or labiodental articulation, backness, implosion. (Others of Henderson's prosodies also correlate fairly indirectly with pronunciation.) There is no suggestion that these features are *universally* linked with one another (Firth himself explicitly disbelieved in linguistic universals), but only that the structure of Vietnamese in particular becomes relatively elegant if these features are regarded as expounding a single prosody in that language. Now, whether we regard elegance of description as a merely aesthetic consideration or as correlating with the relative 'naturalness' of the language described, clearly we must take into consideration not just the simplicity of the statement which tells us how the various prosodies and phonematic units may combine with one another but also the simplicity of the statements relating these units to their respective phonetic exponents; in the Vietnamese case one suspects that the latter statements might be complex enough to outweigh the elegance of the former. But it is characteristic of the Firthian approach to be much more concerned with the 'systems' of choices betwen alternatives which occur in a language than with the details of how particular alternatives are realized. Thus Henderson makes a formal statement of the possible combinations of her Vietnamese prosodies, but she discusses the phonetic realization of the prosodies informally (though in considerable detail), tacitly suggesting that that aspect of her exposition is not part of the analysis proper.

This attitude is precisely the converse of that taken by the generative phonologists, if we think of the prosodic structure of an utterance as occupying roughly the same position in the one theory as underlying phonological structure does in the other: generative phonologists are interested almost exclusively in the rules for deriving surface from deep phonetics, and say little or nothing about the elegance or otherwise of the system of possible underlying phonological shapes in a language. Nowhere in Chomsky and Halle's *Sound Pattern of English*, for instance, will one find a statement of the pattern of possible phonological shapes for English syllables or words. Each of these attitudes seems as one-sided as the other. However, in both cases the weakness is only a weakness, not a fatal flaw. It would be easy enough to supplement a generative phonology with a 'phonological grammar' stating the range of underlying phonological shapes, and likewise there is no reason why one should not formalize the relationship between a prosodic analysis and pronunciation – this might lead to rejection of certain particular prosodic analyses, but not of prosodic analysis in general. Generative phonology is fatally flawed in other respects, but I do not believe that is true of prosodic analysis.[7]

The final point worth mentioning about Firthian phonology, however, is much less easy to defend. Firth insisted that sound and meaning in language were more directly related than they are usually taken to be. He seemed reluctant even to regard expression and content as distinct sides of the same coin, in the Saussurean way (Firth 1951a, p. 227), and he was wholly unwilling to acknowledge the indirectness of the expression/content relationship suggested by Martinet's slogan about 'double articulation'. (Firth nowhere refers to Martinet, as far as I know; Martinet's British academic links were with Oxford more than with London.) For Firth, a phonology was a structure of systems of choices, and systems of choices were systems of meaning (cf. Berry 1975, p. 143, for a recent restatement of this position). Of course it is true that we can use language meaningfully only because we can opt to say one thing rather than another, but Firth meant that each individual choice-point in a grammar had its own individual semantic correlates, and this just cannot be taken seriously; I have already said that Martinet's principle is a trivial truism, which means that a denial of it is trivially false. In English, / n / is one of the options in the system of word-initial consonants, but in isolation the choice of / n / implies nothing whatever about the meaning of an utterance – I might choose that option in order to say the word *nice*, or the word *nasty* or the word *neutral*. There are a few direct correlations – thus for example / fl- / occurs in many English words denoting sudden movement, such as *flick, flicker, flit, flap*, *flurry*, etc., and Firth was interested in such cases; but it would be wishful thinking to imagine that phenomena of this kind were more than peripheral in the language as a whole. This aspect of Firth's thought seems to be a consequence of his odd concept of 'meaning', which we shall explore shortly.

The principle just mentioned did have some heuristic value for the work of the London School. It meant, for instance, that the practitioners of that school were quite happy to introduce grammatical considerations into their phonological analyses where this was convenient, at a time when American Descriptivists of the discovery-procedure persuasion were ruling out such 'mixing of levels' as methodologically illegitimate; but this controversy is now quite rightly a dead issue, and there would perhaps be little to be gained by resurrecting it here.[8] More interestingly, the principle encouraged members of the school to devote a good deal of attention to intonation, which is one area of phonology for which the claim of direct phonological/semantic correlation is more tenable. Linguists of the London School have done much more work on the analysis of intonation than have Americans of any camp, and the British work (e.g. O'Connor and Arnold 1961) is both quite different in kind from and, in the present author's inexpert judgement, more enlightening than, the kinds of analysis current in America.[9] But on the whole this last aspect of Firth's phonological thinking is an unfortunate excrescence which has been properly ignored by many prosodic analysts.

To understand Firth's notion of meaning, we must examine the linguistic ideas of his colleague Bronisław Malinowski (1884–1942), Professor of Anthropology at the London School of Economics from 1927 onwards. Malinowski, a Pole of aristocratic descent, did fieldwork in the very primitive culture of the Trobriand Islands off eastern New Guinea. (His reputation would be secure if for no other reason than unusual felicity in naming his books; there can be few other scholars whose dry academic volumes are graced with titles as alluring in their different ways as *Coral Gardens and their Magic* and *The Sexual Life of Savages*.) The most important aspect of Malinowski's theorizing, as distinct from his purely ethnographic work, concerned the functioning of language.

For Malinowski, to think of language as a 'means of transfusing ideas from the head of the speaker to that of the listener' was a misleading myth (1935, p. 9): to speak, particularly in a primitive culture, is not to tell but to do. 'In its primitive uses, language functions as a link in concerted human activity. . . . It is a mode of action and not an instrument of reflection' (1923, p. 312). Malinowski illustrates his point by referring to a Trobriand fishing expedition: 'A small fleet of canoes moving in concerted action is constantly directed and its movements co-ordinated by verbal utterance. . . . The meaning of a cry announcing a shoal of fish consists in the complete resetting of all the movements of the fleet' (1935, p. 58). 'The manner in which I am using [language] now, in writing these words,' on the other hand, 'is a very far-fetched and derivative use of language' (1923, p. 312). Words are tools, and the 'meaning' of a tool is its use: a view which Ludwig Wittgenstein acquired a considerable reputation by restating long after Malinowski had argued the point at length.

One problem with this view is that even the Trobrianders did spend a good deal of time just chatting, not about activities in which they were jointly engaged. For Malinowski this sort of speech also had to be 'doing' something, and he argues that its function is to create or maintain bonds of sentiment between the speakers; Malinowski coins the term *phatic communion* (1923, p. 315) for speech which serves this function and in which the 'meaning of the words' in the usual sense is irrelevant – he cites 'How do you do?' and 'Nice day today' as English examples. The issue that Malinowski dodges, because he cannot meet it properly, is that 'idle gossip' does not consist exclusively or even chiefly of such empty phrases as these; and it succeeds in forging bonds of sentiment just because it tells the hearers things that interest them and that reassure them about the speaker's attitudes. To put the same point another way: at least in his earlier writing, Malinowski accepts that modern scientific language does consist of telling rather than doing; once one accepts that people can tell each other things, it seems perverse to deny that that is what the Trobrianders do. The utterance of a Trobriander who spots a shoal of fish causes a resetting of the movements of the fleet not because the utterance is a tool for positioning canoes as a hammer is a tool for driving nails, but because the utterance tells the other men about the location of the fish and they take the actions which seem appropriate to them in the light of their new knowledge. Malinowski, clearly, is being led by the behaviourist fallacy of Chapter 3 to try to deny the existence of unobservable thought-processes, although his comments about the use of language in civilized societies show that in 1923 he was not wholly consistent in his 'bad behaviourism'. Later Malinowski realized that he had been inconsistent (1935, p. 58), and he tried to argue that even Western scientific discourse was a matter of 'doing' rather than 'telling', but his attempt was very unconvincing. He stressed the existence of utterances which J. L. Austin was later to call 'performatives' – utterances such as 'I promise to repay you tomorrow' or 'I declare you man and wife' which really do 'do things' rather than stating that something is the case (Malinowski 1935, p. 53); but most utterances are not performatives.

Firth accepted Malinowski's view of language, and indeed the two men probably each influenced the other in evolving what were ultimately very similar views; as a result, Firth uses the word 'meaning', which occurs frequently in his writings, in rather bizarre ways. The meaning of an utterance is what it does, but of course various aspects of utterances do very different kinds of thing. Thus, certain phonetic features which we recognize as constituting an American accent cause us to act in whatever particular ways we feel to be appropriate in the presence of Americans – to become hospitable but defensive, perhaps. One would not normally regard an ordinary sentence (leaving aside shibboleths like *candy* or *bathroom*) as *meaning* something special merely by virtue of being pronounced in an American accent; but, for Firth, 'Surely it is part of the meaning of an American to sound like one' (1951b, p. 192). Firth often reads as if he felt that *any* property of an utterance was part of its meaning; his use of the term is so broad and at the same time so vague that it seems to serve little purpose (cf. the critique by Lyons, 1966).[10]

Malinowski clarifies his idea of meaning by appealing to a notion of 'context of situation' (Malinowski 1923, p. 306). He makes the point that a European, suddenly plunged into a Trobriand community and given a word-by-word translation of the Trobrianders' utterances, would be no nearer understanding them than if the utterances remained untranslated – the utterances become comprehensible only in the context of the whole way of life of which they form part. This is certainly true: it is essentially the same point that I was making in Chapter 4 when I said that one has to study the Bororós' theories before one can understand what they mean by calling themselves parrots, which was an extreme example of a difficulty that recurs constantly in less extreme forms in communication between people leading different ways of life. To understand an utterance in an alien language is not just to equate it with some element of one's own language but is rather to know its position in a complex network of sense-relationships which it contracts with other elements of the alien language. However, once one has become a wholehearted 'bad behaviourist', the notion of describing a semantic system as an unseen network of relationships in speakers' minds is a suspect one (and Firth and Malinowski did not have the alternative of attributing the structure to a *'conscience collective'* – both of them explicitly opposed Durkheimian collectivism). The notion that meaning is to be stated in terms of observables, allied to the fairly flexible concept of 'context', suggests two possible approaches to semantics, and Firth advocated both approaches at different points in his writings.

On the one hand one can think of human behaviour as a series of observable patterns in which speech occurs as a more-or-less predictable gloss at certain points; to quote Lyons's exposition of Firth's view (1966, p. 290), "meaning", or "function in context", is to be interpreted as acceptability or appropriateness in that context: an utterance or part of an utterance is "meaningful" if, and only if, it can be used appropriately in some actual context'. But this seems to imply that utterances are meaningful only insofar as they are predictable, which is the reverse of the truth: some of the most significant remarks we hear are remarks which startle us on first encounter, and the more predictable a phrase such as 'How do you do?' becomes in its context the emptier, i.e. the less meaningful, it is. Firth is forced to describe as 'nonsense' Sapir's example-sentence *The farmer kills the duckling* because he could not envisage a likely context of situation for it (Firth 1935, p. 24); but the truth is that the sentence is perfectly meaningful, in the normal sense, whether or not it is likely to be uttered in practice.

The second approach is to interpret context more narrowly as the words in a text surrounding the word or longer form whose meaning is to be expounded, and to *equate* the meaning of a word with the range of verbal contexts in which it occurs: to quote W. Haas (1954, p. 80), 'substitutions for *cat*, in more comprehensive units such as *The —— caught the mouse, I bought fish for my ——*, etc., display its meaning; its privilege of occurring in those contexts with a certain distribution of frequencies among the occurrences, *is* the linguistic meaning of *cat.*' (Firth was aware of the distinction between these two approaches, cf. Firth 1951b, p. 195, but he followed both.) But this latter notion seems perverse. Apart from anything else, it forces us to claim, say, that in a context such as *Stop that this instant or I'll tan your ——*, the word *podex* is as likely to occur as *backside* – or alternatively to deny that these words are synonyms, which by all normal criteria they are.[11] It might be claimed that this approach has a heuristic value in emphasizing that there is more to the 'force' of an utterance than the strictly 'propositional meaning' that a logician would see in it, but to my mind the notion of meaning as range of possible verbal contexts not merely clashes violently with the layman's use of 'meaning' but obscures, rather than clarifying, the distinction between 'what one says' and 'how one says it'. The results achieved by uttering a given sentence may depend on factors such as the social 'tone' of the words employed, as well as on their logical sense; but, provided we refrain from committing the behaviourist fallacy, we need not be tempted to equate the meaning of a sentence with the visible results achieved by uttering it.

Firth's ideas on meaning seem, in fact, to have very little to offer. Insofar as scholars trained within the London School have contributed to our understanding of semantics, as John Lyons in particular has done, they have achieved this by going beyond the framework of ideas shared by other members of the school. Let me turn now to a consideration of the London approach to syntax. This draws heavily on Firthian principles which we have already encountered in connection with phonological analysis, but the application of these principles to syntax has been carried out by successors of Firth, notably Michael Halliday (b. 1925), once Professor of General Linguistics at University College, London, and at the time of writing Professor at the University of Sydney, and R. A. Hudson (b. 1939), of UCL.

Syntactic analysis in the London style is commonly called 'systemic grammar' (other, less significant terms have also been used). A 'system' in Firthian language, remember, is a set of mutually exclusive options that come into play at some point in a linguistic structure. This is the clue to London School syntax: like

Firthian phonology, it is primarily concerned with the nature and import of the various choices which one makes (consciously or unconsciously) in deciding to utter one particular sentence out of the infinitely numerous sentences that one's language makes available.

To make this clearer, we may contrast the systemic approach with Chomsky's approach to grammar. A Chomskyan grammar defines the class of well-formed sentences in a language by providing a set of rules for rewriting symbols as other symbols, such that if one begins with the specified initial symbol *S* and applies the rules repeatedly the end-result will be one of the target sentences. Such a grammar can succeed in defining a *range* of different sentences, clearly, only because in applying the rules one is often faced with choices. But in a Chomskyan grammar the choice-points are diffused throughout the description, and no special attention is drawn to them. Many choices are made in the constituency base: a given category symbol is expanded by means of braces or commas into alternative rewrites, or brackets are used to show that some element may or may not occur in the rewrite of a category symbol. Other choices arise in applying transformations: certain transformations are optional, others can apply in alternative ways, and (in some versions of transformational theory) there are alternative orders for applying transformations, with the nature of the ultimate result varying according to which order is selected. Often it will be the case that some choice in applying the transformational rules becomes available only if certain options have been selected in the constituency base, but a Chomskyan grammar does nothing to make such interdependences between choices explicit – that is not its aim.

In a systemic grammar, on the other hand, the central component is a chart of the full set of choices available in constructing a sentence, with a specification of the relationships between choices – that is, one is told that a given system of alternatives comes into play if and only if such-and-such an option is chosen in another specified system, and so on. The 'systems' are named, and so are all the alternatives within each system; and it is taken as axiomatic that these choice-elements have semantic correlates. Such semantic correlates will normally not be particular elements of meaning in the 'propositional' or 'logical' sense, since those are determined mainly by choice of lexical items rather than by choice of syntactic structure. The correlates will rather have to do with the sort of characteristics discussed as Functional Sentence Perspective by the Prague School, or they will define the *categories* of logical meaning expressed by a given construction. (Cf. Halliday 1969 and 1970 for relatively accessible accounts of the semantics of his syntactic 'systems'.) To cite a very simple example, Halliday (1967, p. 40) suggests that one system of choices operating in English main clauses, a system which he labels 'transitivity', provides for a choice between 'intensive' (clause with 'ascription' process-type, e.g. *she looked happy*) and 'extensive' (clause with 'action' process-type); if the 'extensive' option is chosen, a choice comes into play between 'descriptive' (clause with 'non-directed action' process-type, e.g. *the prisoners marched*) and 'effective' (clause with 'directed action' process-type); and if 'effective' is chosen there is a further opposition between 'operative' (subject as actor, e.g. *she washed the clothes*) and 'receptive' (subject as goal, e.g. *the clothes were washed*).[12] In a standard transformational grammar, the syntactic differences between these clauses would correlate with choice of rewrite for the category symbol '*VP*' and for certain other symbols in the base, with choice of whether or not to apply the Passive transformation, and with choice of whether or not to apply the transformation which deletes the *by*-phrase produced by Passive. No explicit statement would be found in a transformational grammar pointing out, for example, that the choice of applying the Passive transformation arises only if certain options are chosen when rewriting '*VP*' in the base, and there are certainly no special names given to the alternative structures which result from the various choices. (Occasionally Chomskyans do use a special term to describe some particular syntactic structure, but usually this is a term inherited from traditional philological vocabulary, and traditional terminology provides names for only the most elementary among the many systems defined in a systemic grammar – Chomskyans do not make a point of supplementing this deficiency.) It is clearly much more reasonable to say that each syntactic choice has a direct semantic correlate than it was to make the parallel statement about phonology.

As in the case of prosodic phonology, so in syntax the London School is more interested in stating the range of options open to the speaker than in specifying how any particular set of choices from the range available is realized as a sequence of words. The existence of a regular relationship between the outward syntactic shapes of a group of sentence-types will be relevant to the decision that they constitute alternatives belonging to a single system, but 'systems' are also identified in terms of the analyst's intuitive feeling for semantic relationships; and the rules for realizing given syntactic choices are left relatively informal, whereas the systems of choices and their interrelationships are made very explicit and formal. (London School linguists have no interest in asking what particular types of rules are used in realizing various systemic options, since they are not concerned with the question of linguistic universals.) Again the converse tendency is noticeable with the Chomskyans. In the case of syntax the latter are less one-sided than in the case of phonology, since most Chomskyan grammars include a constituency base defining a range of deep structures as well as a set of transformational rules converting deep into surface structures; but many Chomskyans evince far more interest in the details of the transformational rules than in the details of the base, and some of the younger group of 'generative semanticists' seem to take the constituency base completely for granted (apparently feeling that it is somehow given *a priori* as a matter of logic – cf. McCawley 1968, p. 167; Parret 1974, p. 152), so that they discuss exclusively the rules for converting underlying structures into pronounceable form.

In order to grasp the rationale of systemic grammar, it is important to appreciate that its advocates do not normally suggest that it is more successful than transformational grammar at carrying out the task for which the latter was designed – namely, defining the range of grammatical sentences in a language.[13] Systemic grammar aims rather to provide a taxonomy for sentences, a means of descriptively classifying particular sentences. If a generative linguist armed with a Chomskyan grammar of English is presented with an individual English sentence and asked what kind of sentence it is, he could answer 'A grammatical sentence'; but, pressed to say what kind of grammatical sentence it is, he might be somewhat nonplussed: generative theory is geared to describing languages, not individual sentences. Systemic grammar, on the other hand, provides a battery of descriptive terms which enable the linguist to give a detailed characterization of any given sentence and to show in what ways it resembles and how it differs from other sentences.

Systemic grammarians claim, with some justice, that their sort of theory is much more relevant than the generative approach to the needs of various groups of people who deal with language. (Significantly, one of Halliday's articles is entitled 'Syntax and the Consumer' (1964). Firth made a point of claiming to be a 'hocus-pocus' rather than 'God's-truth' linguist when Householder's distinction – page 72 above – was drawn to his attention (Sebeok 1966, p. 551); it is an important and admirable part of the London tradition to believe that different types of linguistic description may be appropriate for different purposes.)[14] Margaret Berry's introduction to systemic theory makes the astute point that, while Chomskyan linguistics appeals to the psychologist, systemic linguistics is more relevant for the sociologist (Berry 1975, p. 23). The psychologist wants a theory that describes languages, so that he can see what kinds of languages human beings are capable of using. To each individual, on the other hand, his language, as a total range of options, is a more or less fixed given – the sociologist wants to be able to describe any patterns that emerge in the particular choices that given types of individual make in given circumstances from the overall range provided by their language. (This distinction between psychology and sociology is admittedly over-simple, but it is broadly accurate.) Other purposes for which systemic grammar is held to be more relevant than transformational grammar are literary criticism, and language teaching. It is possible to be sceptical as to whether *any* version of theoretical linguistics has much relevance to these activities, which some may feel are best done by informal, intuitive methods. But, if one does need a technical vocabulary in order to discuss the usage of a particular writer or to isolate aspects of French grammar which are proving difficult for a child to master, then it is easy to agree that one will need a theory that allows for the description of individual sentences rather than one designed for the description of whole languages.

At the same time, there are problems about the assumptions underlying systemic theory. One of these is parallel to, though much less serious than, the problem which arose for Firth's claim that phonological choices have direct semantic correlates. A phonological system provides a set of choices which is not, and could not be, even approximately isomorphic to the system of alternative messages that humans want to exchange: therefore most relationships between sound and meaning in any language must be very indirect. To some extent this appears to be true even for syntax: a language provides syntactic possibilities which are exploited in several different ways rather than being used for just one semantic function each. Thus, Berry (1975, p. 142) lists a system of 'finiteness' for the English verbal group, with the choices 'finite' and 'non-finite' (in the traditional senses). Surely there is no particular meaning or category of meaning correlated with non-finiteness? Berry gives, as two examples of non-finite verbal groups, *having finished (the course)* and *to pass (the exam)*. Of these, the former functions adjectivally (*Having finished the course John took a holiday*) while the latter acts as a noun (*To pass the exam is easy*), and other non-finite verbal groups occur in adverbial constructions (*The course having finished, everyone left*). I see no sense in which these various functions can be equated; only the syntactic *form* is constant as contrasted with that of finite verbal groups.[15] Conversely, Hudson points out (1971, pp. 101–2, 304–5) that even the distinction between *He thinks that she's wonderful* and *He thinks she's wonderful* has to be treated as expounding a 'system' (which he calls 'with BINDER' v. 'without BINDER'), although in this case there appears to be no difference in meaning of any kind correlated with the system. (This is a much less serious criticism: paraphrase is a semantic relationship, and it might be quite convenient to have alternative labels available for a syntactic distinction which does exist and may well come to be associated with some slight difference of meaning in the future even if it is not associated with any semantic difference at present.)

There are also certain special problems concerned with Michael Halliday's individual version of systemic theory, and it is perhaps worth briefly alluding to these since Halliday's version is at present by far the best known even if it is not, in my own view, the most attractive version of the theory. Alongside the notion of 'system', Halliday (for example, 1961) introduces into syntax the notions 'rank' and 'delicacy'. 'Rank' refers to a scale of sizes of grammatical unit, roughly speaking: the lowest-ranking unit is the morpheme, the highest-ranking is the sentence, and for any given language there will be a fixed number of intermediate ranks (English is said to have five ranks in all). Any grammatical system will operate at a specific rank. If we think in terms of

Chomskyan hierarchical tree diagrams, Halliday is saying, as it were, that sentences can be represented not merely as trees but as trees which are regimented in such a way that along any branch there are the same number of intermediate nodes between the 'root' and the 'leaf'. For Chomskyan grammars this is quite untrue (see Figure 4, page 139: some morphemes are dominated immediately or almost immediately by the root *S* node, other morphemes are reached only via a long chain of intermediate nodes and branches representing the application of many rules. Halliday *appears*, with his notion of 'rank', to be putting forward a claim about a new and hitherto unsuspected universal of syntactic structure; but we have seen that the London School is not in general interested in linguistic universals, and I believe Halliday simply did not appreciate what he was committing himself to in introducing the term. Matthews (1966) argues in effect that the notion is either empty or, if interpreted so as to make an empirical claim, false; and he seems correct – languages just are not regimented in that particular way.

As for 'delicacy', this is a scale of relative preciseness of grammatical statement. Thus, *car* will be distinguished from *shiny* at a very gross syntactic level, since there are few verbal contexts in which one of the words could be substituted for the other in a syntactically well-formed sentence; on the other hand, *car* and *hovercraft* will be distinguished only at a more delicate level – the two are largely interchangeable syntactically, but *hovercraft* does not take *-s* in the plural. The notion of delicacy might be harmless, except that Halliday's motive for introducing it is to argue that there is in principle no end to the process of increasing the delicacy of a grammar: at a delicate enough level even the words *boy* and *girl*, for instance, would be syntactically distinct (Halliday 1961, p. 267). This is just wrong; unless I have overlooked something, *boy* and *girl* are syntactically equivalent at the most delicate level. What Halliday has in mind is that, for instance, the utterance *This girl is pregnant* is more probable (to put it no more strongly) than *This boy is pregnant*; but that is because of human physiology and because people do not often utter patent untruths, not because the latter sentence is in any way un-English – cf. my *Form*, pp. 80 ff. (If my latter sentence were not English we could not say why it is silly.) According to Halliday (1961, p. 275), 'It is too often assumed that what cannot be stated *grammatically* cannot be stated *formally*: that what is not grammar is semantics, and here ... linguistics gives up'.

(Halliday adds, with a joky allusion to Chomsky's *Syntactic Structures*, that 'the view that the only formal linguistics is grammar might be described as a colourless green idea that sleeps furiously between the sheets of linguistic theory, preventing the bed being made'!) But one of those who hold the view against which Halliday inveighs is the present author, and I find nothing in Halliday's work to suggest that I am wrong. A correct grammar of English is a fully delicate grammar, in the sense that it will distinguish all words whose *syntactic* behaviour is idiosyncratic in any way, and there is no reason why the goal of complete delicacy should not be achieved in practice. 'Indelicacies' such as failure to distinguish *car* from *hovercraft* are simply errors. To distinguish in a grammar between *boy* and *girl*, on the other hand, is not to increase the delicacy of the grammar, but to confuse nonsensicality with ungrammaticality. In more recent work some systemicists have abandoned both the terms 'rank' and 'delicacy' (Hudson 1971, p. 69).[16]

The major difficulty in systemic grammar, for one who cares about the methodological issues discussed in earlier chapters, concerns the essential role that intuition appears to play in systemic analysis. Chomsky and his followers claim to rely on intuition; but I argued in Chapter 6 that a generative grammar could perfectly well be worked out on the basis of normal empirical evidence – what it makes predictions about are the word-sequences which speakers do and do not use, and that is an observable matter. The question whether or not certain constructions express different cases of a single semantic category and therefore belong together in one 'system', on the other hand, may be unavoidably an intuitive decision, in which case 'systemic grammar' cannot hope to rank as a science. But then, neither can sociology (cf. Winch 1958), the subject with which systemic grammar claims affiliation; provided that sociologists understand the logical status of their discourse, the fact that it is not scientific perhaps does no harm. (However, if systemic grammar were to justify itself in this way as a sort of philosophical analysis, it would presumably need at least to be able to claim that the intuitions to which the analysis into 'systems' appeals are reasonably widely shared – this seems much less clearly true of London School grammatical analysis than it is of some sociological or philosophical discourse.) On the other hand, it might be that if systemic linguists render the rules for realizing choices as explicit as the rules for making choices, criteria of overall simplicity might determine the analysis into systems independently of intuitions about meaning (cf. my remarks on prosodic analysis, page 221 above); whether or not systemic analysis would then become indistinguishable from Chomskyan linguistics is a question I do not feel qualified to answer. And although the role of intuition is a serious problem for systemic theory, clearly the Chomskyan school are the very last people who can use this criticism to attack it.

All in all, the London School would appear to have a good deal to offer. Where it fails completely, with respect to its notion of meaning, all other linguistic schools have likewise failed. Systemic syntax seems well worth consideration as an alternative, not necessarily exclusive, to more fashionable approaches. And prosodic phonology is in my judgement more nearly right than any other phonological theory.

Whether the potential contributions of the London School will succeed in finding a permanent place in the international pool of linguistic scholarship is another matter. The discipline of linguistics seems to be peopled largely by intellectual Brahmanists, who evaluate ideas in terms of ancestry rather than intrinsic worth; and, nowadays, the proper caste to belong to is American. The most half-baked idea from MIT is taken seriously, even if it has been anticipated by far more solid work done in the 'wrong' places; the latter is not rejected, just ignored.[17] London and other universities in Britain and the Commonwealth still contain scholars working within the Firthian tradition, but by now these are outnumbered, or at least outpublished, by a later, thoroughly Chomskyanized generation.[18] To the young English linguistic scholar of today, the dignified print and decent bindings of the *Transactions of the Philological Society* smack of genteel, leather-elbow-patched poverty and nostalgia for vanished glories on the North-west Frontier, while blurred stencils hot from the presses of the Indiana University Linguistics Club are invested with all the authority of the Apollo Programme and the billion-dollar economy. Against such powerful magic, mere common sense (of which the London School can offer as much as might be expected from a tradition founded by a Yorkshireman) and meticulous scholarship (in which it compares favourably, to say the least, with the movement that has eclipsed it) are considerations that seem to count for disappointingly little.

10 Conclusion

It is presumptuous to write a conclusion to a survey of a subject which is as lively and as widely practised (if not necessarily as successful) at present as it has ever been. Any overall pattern that I seem to see in the work of the century and more discussed here will soon look very one-sided and idiosyncratic, as new ideas come forward which cause us to recast our views about what was most important in the work of the past. With that proviso, though, it seems worthwhile to round the book off by drawing together some themes which have recurred continually through the period I have surveyed.

The first is the question whether linguistics is a *Geisteswissenschaft* or a *Naturwissenschaft* – an 'art' or a 'science', to use the less explicit contemporary English terms. In fact the question is not often put so uncomprisingly, because many linguists (like, I believe, many laymen) have felt that the study of language properly combines both modes of discourse. Our phonetic habits are not normally under our conscious control, and the phonetic behaviour of speakers of any given language seems to conform to more or less fixed norms – phonetics and phonology seem to be one aspect of human behaviour which is rather clearly describable in terms of statements that predict the non-occurrence of logically possible observable phenomena (e.g. 'German speakers do not produce interdental fricatives'), and is thus scientific. (The fact that such statements involve proper names such as 'German' is suspicious, for a science: a German-speaker may learn English. But that is only a superficial difficulty in the way of treating phonology as a science.) Semantic description, on the other hand, cannot be scientific, because our semantic behaviour is an example *par excellence* of the unregimented, unpredictable working of the conscious human mind. Jerrold Katz tells me that a 'bachelor' is 'by definition' an unmarried adult male; but I am entitled to reply that for me the essence of bachelordom is not one's sex but the free and easy life that bachelors lead (a 'component' of bachelordom not noticed by Katz's analysis) – so that, in the era of Women's Lib, young Samantha is as much a bachelor as old Theophilus ever was. Real words in real languages shift their senses in just this unforeseeable way, so any discussion of the meanings of words can offer only interpretations of what has happened in the past, not predictions about future developments. Semantics cannot be scientific.[1]

Proponents of the logical extremes have not been lacking. The Italian neolinguists, followers of the philosopher Benedetto Croce who identified linguistics with aesthetics, held that there was no room for scientific discourse in any branch of linguistics at all. My limited knowledge has prevented me from devoting the space to this group that they clearly deserve; though, that having been said, I will add that from what little I have seen of the writings of Bàrtoli and Bonfante I judge it unlikely that I would ultimately be convinced. American linguists, by contrast, have argued that all aspects of language can be treated scientifically (this was as true in principle of Bloomfield as it is of Chomsky – Bloomfield thought merely that there were practical difficulties in applying the scientific method to semantics). But this does not mean that the Americans have judiciously concluded that semantics falls on the scientific side of the arts/science divide: for them there is no divide, they are believers in the fallacy of scientism. (Bloomfield makes his adherence to the logical-positivist faith – that is, Carnap's as opposed to Popper's version of inter-war Viennese philosophy – very explicit; and Chomsky dismisses the notion of intrinsically unscientific *Geisteswissenschaften* as an implausible 'counsel of despair', cf. Mehta 1971, p. 212.) Of the non-extreme positions, a very attractive one was articulated by Schleicher (1850, pp. 3–4), who located the boundary between science and art as coinciding with that between morphology and syntax – it being understood that phonology was in the same boat as morphology and semantics in the same boat as syntax. Intuitively it seems very reasonable to say that we accept the words of our language as a fixed given, but use our creative intelligence in deciding how to string them together. Saussure, on the other hand, seems to have felt that even morphology belonged on the arts side of the divide (though he was not very explicit, and if he meant to say this he was surely wrong).² In our own time Chomsky has shown us how syntax can be a science, and I believe he is right. We deceive ourselves when we imagine that we are free to string words together as we wish. Our syntactic structures follow fixed, conventional rules of which most of us remain unconscious; where we exercise our intelligence is in deciding how to understand the grammatical sentences of our language, and hence where to draw the line between sensible statements and grammatical nonsense – those are issues of semantics, not of syntax. This achievement of Chomsky's in showing us how syntax can be described scientifically is a great contribution to the discipline, and one regrets that Chomsky has chosen not to participate in constructing the science whose place in the intellectual arena he has mapped out for us.

Chomsky has not in practice helped to inaugurate a scientific approach to syntax, because of his belief that it is possible and appropriate to make scientific, predictive statements on a foundation of intuitive data rather than of observation. It is difficult to know what one can usefully respond to such an idea. It is true, of course, that potentially-scientific topics in their initial stages are often approached in a relatively intuitive, non-falsificationist spirit: we have seen that this is true of some of the work of the Prague School, for instance. (Other aspects of Prague School work, such as their literary criticism, are presumably intrinsically *geisteswissenschaftlich*.) But the proper response to that situation, if there seems to be merit in the embryonic ideas, is to try to sharpen them up into empirical, testable theories and to test them – we have seen that André Martinet, William Labov, and others have pushed this programme forward to a greater or lesser extent in the case of Prague School thought. It is true, also, that hypotheses even in a mature science come from the scientist's imagination rather than by induction from his data; but what makes a theory empirical is a question not of where the theory comes from but of how it is tested. When Chomsky argues that a fully mature scientific discipline ought *in principle* to be treated as answerable to intuitions rather than to observation, fruitful dialogue seems impossible.

The final issue is the question of language universals. This question is of course closely related to the science-v.-art question. To say that such-and-such is a universal feature of human language is to say that no human language can lack that feature, which is to make a testable, scientific statement. The difference is one of level: when I asked how far linguistics could be scientific I was asking what parts of the structure *of any individual* language are open to scientific analysis, whereas here I am asking what aspects of human language as a general phenomenon can be treated predictively. The questions at either level are connected: if it is in principle impossible to describe scientifically the semantic structure of any given language, then it follows (surely?) that one cannot make true predictions about semantic universals. On the other hand, from the fact (if it is a fact) that phonological and syntactic structures of individual languages can be described scientifically it does not follow that there are scientific theories of phonological or syntactic universals waiting to be discovered – languages might just differ unpredictably in the nature of the fixed phonological and syntactic structures which they severally display.

With respect to phonology, as the reader will have gathered, I believe that that is exactly the situation. Of course it is uncontroversial that 'phonological universals' of a kind exist: thus a language with a system of just three vowels will have roughly the vowels [i u a] (rather than, say, [e ẽ ɯ]), because [i u a] are the 'furthest apart' vowels in both articulatory and acoustic terms, so that speech is easier and more efficient if [i u a] are the vowels used. Universals of that sort give us no grounds at all to posit the inheritance of complex fixed mental machinery for language-processing, because such universals are entirely predictable without a hypothesis about innate mental structure, given the facts of physics and human physiology. (There is no dispute about the fact that our physiology is largely innately determined; empiricists believe that mind differs from body in this respect.) An argument from linguistic universals to innate mental mechanisms could only possibly work provided that the linguistic universals were not ones for which more obvious explanations are available, and I remain to be convinced that there are any such universals in the field of phonology.

I believed, at the time I began writing this book, that the situation was rather different in syntax. Certainly, as I indicated in Chapter 6, many alleged syntactic universals either are not universal or are vacuous. Furthermore, a number of universal claims which do constitute falsifiable statements and which have survived testing turn out to be 'explainable-away' rather as the [i u a] universal could be explained away, although the explanations tend to be rather subtler in syntax than in phonology. (Thus Schachter 1977 explains away – in my view, convincingly – a syntactic universal that had seemed for some time as impressively arbitrary as the 'A-over-A' principle discussed in Chapter 6; I think it likely that the latter phenomenon will yield to a similar explanation in terms of need to ensure that sentences are comprehensible.) However, the basic fact of the centrality of hierarchical structure in the syntax of all human languages, which seems to be a true and empirically-testable phenomenon (and not merely a matter of the way individuals choose to describe syntax, as has sometimes been suggested by those unfamiliar with the mathematical side of linguistics) appeared to me until recently to be resistant to 'explaining-away' as a predictable consequence of known principles, and therefore to constitute good *prima-facie* evidence for a rationalist account of mind. (I have criticized various standard attempts to 'explain away' the ubiquity of hierarchical structure in my *Form*, chs. 6–7.)

I have ceased to believe this, since reading an article (which seems to be unfamiliar to most linguists though published some time ago) by Herbert Simon, Professor of Computer Science and Psychology at the Carnegie-Mellon University (Simon 1962). I have no space to do justice to Simon's argument here; I have discussed its application to linguistics in two recent works (Sampson 1978, 1980). Briefly, Simon is concerned with the distinction, among complex structures, between those which have been planned and produced from scratch 'in one go' by a guiding intelligence, and those which are the outcome of a process of step-by-step trial-and-error evolution from simple beginnings, in other words processes formally akin to Darwinian evolution. Structures of the former class may take whatever form their creator thinks up; but Simon demonstrates mathematically that structures of the latter class must be organized hierarchically, even though hierarchical organization may do nothing to make them more 'fit', useful, or likely to survive once they have appeared. Nothing seems more plausible than to suppose that human language, like other complex social institutions, has evolved from the simple signalling-systems of beasts through a long process of cultural transmission, modification, and competition in terms of efficiency between alternative usages. Given that assumption, it turns out that Simon's argument predicts very accurately the various syntactic universals discussed by Chomsky which had seemed to argue for an innate *faculté de langage*. I conclude, therefore, that the empiricist account of human nature is correct, and there are no grounds for thinking that the human infant has any tacit 'knowledge of knowledge' when he comes into the world (indeed, Simon's argument provides positive reasons to believe that the infant does *not* have such knowledge). We learn to speak, as we learn everything else, because we are good at picking things up rather than because in a sense we knew how already; and the only limits to the diversity of human languages are those imposed by our bodies (rather than our minds) and by the unsurprising tendency for all human activities (not just speech) to be carried out efficiently rather than inefficiently when alternative methods are available.

The true general theory of language is that there is no general theory of language; the only features common to all human languages are predictable consequences of principles belonging to other, established disciplines, so that there is no room in the intellectual arena for an independent theoretical subject called 'general linguistics'.

Thus, with a certain elegance, we end where we began in Chapter 1: in biology. Schleicher has often been called naïve and worse for his treatment of linguistics as a branch of Darwinism, but it seems that he was not far from the truth.

Schleicher went wrong, perhaps, by thinking in terms of a struggle for survival between languages of different morphological rather than different syntactic characteristics (from what I have said about Schleicher's view of syntax it is entirely understandable that he did not discuss syntax in connection with Darwinism); the relative efficiency of languages has more to do with syntax than with morphology, but from the evolutionary point of view all extant languages (modern and classical) are much of a muchness – in terms of Simon's argument, the contemporary 'glossosphere' looks less like the contemporary biosphere than like a biosphere in which the struggle for survival had continued to the point at which one species had eliminated all the others. (Here, however, one has to reckon with disanalogies between linguistics and the other branches of biology.) That is one reason why we cannot confirm the operation of the survival of the fittest by data about expansion and contraction of languages like English and Welsh: from the Darwinian point of view one is as good as another, so men choose in terms of fashion or politics, or other criteria having nothing to do with the intrinsic structure of the languages.

Doubtless Schleicher was wrong, too, in assuming that if Darwinism was to be applicable to linguistics then languages had to be seen as genetically-determined living 'organisms'. Darwinian theory applies to individual features of organisms, as well as to organisms as wholes; and modern ethologists realize that behaviour-patterns are just as much open to Darwinian analysis as are features such as the foot or the eye. Furthermore, the application of Darwinism to linguistics does not commit us to the view that individual humans inherit an 'instinct for language'; trial-and-error learning by an individual mind who begins mentally as a 'blank slate' is as much a Darwinian process as is evolution by genetic mutation within a species.

In general, though, Schleicher was right; and I venture to predict (with the very limited confidence that one is entitled to place in predictions about intellectual progress) that as the linguistics of the immediate past has been psychological linguistics, so the linguistics of the near future will be biological linguistics.

Notes

1 Prelude: the nineteenth century

1 The term *philology* and its cognates in the European languages embody an awkward ambiguity. On the Continent – as, originally, in English – *Philologie* refers to the study of a culture through its literature: 'classical philology' concerned itself with the Latin and Greek languages only as means to a better understanding of Roman and Greek civilization, and when, during the Romantic period, scholars in Central Europe began to study the early forms of their own languages, as ends in themselves rather than as literary vehicles (which they were not), they tended to distinguish this new approach to language-study as *Sprachwissenschaft* or *Linguistik*. In English, on the other hand, *philology* shifted its meaning to cover the newer subject; the term *linguistics* did not become current, at least in Britain, until after the subsequent re-orientation within the new subject discussed in the text, so that in modern English usage *linguistics* normally means linguistics in the twentieth-century style – therefore primarily synchronic linguistics – while *philology*, if used at all, refers (often slightly patronizingly) to historical linguistics as practised in the nineteenth century. On the conflicting senses of *philology* (usage has varied even between Britain and America), cf. Bolling (1929).

2 The term 'Indo-European' refers to the family of languages to which English and most languages of Europe and Northern India belong. All these languages are held to descend ultimately from a hypothesized 'Proto-Indo-European' language ('PIE'). From PIE descended Sanskrit, Latin, Greek, 'Proto-Germanic', and various other known or hypothesized ancient languages, and different modern languages in turn derive from these: thus Latin is the ancestor of French, Italian, Rumanian, etc.; from Proto-Germanic derive English, Dutch, German and the Scandinavian languages; and so on for the other branches.

3 As a *prescription* for how the scientist should choose between theories, Kuhn's views leave much to be desired, but as a *description* of what happens in practice they are more satisfactory. (Cf. page 159 below.)

4 Corresponding to English *door* we find German *Tür*; that is because, after Proto-Germanic had split into the ancestors of the various modern Germanic languages, a further consonant-shift in the German branch altered (among other things) [d] to [t].

5 The term *idiolect* refers to the habits of speech of a single person.

6 An *isogloss* is a line delimiting the territorial range of some single feature with respect to which dialects differ.

7 Independently of Schmidt's arguments, however, there is evidence that structural features of languages may spread across boundaries between languages which are only distantly or not at all related. Schleicher was aware of this phenomenon (1848, p. 29), but he did not appreciate how damaging it was for his Darwinist view of language: it has no analogue in biology, since unions between members of distantly related species are infertile. The family-tree view of linguistic relationships was rejected by the Italian school of 'neolinguists' (Bonfante 1946; also see Jakobson 1931 and Vachek 1966, p. 26, on the Prague School notion of *Sprachbünde* or 'language unions'), but family trees remained axiomatic for the mainstream linguistic tradition inherited by America from Germany; within that tradition, non-genetic relationships between languages were first discussed in detail only by Emeneau (1956), though cf. Boas (1929).

8 One point uniting zoology and botany as against linguistics is that, if we go far enough back in time, *all* plant and animal species are held to share a common origin: however far back we trace the evolution of languages, we will encounter only older languages, never algae or the like. But it cannot be a defining trait of biology that all its subject-matter shares a common ancestry: if life turns out to have originated and evolved independently on Mars, for instance, the biologist will not refuse to admit Martian life into his purview. Schleicher gave his own answer to the objection that languages are not 'things' in a supplement to *Darwin's Theory and Linguistics* published in 1865.

9 Jespersen (1922, p. 36), referring to A. W. von Schlegel (1818). The three-way classification is still commonly used today, although with no suggestion that the different types are of unequal merit. The distinction between isolating and agglutinating types, however, seems relatively superficial: the only reason why we say that Turkish has words several morphemes long while in Vietnamese words are not distinct from morphemes is because Turkish has vowel-harmony, and it is convenient to use the term 'word' for the domain over which vowel-harmony operates. (Cf. Matthews 1974, p. 170.) The terms *morpheme* and *vowel harmony* are explained in n. 14, page 247, and n. 7, page 255, respectively. The distinction between these two types taken together and the inflecting type, on the other hand, does seem a basic one, though the distinction is gradient rather than sharp.

10 Schleicher had answers (though in my view quite unsatisfactory ones) to the former point; but the latter point seems to have been a clear and unresolved contradiction in his thought: cf. Jespersen (1922, pp. 72–3) on the introductions to the two volumes of Schleicher's *Sprachvergleichende Untersuchungen* (1848, 1850), or Kurt Jankowsky's disagreement (1972, p. 101) with Delbrück on the relation between Schleicher's Hegelianism and his view of linguistics as biology.

11 Cf. Catford (1974), Householder (1977, pp. 560–3). The notion of directionality in grammatical change has recently been revived (see, for example, Li 1975); it remains to be seen how successful this revival will be.

12 One problem in interpreting comments like this last one is that history was thought of as the *Geisteswissenschaft par excellence*, which led to a measure of confusion between the diachronic/synchronic and the arts/science distinctions.

13 Paul would not have accepted this point as robbing his objection to Schleicher of its force. Paul's disagreement with his predecessors was based not merely on a different view of social phenomena, but on novel presuppositions about the nature of science in general. He was influenced by the 'descriptivist' view of science, advocated in his time by the physicist and philosopher Ernst Mach, according to which only observables really exist, while theoretical entities – atoms, for instance – are convenient fictions introduced to abbreviate statements about observables. Thus, for Paul, the biologist who hypostatizes a species 'carrot' might well be accused of mysticism (cf. for example, Paul 1880, p. 37). However, descriptivism (on which see, for example, Nagel 1961, ch. 6; Sampson 1975a, pp. 27–9) does not seem to most modern philosophers to provide an adequate account of the nature of scientific theories.

14 It has recently been revived by William Wang (1969).

15 Interestingly enough, those who argue that *grammatical* change is a process of simplification are not similarly forced to postulate perversely complex proto-languages. E.H. Sturtevant (1947, pp. 107–9) points out that it is in the nature of sound-change to create grammatical irregularity; thus, once one accepts the axiom that sound-changes occur, one can claim that *other* linguistic changes are motivated by a tendency towards simplicity while the overall complexity of a language remains more or less constant.

16 '... utility [*Zweck*] plays the same role in the evolution of linguistic usage as Darwin attributed to it in the evolution of organic nature: the greater or lesser fitness [*Zweckmässigkeit*] of newly arising forms is decisive for their retention or extinction' Paul 1880, p. 32).

17 Recently there have been renewed attempts to produce general scientific theories of linguistic change. See, for example, Weinreich *et al.* (1968), Li (1975). For a recent discussion of the motivation of Grimm's Law, see Lass (1974).

2 Saussure: language as social fact

1 Philosophically this is arguable: just as one postulates a system called an 'idiolect' underlying the diverse utterances a man is observed to produce, so, it might be suggested, one postulates a physical object to explain the orange-coloured visual stimuli, etc., that one receives on looking towards the

kitchen table. But physical objects are so much more straightforward a category of entities than idiolects that for practical purposes the disanalogy between linguistics and biology is undeniable.

2 Page references in connection with Saussure are to the *Cours* (Saussure 1916).

3 'RP' (Received Pronunciation) refers to the version of spoken English widely accepted as 'correct' in England.

4 Saussure did not invent the term 'phoneme' – it was first used by the French phonetician A. Dufriche-Desgenettes in 1873; but it seems to have been Saussure's *Mémoire* of 1878 that brought the term into common use to indicate an element of the sound-system of a language as opposed to a speech-sound considered apart from its role in the phonology of a particular language. It is usual to enclose phonetic transcription in square brackets and phonemic transciption in solidi. Thus, in R P, we distinguish between the *phones* [l] and [lᵘ], but regard them both as members of the *phoneme* / l /; the members of one phoneme are its *allophones*. All phonetic transcription in this book uses the phonetic alphabet of the International Phonetic Association.

5 Even this much might not happen. RP has a non-distinctive variation in vowel duration, whereby a vowel such as / i / is shorter before a voiceless consonant like / f / than before voiced consonants or in final position. If this variation survived the disappearance of final / f v / it might become distinctive, so that (short) [li] for *leaf* would still sound different from (long) [li:] for *leave* or *lee*. This, incidentally, illustrates Saussure's point about the unexpected repercussions of an individual change to the system: here, loss of certain final consonants automatically introduces to the system distinctive vowel quantity, previously almost unknown in English.

6 In reality a chess game played like this would result in a rapid win for the man who could see what he was doing; but this obviously stretches the analogy too far, since there is no analogue in language of 'winning', and we must rather think of the two players as maintaining some sort of state of equilibrium in a game which never ends.

7 At one point in the *Cours* (p. 79), Saussure gives what seems intended as a third, independent reason for separating synchronic from diachronic linguistics. He says that most sciences (his instances are astronomy, geology, law, and political science) do not need to make such a distinction: linguistics and economics do (economic history is a discipline sharply distinct from political economy, according to Saussure), and the common factor in these two subjects is that they both deal with systems of *value* (economics relates money to goods, linguistics relates sounds to meanings). But it is unclear to me what connection there is supposed to be between the notion of value and the need to separate synchrony from diachrony; and I am also not clear that the latter distinction is as unimportant in subjects such as astronomy as

Saussure suggests (thus, are celestial mechanics and the theory of stellar evolution not rather sharply distinct branches of astronomy which are opposed to one another very much as synchronic to diachronic linguistics?). So, despite its prominent position in the *Cours*, I regard this passage as simply a mistake.

8 As it happened, the individualism/collectivism issue played only a small part in that final debate.

9 Koerner's remarks seem to stem from an exaggerated concern with the (surely relatively trivial) issue of where scholars borrow their technical terms from. At one point, for instance, Koerner (1973, p. 90) discusses Saussure's use of the word 'zero', and describes it as 'a term which we [i.e. Koerner] believe he took over from mathematics' – a safe bet, one feels.

10 Robert Godel (1969) identifies a 'Geneva School' or 'Saussurean School' of linguists, but these scholars are singled out because they work at Saussure's university and because several of them have been engaged in editing Saussure's papers and in exegesis of Saussure's ideas, rather than because their own original work is influenced by Saussure's thought in a way that the work of other linguists is not. Iordan-Orr (1937, pp. 279 ff.) identifies a 'French School' which was particularly concerned to develop the notion of language as social fact.

11 Rulon Wells's critique of Saussure (1947) virtually ignores this aspect of the *Cours* (see especially section 60 of Wells's article); one wonders whether collectivist thought may have been so alien to Wells that he simply did not recognize it for what it was.

12 Chomsky's thought is discussed at length in Chapter 6. However, his standing in the discipline at present is such that the reader is more likely to have encountered Chomsky's ideas than those of most of the other figures who appear in this book, and I shall allow myself to anticipate Chapter 6 by occasional earlier references to Chomsky's work when this is convenient.

13 One might suppose that 'water' means *both* H_2O and XYZ in English (and in Twin-Earth language), since an Englishman without special knowledge of chemistry would call a sample of XYZ 'water' (and *vice versa* for the Twin-Earther). But once the Englishman was told that the sample was chemically quite different from the stuff in lakes etc. he would agree that *he had been mistaken all along* in calling it 'water': this is what shows that 'water' does not mean XYZ in English.

14 A 'morpheme' is a minimum meaningful unit: thus the word *cat* consists of a single morpheme, but *unlovable*, for example, is made up of three morphemes, *un-*, *love*, and *-able*. (Some) morphemes are said to have 'allomorphs', as phonemes have allophones: e.g. the *bett-* of *better* is an allomorph of the morpheme whose principal allomorph is *good*.

15 Syntagmatic relationships exist between phonemes as well as between morphemes or other meaningful units. Thus, the fact that, in English, vowels such as / æ ʊ / can occur only before a consonant whereas / ɑ u /, for example, can occur in final position is a syntagmatic fact; the fact that English [l] contrasts with [r] but is in complementary distribution with [lʷ] is a paradigmatic fact.

16 For further discussion of the relevance of the knowing-how/knowing-that distinction for linguistics, cf. Sampson (1975, pp. 74–5, 204) and references cited there.

3 The Descriptivists

1 Edward Sapir, another influential early Descriptivist, will be discussed in Chapter 4.

2 The term 'grammar' is used for a linguist's formal description of the structure of a language.

3 Even this statement yields more ground than necessary to the point of view I am opposing; for instance, behaviourist methodology in no way requires us to reject the notion of free will.

4 The argument that follows concerns the proper analysis not only of fricatives but of consonants with two other manners of articulation; but nothing is lost by restricting the discussion to the fricatives for ease of exposition.

5 The principle tacitly presupposed by phonemic analysis is actually rather subtler than is suggested above. For instance, a Descriptivist would have seen nothing problematical about a language in which twenty consonants contrast prevocalically but only the single consonant [s] can occur in a cluster before another consonant. Perhaps one should say that phonemic analysis assumes that the number of alternatives found in one environment will be either identical to or *very* different from that found in another environment; or perhaps it assumes that '___i' and '___u' are 'comparable' environments in a sense in which '___V' and '___C' are non-comparable.

6 Miller (1973) rightly argues that the extent to which the Descriptivist school as a whole was concerned with discovery procedures has been considerably exaggerated in recent discussion.

7 In his most recent writing (1976) Chomsky has made his position more consistent by arguing (to put it over-simply) not that children learn languages by making imaginative leaps but that Einsteins invent scientific theories by following innate rules of thumb. I discuss Chomsky's position at length in my *Liberty and Language* and *Making Sense*; I find it difficult to take his current views on the nature of original thought seriously. For the evolution of Chomsky's ideas on the discovery-procedure issue, see Sampson (1979b).

8 For an outstanding book-length treatment of the history of the Descriptivist tradition and subsequent scholars' reinterpretation of it, see Hymes and Fought (1975).

4 The Sapir–Whorf hypothesis

1 Sapir has been cited by members of the modern, Chomskyan school as a fore-runner of their own movement. I find this judgment somewhat forced; Sapir did not construct explicit arguments *against* the behaviourist principle, as Chomsky has done, he merely remained uninfluenced by the arguments *for* behaviourism (Sapir was interested in questions of substance rather than of methodology).

2 The following English parallel may be worth mentioning. In conservative dialects of English, including my own, animateness is a covert category in that only animate nouns may take the 'Germanic genitive' (*N's* as opposed to *of N*; innovating dialects permit expressions such as *the car's wheels, the theory's influence*, but these phrases are ill-formed for me). I have been mildly disturbed to notice that the one noun in my own speech which consistently takes the Germanic genitive in *prima facie* violation of this rule is the noun *computer*.

3 One wonders whether Sigmund Freud may have had in mind Lévy-Bruhl's account of the primitive mentality when he discussed the 'id' (Freud 1932, pp. 73–4).

4 I argued in Chapter 3, following Boas, that languages cannot be distinguished as 'primitive' or 'advanced' in terms of their (phonological or grammatical) structure, which is relatively durable and independent of speakers' culture; vocabulary, on the other hand, certainly does reflect cultural level.

5 Homeric Greek is the only dead language discussed by Berlin and Kay. It is a particularly interesting case, because its extreme poverty of colour terms led no less a personage than W. E. Gladstone to argue for a Whorfian approach to this area of vocabulary (Gladstone, 1858, pp. 457–99). Berlin and Kay mention Gladstone's analysis but seem not to have read it; they subscribe (p. 148) to the common misunderstanding that Gladstone thought the ancient Greeks were colour-blind, whereas Gladstone explicitly rejected this hypothesis, arguing instead (as Berlin and Kay argue more than a century later) that sophisticated colour vocabularies go with technically sophisticated cultures.

6 Note that Berlin and Kay (p. 109) supposed that what they had discovered was a mental rather than merely physical or physiological phenomenon. For further discussion of Berlin and Kay's and other arguments for semantic universals, see Sampson (1978, 1980).

5 Functional linguistics: the Prague School

1 Trubetzkoy seems to turn his notion of 'archiphoneme' into an empirical hypothesis when he claims (1939, pp. 79–80) that only 'bilateral' oppositions can be neutralized, and furthermore that neutralizations of 'privative' oppositions are always realized by the 'unmarked' member of the opposition.

But these claims (although true of German / t / ~ / d /) seem to be false in general unless interpreted so as to become vacuous (Vachek 1966, pp. 61–2).

2 Stress is called a 'suprasegmental' feature because it coexists with a sequence of phonemes (a syllable, in this case) rather than occupying an individual slot in the phoneme-sequence.

3 I borrow this example from a lecture by Charles Fries.

4 True, Darwin showed us how evolution which appears to be directed towards a goal of increased fitness is perfectly compatible with the idea that each individual mutation occurs at random; but Saussure seems to say (he does not discuss Darwinism explicitly) that linguistic mutations not only occur at random but are retained at random – in biology, only mutations that happen to be favourable are retained.

5 Apart from the therapeutic theory of sound-change, Martinet is known for making the point that language has a 'double articulation' (Martinet 1949; 1955, pp. 157 ff.). By this he means that no human language divides the continuum of human speech-sound into a set of units which can be put into a one-for-one correspondence with the elements of meaning to which humans wish to refer (there are always far fewer phonemes than morphemes in a language); therefore a language divides up the sound-continuum in a semantically arbitrary way, and uses arbitrary combinations of the sound-segments resulting from this 'second articulation' in order to represent the units produced by the articulation of meaning (or 'first articulation'). This is perhaps worth saying, because Saussure's doctrine of a language as a set of signs, each of which was the union of a *signifiant* with a *signifié*, seemed to suggest that languages exhibited a relatively direct correspondence between articulation of the sound medium and articulation of meaning. However, Martinet's point seems a rather trivial truism which does not merit extended discussion.

6 One might suppose that Martinet's theory was refuted by the work of another of his predecessors at the École des Hautes Études, the Swiss Jules Gilliéron (1854–1926), who argued that lexical development is motivated by 'intolerable' homonymy produced by sound-changes (Iordan-Orr 1937, pp. 157 ff.). Martinet's principle appears to imply that sound-changes which would lead to intolerable homonymy should not occur. Martinet (1955, pp. 26–7) claims, however, that his and Gilliéron's views are not incompatible. A further point which might be counted a difficulty for Martinet's theory is that it seems to have no applicability at all to sound-changes such as Grimm's Law which leave the system of phonological contrasts unaltered.

7 What led Jakobson to the hypothesis that all parameters are 'binary' seems to have been the mathematical notion that a transmission-code is more efficient when it uses only independent binary choices (cf. page 193 below). This concern with relative efficiency is one respect in which Jakobson shares the functional outlook of the other members of the Prague School.

8 This aspect of Jakobson's theory was related to his belief about the primacy of acoustic over articulatory phonetics discussed on page 193 below.

9 It is not clear whether Jakobson *et al*. meant to suggest that *all* articulatory parameters would ultimately be assignable to one or other of their twelve features (a programme which they certainly did not carry out fully in their book), or whether they believed that some articulatory parameters were doomed never to be used distinctively in any language and therefore did not belong to any of the twelve features.

10 These observations equally argue against the alternative explanation for the priority of labials in child speech, namely that they are the consonants whose mechanism of production is most open to inspection.

6 Noam Chomsky and generative grammar

1 The view that grammaticality is *not* a well-defined property has been argued as against Chomsky by Hockett (1968); cf. my *Form of Language* (Sampson 1975a, pp. 53–9 – I shall refer to this work from here onwards as '*Form*'). Chomsky's MIT colleague J. R. Ross (e.g. 1972a) has argued that grammaticality is a gradient rather than a yes-or-no property, but this, as we have seen, is a separate and far less crucial question.

2 Harris did *not* think of his formulae in this light; although Chomsky regarded his own approach to grammar (with some justice) as a logical development of his teacher's ideas, once Chomsky had pressed these ideas to their logical conclusion, making explicit the assumption that grammaticality in a language is a well defined property, Harris rejected this assumption (Harris 1965, p. 370).

3 R. A. Hudson tells me that he believes the particular category 'nominal phrase' was first identified only in this century, by linguists of the Descriptivist school. It is nevertheless true that traditional parsing assumed a view of syntax broadly similar to constituency grammar.

4 Thus we might define the class which comprises, say, each sequence of English morphemes that obeys the rule 'sequences whose length is even contain at least one repeated morpheme; sequences whose length is odd contain no repeated morpheme'. Clearly the 'language' defined by a rule of this sort will have very little resemblance to a real human language. For other examples of hypothetical non-constituency languages, cf. my *Form*, pp. 41–2.

5 In practice we do find valleys which superficially do not fall neatly into either category, which is an additional reason for using a relatively flexible map-notation. Even this has a parallel in Chomskyan linguistics; a Chomskyan might say that events such as earthquakes or landslips which interfere with pristine U or V configurations are 'performance errors' by Nature whose effects should be ignored in drawing maps (cf. p. 153 below). The main point, however, is that even if all valleys really were perfect

examples of the U or V categories, there would still be no reason to object to a map-notation which potentially allowed for a wider range of possibilities.

6 Claude Hagège (1976, p. 17 n. 1) suggests, as one reason for the wide success of Chomskyan linguistics, that the 'applied linguistics' industry which grew up suddenly in the 1960s was attracted to a theory of language which used familiar grammatical terms that teachers already knew, rather than novel terminology (such as Fries's 'Class 1 words', etc.) worked out for Modern English rather than inherited from Greek. I believe Hagège is right, and I suspect that with hindsight the 'applied linguists' wish that they had looked rather harder before they leapt; Chomsky's school seems to be the very last to have anything to offer to the language-teacher (as Chomsky himself readily agrees).

7 Before we move on, it is worth considering the following point. Aristotle, one of the first thinkers known to have approached the question of grammatical categories, postulated a system much cruder than that evolved by Thrax two and a half centuries later: Aristotle had a single category of *syndesmoi* covering at least conjunctions, pronouns, and the article (Robins 1967, p. 26), although such a grouping can be justified neither on logical nor on linguistic grounds. If, as Chomsky and Langendoen argue, such classifications are made by the pure light of introspective reason rather than requiring education and experience, this seems to imply that Aristotle's mind was defective to a degree that one would not expect to encounter in a freshman class of an American college.

8 In my *Form* (pp. 156 ff.) I suggested that the empirical evidence might possibly be adequate to confirm a theory of 'grammar-meaning' although not of 'word-meaning'. I realize now that that was hopelessly optimistic.

9 The fact that the scientistic prejudice embodies an error has been demonstrated by Karl Popper, in intuitive terms (1957, pp. v–vii) and formally (1950).

10 The link between Chomsky's 'absolutist' political views and his approach to linguistics, which I discuss in detail in my *Liberty and Language*, was hinted at by Chomsky's teacher Harris in 1965 (Harris 1965, p. 365 n. 6).

11 I have been blurring the morphology/syntax distinction somewhat, and it is characteristic of American linguistics (of both Descriptivist and Chomskyan varieties) to blur the distinction. The decision to treat sentences as *sequences* of morphemes implies a decision to treat all languages as if they were of the isolating or agglutinating kind (cf. page 22, above), whereas the distinction between morphology and syntax is most salient in languages having elements of the inflecting type.

12 The course which Halle's and Chomsky's department offers on non-Chomskyan linguistics (i.e. on all the material surveyed in this book

other than in the present chapter and Chapter 8) is popularly known, by staff and students alike, as 'The Bad Guys'. Obviously the name is not intended too seriously, but it is nevertheless indicative. For a non-jocular expression of a similar attitude, see a remark of Chomsky's quoted by Mehta (1971, p. 191).

13 This system, under which it is generally acknowledged that much of what counts as important doctrine is not publicly available, has been a distinctive characteristic of Chomskyan linguistics from its earliest beginnings (cf. Sampson 1979b).

14 One striking piece of evidence *against* the view that human linguistic ability depends on innate psychological structure is the considerable success that has attended various recent experiments in teaching communication-systems syntactically similar to human languages to members of another species (chimpanzees). I have attempted to construct a defence of Chomskyan rationalism against these findings (*Form*, pp. 126–9), but I do not myself think the defence altogether successful; Chomsky, together with his followers, simply ignores the chimpanzee experiments entirely – which is consistent with his policy of preferring intuitive to experimental evidence, if almost scandalous by normal standards of empirical scholarship. The chimpanzee experimenters very understandably dismiss Chomskyan linguistics as a new scholasticism (Linden 1974, p. 246).

7 Relational grammar: Hjelmslev, Lamb, Reich

1 I use the term 'relational grammar' to cover the theory initiated by Hjelmslev and H. J. Uldall and developed by Sydney Lamb and Peter Reich. Hjelmslev and Uldall called their theory 'glossematics' or 'immanent grammar', and the term 'stratificational grammar' is associated with Lamb's work; none of these latter names seem particularly apt, and the suggestion that Hjelmslev and Lamb belong to distinct 'schools' is quite misleading. A further source of potential confusion stems from the use in the last few years of the term 'relational grammar' to denote a variant of Chomskyan linguistics which lays more stress than Chomsky himself does on concepts such as 'subject' and 'object': this latter theory has not seemed to me different enough from Chomsky's to warrant separate treatment in this book (and Reich has established a prior claim to the term 'relational grammar').

2 Although the diagrammatic notation is commonly thought to be specifically Lamb's contribution to relational grammar, Lamb in fact borrowed the notation from the German linguist Alfred Hoppe; see, for example, Hoppe (1964).

3 The critique of Lamb's theory which follows is based on a fuller discussion in Sampson (1974b).

8 Generative phonology

1 I have argued that it should (Sampson 1970).

2 The difference between Jakobson's and Halle's application of the concept of 'universal phonetic system' to phonological contrasts and to morphophonemic phenomena, respectively, is another example of European emphasis on paradigmatic relations in language versus American emphasis on syntagmatic relations.

3 It should be said that, although Halle (e.g. 1962) writes as if there is no question that phonological structures and processes operate in terms of 'natural classes' of sounds which have simple definitions in terms of phonetic features, one can find plenty of counter-examples: e.g. Hockett (1942, section 9); Martinet (1955, p. 51); Zwicky (1970). On balance, however, the weight of the evidence seems to argue for Halle's approach (indeed, the point was made already by Eduard Sievers, 1876, p. 4).

4 Consider, for example, the following point. Given a system of four pitch-levels, say '1 2 3 4' (with 1 highest), a binary-feature treatment will obviously include a feature High v. Low such that 1 and 2 are High and 3 and 4 Low; but the other feature might be either 2 & 3 = Central v. 1 & 4 = Extreme, or 1 & 3 = Raised v. 2 & 4 = Diminished. Jakobson and Halle opt for the latter analysis on the grounds that one West African tribe who speak a four-pitch language and who transpose the tones of their language into drum signals use, as names for the signals, 'smaller little bird', 'larger little bird', 'smaller big bird', and 'larger big bird', respectively. This seems slender evidence on which to base a claim about languages many of which are spoken thousands of miles away from Africa.

5 Paul Kiparsky at one time argued that generative-phonological analyses of sound-systems led to testable predictions about subsequent sound-changes (Kiparsky 1968), in which case they could hardly be treated as mere reconstructions of history (unless we are prepared to admit the unreasonable-seeming concept of action at a distance in time, i.e. to allow that an event at time *t* might cause an event at a later time *t'* while having no reflection in the situation obtaining at a date between time *t* and *t'*). However, Kiparsky was later (1971) forced by the pressure of counter-examples to replace his original universal principles of sound-change by principles which say in effect that languages tend to lose phonological alternations which are relatively irregular and therefore difficult to master: clearly we do not need generative phonology in order to predict that. Again, Paul Postal (1968, pp. 55 ff.) has argued that generative phonology is a relatively 'strong' theory of phonology because it incorporates a 'naturalness condition' according to which only phonetically-meaningful units can be mentioned at any phonological level, whereas Descriptivist and other theories allow themselves considerable freedom to posit morphophonemes (such as the |F| v. |f| discussed above) with no direct phonetic interpretation. Postal's naturalness condition certainly is a methodologically desirable

characteristic, but he is wrong to suggest that generative analyses obey it; all generative phonologists have found it necessary to use phonetically meaningless features such as the feature Romance v. Germanic which decides whether a given | k | becomes [s] before a non-open front vowel in English. In his efforts to reconcile this fact with his claim about the 'naturalness condition', Postal ends (p. 124) by converting the latter from an empirical ·claim into an empty verbal stipulation.

6 Compare J. van Ginneken's description of the language development of a Dutch child as proceeding 'from general human language to Dutch', quoted by Jakobson (1941, p. 51), and cf. Stampe (1969).

7 The term 'harmony' refers to limitations (which are found in many languages) on the extent to which sounds occurring in the same word may differ. Thus, in a vowel-harmony language, the vowels of any given word must be (say) either all front or all back; a consonant-harmony language might require all the consonants of a word to share a single place of articulation.

9 The London School

1 It is odd that nowadays, when everything from our weights and measures to our patterns of division of labour between the sexes are being transformed overnight by reformers who, rightly or wrongly, give no weight at all to the claims of tradition, those who advocate simplification of our enormously cumbersome spelling system are regarded as cranks or worse. In the nineteenth century, spelling reform was a serious, live issue. As recently as 1937, J. R. Firth (see below) wrote that 'English spelling is ... so preposterously unsystematic that some sort of reform is undoubtedly necessary' (Firth 1937, p. 48). I suspect that the change in attitude may be linked with the frighteningly complete, and uncharacteristic, loss of national self-confidence which England has suffered since the Second World War. We see ourselves now as following the lead of others rather than as the model to which foreigners aspire; since even the Eurocrats of Brussels have not yet presumed to reform our own language for us, we instinctively suppose that change must be inappropriate or impossible (though in fact many nations with spelling-systems much less awkward than ours have reformed them very successfully).

2 There is some excuse for American phonetic vagueness. Mastery of the cardinal vowels, for instance, is a skill transmitted through intensive personal training by men who acquired it directly or indirectly from Jones himself, and an 'ear' for the cardinal vowels has to be kept in tune through periodic checks with other bearers of the tradition. This sort of thing is more feasible within the tight circle of British linguistics than it would be in the much more diffuse American academic world. Alas, since the great university expansion of the 1960s the tradition seems to be breaking down even in Britain.

3 The proposal for such an institute was originally made by the Marquess of Wellesley shortly after he became Governor-General of British India in 1798.

4 This example would not quite work for speakers who pronounce a few inflected forms such as *dreamt* as [dremt] rather than [drempt]. I shall ignore this problem, rather choosing a more perfect but inevitably more *recherché* example.

5 Firth (1948, p. 123) somewhat pedantically insisted on the etmyologically-correct derivative *phonematic* (rather than the American *phonemic*) from *phoneme*, in the same article in which he repeatedly used the form (*mono/poly-*)*systemic*, rather than *systematic*.

6 Firthians sometimes talk of prosodies as having a particular segment as their 'focus', so that it may be unfair of me to suggest that prosodic analysis was misapplied in the lecture just discussed; but prosodic analysis is specially persuasive only in the cases where no individual segment can be selected as 'focus'.

7 The difference of approach as between generative phonologists and prosodic analysts discussed above is not quite the same as the syntagmatic/paradigmatic contrast between American and European linguistics discussed earlier. Firthian 'systems' are paradigms, but the corresponding syntagmatic relationships would be represented by rules for constructing phonologically possible words, and I have just pointed out that generative phonologists do not discuss these. What the latter group are interested in, namely the rules relating 'deep' and 'surface' representations, is a third category of phenomena distinct from both paradigmatic and syntagmatic facts (although perhaps connected more closely with the latter). One American approach which does provide for exhaustive analysis of syntagmatic relationships in phonology is Lamb's stratificational grammar (a Lamb grammar has a 'tactic pattern' at the phonological level as well as at other levels). However, the kind of generalization which I argue is missed by a generative phonology lacking syllable-construction rules (Sampson 1970) is equally missed by a Lamb grammar, since it involves structure-dependent modification of syllables, of which Lamb grammars are no more capable at the phonological level than at the syntactic level.

8 To explain with a brief illustration: in English the forms *nitrate* and *night rate* differ in pronunciation, although they would normally both be regarded as consisting of the phoneme-sequence / n a i t r e i t /. The common-sense explanation is that the allophonic realization of a phoneme will often depend on its position in a word; but, since 'word' is a grammatical concept, opponents of level-mixing were forced to posit some quite artifical *phonemic* distinction in cases of this kind.

9 This may not be as serious a criticism of American linguistics as it seems. Intonation appears to be one respect in which American English and R P

are very different languages, so perhaps American analysis of intonation is more satisfactory for American English than it would be for RP.

10 Firth's very loose use of 'meaning' perhaps makes his notion, criticized above, of a direct relationship between sound and meaning somewhat less unreasonable, in his own terms.

11 It may be that there are some subtle respects in which the words in question are not quite exactly synonymous, but that is not why one of them is more probable than the other in the quoted frame.

12 Halliday later argues that the English transitivity system is in fact considerably more complex than this.

13 In fact, this *has* now been claimed by Hudson (1976); but Hudson's claim is not typical of the tradition within which he works, and to my mind systemic theory is most interesting when it sets out to do something that generative grammarians have never pretended to do.

14 I argued in Chapter 3 that the 'hocus-pocus' approach was an unsatisfying stance for the pure linguist to adopt. The situation changes, however, when we think of linguistics as a service discipline providing grammars for the use of 'consumers' in other fields. The geologist wants to know whether the accepted theory of valley-formation is right or wrong, and he will not be content to allow rival theories to co-exist indefinitely; but that does not mean that he thinks there should be only one kind of map, so that it is inappropriate for the maps used by motorists to differ from those used on army manoeuvres.

15 This kind of problem occurs also with 'tagmemic' grammar (see page 79 above), which resembles the systemic approach fairly closely.

16 Linguists often make the point that no fully complete formal grammar of a language has even been produced, and tacitly or overtly suggest that it is improbable that one ever could be. There are two problems here. One is that many linguists (we have seen that this is true both of the Chomskyans and of Halliday) confuse the ungrammaticality of some word-sequences with the nonsensicality of some grammatical word-sequences, and thus greatly exaggerate the number of facts that a complete grammar would have to account for. (The task of saying which grammatical sentences might in some circumstances have a sensible use really is impossible in principle, because it depends wholly on how imaginative one is in constructing hypothetical circumstances, and there are no bounds to the fertility of human imagination.) The other point is that linguists who aim at a complete account of the range of *syntactically* well-formed sentences face a problem of diminishing returns. Once the main clause-types and phrase-types have been discussed, there are all sorts of specialized quirks of usage involving particular vocabulary items or small classes of items; thus, additions to the grammatical description add fewer and fewer extra sentences to the class

defined as grammatical. Theoretically minded linguists, in particular, tend to lose heart as soon as returns begin to diminish appreciably. But I cannot see that either of these points should lead us to conclude that there is no end in *principle* to the work of describing the syntax of a language.

17 In the present connection, consider, for example, Langendoen's treatment of Robins's view that prosodic analysis needs to be supplemented for practical purposes by a phonemic 'reading transcription' – 'presumably at no extra cost', Langendoen comments dismissively (1968, p. 59). When exactly the same point is made by Morris Halle of MIT in connection with his feature-matrix notation (for example, Halle 1962, p. 56 n. 2), it is hailed as an important insight. As *Schools of Linguistics* was being written, prosodic analysis began to be re-invented by MIT linguists under the name 'auto-segmental phonology' (see, for instance, Goldsmith 1976) – needless to say, without acknowledgement to Firth.

18 One of the many consequences of the excessive and over-sudden expansion of British higher education which occurred in the 1960s is that, since the fashionability of Chomskyan linguistics was at its height at that period, our universities and polytechnics are full of staff with a vested interest in that particular brand of the subject. Should our current economic decline end by putting much of our establishment of higher education out of business, one can at least hope that any subsequent recovery will be gradual enough to allow the scholarly community to reflect a greater diversity of views.

10 Conclusion

1 It would of course be quite possible for a Chomskyan semantician to claim that what he was doing was describing past usage rather than predicting future usage. But if that is what the Chomskyan semanticians are trying to do, it is already being done: when the words discussed are ones of special philosophical importance the activity is called 'analytic philosophy' (as practised notably at Oxford in the middle decades of this century), when they are ordinary words it is called 'lexicography'. In neither case does the Chomskyans' apparatus of quasi-mathematical formalism add anything to the quality of semantic description – quite the reverse, in fact.

2 However, cf. Matthews (1979, pp. 25–31).

Bibliography

The following is a list of books and articles quoted in this book; it does not set out to be a comprehensive bibliography of linguistics. In my text I have normally quoted works by the date of their first publication, since that is often a relevant piece of information in a historical survey such as this. Page-numbers, on the other hand, refer to the pagination of whichever edition is detailed below (which is not always the same as that of the first edition).

Place of publication is given (in brackets) only when it is not London. Happily for the hard-pressed typist of bibliographies, Harmondsworth, Middlesex, is now within the London boundary.

Abbreviations are used for certain frequently cited periodicals, as follows:

F L   *Foundations of Language*
I J A L *International Journal of American Linguistics*
J L   *Journal of Linguistics*
Lg.   *Language*
L I   *Linguistic Inquiry*

Also, 'J.' abbreviates *Journal* in the titles of periodicals otherwise given in full.

AGINSKY, B., and AGINSKY, E. (1948), 'The importance of language universals', *Word*, vol. 4, pp. 168–72
ANTTILA, R. (1975), 'Revelation as linguistic revolution', in A. and V. B. Makkai (eds.), *The First L A C U S Forum*. Hornbeam Press (Columbia, S.C.)

BACH, E. W. (1971), 'Questions', *L I*, vol. 2, pp. 153–66
BACH, E. W. (1974) 'Explanatory inadequacy', in D. Cohen (ed.), *Explaining Linguistic Phenomena*, John Wiley & Sons
BACH, E. W., and HARMS, R. T., eds. (1968), *Universals in Linguistic Theory*, Holt, Rinehart & Winston
BAR-HILLEL, Y. (1970), *Aspects of Language*, Magnes Press (Jerusalem)
BAUDOUIN DE COURTENAY, J. I. N. (1893), *Vermenschlichung der Sprache*, R. Virchow and W. Wattenbach (eds.), *Sammlung gemein-*

verständlicher wissenschaftlicher Vorträge, Neue Folge, 8. Serie, Heft 173, Verlags-anstalt und Druckerei A. G. (Hamburg)
BENVENISTE, E. (1958), 'Categories of thought and language', reprinted in *Problems in General Linguistics* (*Miami Linguistics Series*, 8), University of Miami Press (Coral Gables, Fla.), 1971
BERLIN, B., and KAY, P. (1969), *Basic Color Terms*. University of California Press (Berkeley & Los Angeles)
BERRY, M. (1975), *An Introduction to Systemic Linguistics 1: Structures and Systems*, Batsford
BLACK, M. (1959), 'Linguistic relativity: the views of Benjamin Lee Whorf', reprinted in *Models and Metaphors*, Cornell University Press (Ithaca, N.Y.), 1962
BLOOMFIELD, L. (1933), *Language*, Holt (New York)
BLOOMFIELD, L. (1939), *Linguistic Aspects of Science* (*International Encyclopedia of Unified Science*, vol. 1, no. 4), University of Chicago Press
BOAS, F. (1889), 'On alternating sounds', *American Anthropologist*, vol. 2, pp. 47–53
BOAS, F. (1897), Review of P. Ehrenreich, *Anthropologische Studien über die Ureinwohner Brasiliens. Science*, n.s., vol. 6, pp. 880–3
BOAS, F., ed. (1911), *Handbook of American Indian Languages, Part I* (Bureau of American Ethnology, Bulletin 40), Smithsonian Institution (Washington, D.C.)
BOAS, F. (1929), 'Classification of American Indian languages', *Lg.*, vol. 5, pp. 1–7
BOLINGER, D. (1977), 'Another glance at main clause phenomena', *Lg.*, vol. 53, pp. 511–19
BOLLING, G.M. (1929), 'Linguistics and philology', *Lg.*, vol. 5, pp. 27–32
BONFANTE, G. (1946), '"Indo-Hittite" and areal linguistics', *American J. of Philology*, vol. 67, pp. 289–310
BONFANTE, G. (1947), 'The neolinguistic position', *Lg.*, vol. 23, pp. 344–75
BOPP, F. (1827), 'Über J. Grimm's deutsche Grammatik', reprinted in *Vocalismus* . . . , Nicolaische Buchhandlung (Berlin), 1836
BOTHA, R. P. (1968), *The Function of the Lexicon in Transformational Generative Grammar* (*Janua Linguarum*, series maior, 38), Mouton (The Hague)
BRAINE, M. D. S. (1976), Review of Smith (1973), *Lg.*, vol. 52, pp. 489–98
BRESNAN, J. W. (1971), 'Sentence stress and syntactic transformations', *Lg.*, vol. 47, pp. 257–81
BROADBENT, D. E. (1961), *Behaviour*, Eyre & Spottiswoode
BROSNAHAN, L. F. (1961), *The Sounds of Language*, W. Heffer & Sons (Cambridge)

BRUCK, A., *et al.*, eds. (1974), *Papers from the Parasession on Natural Phonology*, Chicago Linguistic Society (Chicago)

BÜHLER, K. (1934), *Sprachtheorie*, Gustav Fischer (Jena)

CATFORD, J. C. (1974), '"Natural" sound changes: some questions of directionality in diachronic phonetics', in Bruck *et al.* (1974)

CHAO Y.-R. (1934), 'The non-uniqueness of phonemic solutions of phonetic systems', reprinted in Joos (1957)

CHOMSKY, A. N. (1957), *Syntactic Structures* (*Janua Linguarum*, series minor, 4), Mouton (The Hague)

CHOMSKY, A. N. (1959), 'On certain formal properties of grammars', *Information and Control*, vol. 1, pp. 91–112

CHOMSKY, A. N. (1964), *Current Issues in Linguistic Theory* (*Janua Linguarum*, series minor, 38), Mouton

CHOMSKY, A. N. (1965), *Aspects of the Theory of Syntax*, MIT Press (Cambridge, Mass.)

CHOMSKY, A. N. (1966), *Cartesian Linguistics*, Harper & Row

CHOMSKY, A. N. (1968), *Language and Mind*, Harcourt, Brace, & World (New York)

CHOMSKY, A. N. (1970), 'Phonology and reading', in H. Levin & J. Williams (eds.), *Basic Studies in Reading*, Basic Books (New York)

CHOMSKY, A. N. (1972a), 'On interpreting the world', in *Problems of Knowledge and Freedom*, Fontana

CHOMSKY, A. N. (1972b), 'Some empirical issues in the theory of transformational grammar', in Peters (1972)

CHOMSKY, A. N. (1976), *Reflections on Language*, Temple Smith

CHOMSKY, A. N., and HALLE, M. (1968), *The Sound Pattern of English*, Harper & Row

CLARK, T. N. (1969), Introduction to Tarde (1969)

COHEN, L. J. (1962), *The Diversity of Meaning*, Methuen

COLE, D. T. (1955), *Introduction to Tswana Grammar*, Longman

COLLIER, G. A. (1973), Review of Berlin and Kay (1969), *Lg.*, vol. 49, pp. 245–8

COLLITZ, H. (1918), Review of A. Meillet, *Caractères généraux des langues germaniques*, American J. of Philology, vol. 39, pp. 409–18

DELBRÜCK, B. (1880), *Einleitung in das Studium der Indogermanischen Sprachen*, 4th ed., Breitkopf & Härtel (Leipzig), 1904

DERWING, B. L. (1973), *Transformational Grammar as a Theory of Language Acquisition* (*Cambridge Studies in Linguistics*, 10), Cambridge University Press

DIK, S. C. (1968), *Coordination*, North-Holland (Amsterdam)

DINGWALL, W. O., ed. (1971), *A Survey of Linguistic Science*, University of Maryland Linguistics Program (College Park, Md)

262   Bibliography

DOROSZEWSKI, W. (1933), 'Quelques remarques sur les rapports de la sociologie et de la linguistique: Durkheim et F. de Saussure', *J. de Psychologie*, vol. 30, pp. 82–91

DOROSZEWSKI, W. (1958), 'Le structuralisme linguistique et les études de géographie dialectale', in *Proceedings of the Eighth International Congress of Linguists*, Oslo University Press (Oslo)

DURKHEIM, É. (1895), *The Rules of Sociological Method*, English ed., Collier-Macmillan, 1966

EISELEY, L. (1958), *Darwin's Century*, Doubleday (Garden City, N.Y.), 1961

EMENEAU, M. B. (1956), 'India as a linguistic area', *Lg.*, vol. 32, pp. 3–16

FIRTH, J. R. (1935), 'The technique of semantics', reprinted in Firth (1957)

FIRTH, J. R. (1937), *The Tongues of Men*, reprinted in *The Tongues of Men and Speech*, Oxford University Press, 1964

FIRTH, J. R. (1948), 'Sounds and prosodies', reprinted in Firth (1957)

FIRTH, J. R. (1951a), 'General linguistics and descriptive grammar', reprinted in Firth (1957)

FIRTH, J. R. (1951b), 'Modes of meaning', reprinted in Firth (1957)

FIRTH, J. R. (1957), *Papers in Linguistics 1934–1951*, Oxford University Press

FIRTH, J. R. (1966), *In Memory of J. R. Firth*, ed. C. E. Bazell *et al.*, Longman, Green & Co.

FISCHER-JØRGENSEN, E. (1967), Introduction to 2nd ed. of Uldall (1957)

FLEMING, I. (1967), 'Omission of the determined elements: a type of aphasic error', paper read to Summer Meeting of the Linguistic Society of America.

FODOR, J. A. (1974), 'Special sciences', *Synthese*, vol. 28, pp. 97–115.

FODOR, J. A. and GARRETT, M. (1966), 'Some reflections on competence and performance', in J. Lyons and R. J. Wales (eds.), *Psycholinguistics Papers*, Edinburgh University Press (Edinburgh)

FREUD, S. (1932), 'New introductory lectures on psychoanalysis', in *The Complete Psychological Works of Sigmund Freud*, ed. J. Strachey, vol. 22, Hogarth Press, 1964

FRIES, C. C. (1952), *The Structure of English*, Harcourt, Brace & World (New York)

GARVIN, P. L., ed. (1964), *A Prague School Reader in Esthetics, Literary Structure, and Style*, Georgetown University Press (Washington DC)

GLADSTONE, W. E. (1858), *Studies on Homer and the Homeric Age*, vol. 3, Oxford University Press (Oxford)

GLEASON, H. A. (1969), *An Introduction to Descriptive Linguistics*, rev. ed., Holt, Rinehart & Winston

GODEL, R. (1969), *A Geneva School Reader in Linguistics*, Indiana University Press

GOLDSMITH, J. A. (1976), 'An overview of autosegmental phonology', *Linguistic Analysis*, vol. 2, pp. 23–68

GOYVAERTS, D. L., and PULLUM, G. K., eds. (1975), *Essays on the Sound Pattern of English*, E. Story-Scientia (Ghent)

GRIMM, J. L. K. (1819), *Deutsche Grammatik*, vol. 1, Dieterichsche Buchhandlung (Göttingen)

GRIMM, J. L. K. (1848), *Geschichte der deutschen Sprache*, vol. 1, Weidmannsche Buchhandlung (Leipzig)

GUNDERSON, K., ed. (1975), *Language, Mind, and Knowledge*, Minnesota Studies in the Philosophy of Science (ed. H. Feigl and G. Maxwell), vol. 7, University of Minnesota Press (Minneapolis)

HAAS, W. (1954), 'On defining linguistic units', *Transactions of the Philological Society, 1954*, pp. 54–84.

HAGÈGE, C. (1976), *La grammaire générative: réflexions critiques*, Presses Universitaires de France (Paris)

HALL, E. T. (1959), *The Silent Language*, Doubleday

HALL, R. A. (1946), 'Bartoli's "Neolinguistica"', *Lg.*, vol. 22, pp. 273–83

HALL, R. A. (1950), *Leave Your Language Alone!*, Linguistica (Ithaca, N.Y.)

HALLE, M. (1959), *The Sound Pattern of Russian*, Mouton (The Hague)

HALLE, M. (1962), 'Phonology in generative grammar', *Word*, vol. 18, pp. 54–72

HALLE, M. (1973), 'Prolegomena to a theory of word formation', *LI*, vol. 4, pp. 3–16

HALLIDAY, M. A. K. (1961), 'Categories of the theory of grammar', *Word*, vol. 17, pp. 241–92

HALLIDAY, M. A. K. (1964), 'Syntax and the consumer', in C. I. J. M. Stuart (ed.), *Report of the Fifteenth Annual Round Table Meeting on Linguistics and Language Studies* (*Monograph Series on Languages and Linguistics*, 17), Georgetown University Press (Washington, D.C.)

HALLIDAY, M. A. K. (1967), 'Notes on transitivity and theme in English, Part I', *JL*, vol. 3, pp. 37–81

HALLIDAY, M. A. K. (1969), 'Options and functions in the English clause', reprinted in Householder (1972)

HALLIDAY, M. A. K. (1970), 'Language structure and language function', in J. Lyons (ed.), *New Horizons in Linguistics*, Penguin

HANSON, N. R. (1958), *Patterns of Discovery*, Cambridge University Press

HARMAN, G., ed. (1974), *On Noam Chomsky: Critical Essays*, Anchor Books (Garden City, N.Y.)

HARRIS, Z. S. (1951), *Methods in Structural Linguistics*, University of Chicago Press

HARRIS, Z. S. (1965), 'Transformational theory', *Lg.*, vol. 41, pp. 363–401

HAVRÁNEK, B. (1936), 'Zum Problem der Norm in der heutigen Sprachwissenschaft und Sprachkultur', reprinted in Vachek (1964)

HAYEK, F. A (1955), *The Counter-Revolution of Science: Studies on the Abuse of Reason*, Collier-Macmillan

HAYEK, F. A. (1960), *The Constitution of Liberty*, Routledge & Kegan Paul

HEGEL, G. W. F. (1837), *The Philosophy of History*, English ed., Constable & Co., 1956

HENDERSON, E. J. A. (1966), 'Towards a prosodic statement of Vietnamese syllable structure', in Firth (1966)

HERMAN, D. T., *et al.* (1957), 'Variables in the effect of language on the reproduction of visually perceived forms', *Perceptual and Motor Skills*, vol. 7, Monograph Supplement 2, pp. 171–86

HILL, T. (1966), 'The technique of prosodic analysis', in Firth (1966)

HJELMSLEV, L. (1943), *Prolegomena to a Theory of Language*, 2nd English ed., University of Wisconsin Press (Madison, Wis.), 1961

HJELMSLEV, L. (1963), *Language: An Introduction*, English ed., University of Wisconsin Press (Madison, Wis.), 1970

HOCKETT, C. F. (1942). 'A system of descriptive phonology'. *Lg.*, vol. 18, pp. 3–21

HOCKETT, C. F. (1954), 'Two models of grammatical description', *Word*, vol. 10, pp. 210–31

HOCKETT, C. F. (1955), *A Manual of Phonology (Indiana University Publications in Anthropology and Linguistics*, Memoir 11), supplement to *I J A L*, vol. 21

HOCKETT, C. F. (1968), *The State of the Art (Janua Linguarum*, series minor, 73), Mouton (The Hague)

HODGE, C. T. (1970), 'The linguistic cycle', *Language Sciences*, vol. 13, pp. 1–7

HONEY, P. J. (1956), 'Word classes in Vietnamese', in Householder (1972)

HOPPE, A. (1964), 'Schwierigkeiten und Möglichkeiten der maschinellen Übersetzung', in H. Frank (ed.), *Kybernetische Maschinen*, S. Fischer (Frankfurt a. M.)

HOUSEHOLDER, F. W., ed. (1972), *Syntactic Theory 1: Structuralist*, Penguin

HOUSEHOLDER, F. W. (1974), Review of R. P. Stockwell and R. K. S. Macaulay (eds.), *Linguistic Change and Generative Theory, Lg.*, vol. 50, pp. 555–68

HOUSEHOLDER, F. W. (1978), Review of A. and V. B. Makkai (eds.), *The First LACUS Forum 1974*, *Lg.*, vol. 54, pp. 170–6

HUDSON, R. A. (1971), *English Complex Sentences* (*North-Holland Linguistic Series*, 4), North-Holland (Amsterdam)

HUDSON, R. A. (1976), *Arguments for a Non-Transformational Grammar*, University of Chicago Press

HUMBOLDT, W. (1836), 'Ueber die Verschiedenheit des menschlichen Sprachbaues und ihren Einflusz auf die geistige Entwickelung des Menschengeschlechts', in *Wilhelm von Humboldt's gesammelte Werke*, vol. 6, G. Reimer (Berlin), 1848

HURFORD, J. R. (1977), 'The significance of linguistic generalizations', *Lg.*, vol. 53, pp. 574–620

HYMES, D., and FOUGHT, J. (1975), 'American structuralism', in T. A. Sebeok (ed.), *Current Trends in Linguistics*, vol. 13, Mouton (The Hague)

IORDAN-ORR (1937), I. Iordan, *An Introduction to Romance Linguistics*, translated, revised, and augmented by J. Orr, Methuen

JAKOBSON, R. O. (1931), 'Über die phonologischen Sprachbünde', *Travaux du Cercle Linguistique de Prague*, vol. 4, pp. 234–40

JAKOBSON, R. O. (1941), *Child Language, Aphasia, and Phonological Universals*, English ed. (*Janua Linguarum*, series minor, 72), Mouton (The Hague), 1968

JAKOBSON, R. O., FANT, C. G. M., and HALLE, M. (1952), *Preliminaries to Speech Analysis*, 6th printing, MIT Press (Cambridge, Mass.), 1965

JAKOBSON, R. O., and HALLE, M. (1956), *Fundamentals of Language* (*Janua Linguarum*, 1), Mouton (The Hague)

JANKOWSKY, K. R. (1972), *The Neogrammarians* (*Janua Linguarum*, series minor, 116), Mouton (The Hague)

JESPERSEN, O. (1922), *Language, its Nature, Development, and Origin*, Allen & Unwin

JESPERSEN, O. (1941), 'Efficiency in linguistic change', Kongelige Danske Videnskabernes Selskab, *Historisk-filologiske meddelser*, vol. 28, no. 4 (Copenhagen)

JOOS, M., ed. (1957), *Readings in Linguistics*, American Council of Learned Societies (New York)

KATZ, J. J., and FODOR, J. A. (1963), 'The structure of a semantic theory', *Lg.*, vol. 39, pp. 170–210

KAYE, J., and PIGGOTT, G. (1973), 'On the cyclical nature of Ojibwa T-Palatalization', *LI*, vol. 4, pp. 345–62

KING, R. D. (1967), 'Functional load and sound change', *Lg.*, 43, pp. 831–52

266   *Bibliography*

KING, R. D. (1969), *Historical Linguistics and Generative Grammar*, Prentice-Hall

KING, R. D. (1973), 'Rule insertion', *Lg.*, vol. 49, 551–78

KIPARSKY, P. (1968), 'Linguistic universals and linguistic change', in Bach and Harms (1968)

KIPARSKY, P. (1971), 'Historical linguistics', in Dingwall (1971)

KISSEBERTH, C. W. (1970), 'On the functional unity of phonological rules', *LI*, vol. 1, pp. 291–306

KOERNER, E. F. K. (1973), *Ferdinand de Saussure (Schriften zur Linguistik,* 7), Vieweg (Brunswick)

KOERNER, E. F. K., ed. (1975), *The Transformational-Generative Paradigm and Modern Linguistic Theory (Amsterdam Studies in the Theory and History of Linguistic Science,* series 4, vol. 1), John Benjamins (Amsterdam)

KUČERA, H. (1974), Review of R. Meyerstein, *Functional Load, Lg.*, vol. 50, pp. 169–75

KUHN, T. S. (1962), *The Structure of Scientific Revolutions (International Encyclopedia of Unified Science,* vol. 2, no. 2), University of Chicago Press

LABOV, W. (1966), *The Social Stratification of English in New York City*, Center for Applied Linguistics (Washington, D.C.)

LABOV, W. (1971), 'Methodology', in Dingwall (1971)

LABOV, W. (1975), 'Empirical foundations of linguistic theory', in R. Austerlitz (ed.), *The Scope of American Linguistics*, Peter de Ridder Press (Lisse)

LADEFOGED, P. (1967), 'The nature of vowel quality', in *Three Areas of Experimental Phonetics*, Oxford University Press

LADEFOGED, P. (1971), *Preliminaries to Linguistic Phonetics*, University of Chicago Press

LAKATOS, I. (1970), 'Falsification and the methodology of scientific research programmes', in I. Lakatos and A. Musgrave (eds.), *Criticism and the Growth of Knowledge*, Cambridge University Press

LAKATOS, I. (1976), *Proofs and Refutations*, ed. J. Worrall and E. Zahar, Cambridge University Press

LAMB, S. M. (1966), *Outline of Stratificational Grammar*, Georgetown University Press (Washington, D.C.)

LANE, G. S. (1959), Review of works by O. Höfler, *Lg.*, vol. 35, pp. 315–21

LANGENDOEN, D. T. (1968), *The London School of Linguistics (Research Monograph* no. 46), MIT Press (Cambridge, Mass.)

LANGENDOEN, D. T. (1969), *The Study of Syntax*, Holt, Rinehart & Winston

LASS, R. (1974), 'Strategic design as the motivation for a sound shift: the rationale of Grimm's Law', *Acta Linguistica Hafniensia*, vol. 15, pp. 51–66

LENNEBERG, E. H., and ROBERTS, J. M. (1956), *The Language of Experience* (*Indiana University Publications on Anthropology and Linguistics*, Memoir 13), Supplement to *IJAL*, vol. 22

LESKIEN, A. (1876), *Die Declination im Slavisch-Litauischen und Germanischen* (*Preisschriften gekrönt und herausgegeben von der Fürstlich Jablonowski'schen Gesellschaft zu Leipzig*, no. 19), S. Hirzel (Leipzig)

LÉVY-BRUHL, L. (1910), *Les fonctions mentales dans les sociétés inférieures*, Félix Alcan (Paris)

LI, C. N., ed. (1975), *Word Order and Word Order Change*, University of Texas Press

LILJENCRANTS, J., and LINDBLOM B. (1972), 'Numerical simulation of vowel quality systems', *Lg.*, vol. 48, pp. 839–62

LINDEN, E. (1974), *Apes, Men, and Language*, Penguin ed., 1976

LIPKA, L. (1975), 'Prolegomena to "Prolegomena to a theory of word formation"', in Koerner (1975)

LOCKWOOD, D. G. (1972), *Introduction to Stratificational Linguistics*, Harcourt Brace Jovanovich (New York)

LOVEJOY, A. O. (1936), *The Great Chain of Being*, Oxford University Press

LYELL, C. (1863), *The Geological Evidences of the Antiquity of Man*, John Murray

LYONS, J. (1962), Review of C. Mohrmann (ed.), *Trends in European and American Linguistics*, *American Anthropologist*, vol. 64, pp. 1117–24

LYONS, J. (1966), 'Firth's theory of "meaning"', in Firth (1966)

McCAWLEY, J. D. (1967), 'Le rôle d'un système de traits phonologiques dans une théorie du langage', *Langages*, vol. 6, pp. 112–23

McCAWLEY, J. D. (1968), 'The role of semantics in a grammar', in Bach and Harms (1968)

McCAWLEY, J. D., ed. (1976), *Notes from the Linguistic Underground* (*Syntax and Semantics*, vol. 7), Academic Press

McNEILL, N. (1972), 'Colour and colour terminology', *JL*, vol. 8, pp. 21–33

MALINOWKSI, B. (1923), 'The problem of meaning in primitive languages', supplement to C. K. Ogden and I. A. Richards, *The Meaning of Meaning*, Routledge & Kegan Paul

MALINOWSKI, B. (1935), *Coral Gardens and their Magic*, vol. 2, Allen & Unwin

MARTINET, A. (1949), 'La double articulation linguistique', *Travaux du Cercle Linguistique de Copenhague*, vol. 5, pp. 30–7

MARTINET, A. (1955), *Économie des changements phonétiques*, A. Francke (Bern)

MATHESIUS, V. (1911), 'On the potentiality of the phenomena of language', English translation in Vachek (1964)

MATHESIUS, V. (1928), 'On the linguistic characterology of Modern English', English translation in Vachek (1964)

MATHESIUS, V. (1961), *A Functional Analysis of Present-Day English on a General Linguistic Basis*, English ed., Academia (Prague), 1975

MATTHEWS, P. H. (1966), 'The concept of rank in "Neo-Firthian" grammar', *JL*, vol. 2, pp. 101–10

MATTHEWS, P. H. (1974), *Morphology*, Cambridge University Press

MATTHEWS, P. H. (1979), *Generative Grammar and Linguistic Competence*, Allen & Unwin

MEHTA, V. (1971), *John Is Easy to Please*, Secker & Warburg

MEILLET, A. (1905), 'Comment les mots changent de sens', reprinted in *Linguistique historique et linguistique générale*, vol. 1, Champion (Paris), 1965

MEYER, H. (1901), 'Über den Ursprung der Germanischen Lautverschiebung', *Zeitschrift für deutsches Altertum und deutsches Litteratur*, vol. 45, pp. 101–28

MILLER, J. (1973), 'A note on so-called "discovery procedures"', *FL*, vol. 10, pp. 123–39

MORAVCSIK, J. M. E. (1969), 'Competence, creativity, and innateness', *Philosophy Forum*, vol. 1, pp. 407–37

MÜLLENHOFF, K. (1892), *Deutsche Altertumskunde*, vol. 3, Weidmannsche Buchhandlung (Berlin)

NAGEL, E. (1961), *The Structure of Science*, Routledge & Kegan Paul

NEWMAN, P. (1978), Review of Hagège (1976), *Lg.*, vol. 54, pp. 925–9

NEWMEYER, F. (1975), Review of E. Hamp (ed.), *Themes in Linguistics*, *Lg.*, vol. 51, pp. 163–9

O'CONNOR, J. D., and ARNOLD, G. F. (1961), *Intonation of Colloquial English*, Longman

OERTEL, H. (1902), *Lectures on the Study of Language*, C. Scribner's Sons (New York)

OHALA, J. J. (1974), 'Phonetic explanation in phonology', in Bruck *et al.* (1974)

O'NEILL, J., ed. (1973), *Modes of Individualism and Collectivism*, Heinemann

OSTHOFF, H. (1879), *Das physiologische und psychologische Moment in der sprachlichen Formenbildung*, ed. R. Virchow and F. von Holtzendorff, *Sammlung gemeinverständlicher wissenschaftlicher Vorträge*, 14. Serie, Heft 327, Carl Habel (Berlin)

OSTHOFF, H., and BRUGMAN, K. (1878), *Morphologische Untersuchungen* . . . , 1. Theil, S. Hirzel (Leipzig)

PARRET, H. (1974), *Discussing Language* (*Janua Linguarum*, series maior, 93), Mouton (The Hague)

PAUL, H. (1880), *Prinzipien der Sprachgeschichte*, 8th ed., Max Niemeyer (Tübingen), 1968

PAUL, H. (1891), 'Geschichte der Germanischen Philologie', in H. Paul (ed.), *Grundriss der Germanischen Philologie*, vol. 1, Karl J. Trübner (Strassburg)

PEDERSEN, H. (1924), *The Discovery of Language*, English ed., Indiana University Press, 1962

PERCIVAL, W. K. (1976), 'The applicability of Kuhn's paradigms to the history of linguistics', *Lg.*, vol. 52, pp. 285–94

PERLMUTTER, D. M. (1970), 'Surface structure constraints in syntax', *LI*, vol. 1, pp. 187–255

PETERS, S., ed. (1972), *Goals of Linguistic Theory*, Prentice-Hall

POPPER, K. R. (1945), *The Open Society and its Enemies*, vol. 1, Routledge & Kegan Paul

POPPER, K. R. (1950), 'Indeterminism in quantum physics and in classical physics', *British J. for the Philosophy of Science*, vol. 1, pp. 117–33, 173–95

POPPER, K. R. (1957), *The Poverty of Historicism*, Routledge & Kegan Paul

POSTAL, P. M. (1964), *Constituent Structure: A Study of Contemporary Models of Syntactic Description* (*Indiana University Publications in Anthropology and Linguistics*, Memoir 30), supplement to *IJAL*, vol. 30

POSTAL, P. M. (1968), *Aspects of Phonological Theory*, Harper & Row

POSTAL, P. M. (1972), 'The best theory', in Peters (1972)

POTT, A. F. (1833), *Etymologische Forschungen . . .* , vol. 1, Meyersche Hof-Buchhandlung (Lemgo)

PUTNAM, H. (1973), 'Meaning and reference', *J. of Philosophy*, vol. 70, pp. 699–711

PUTNAM, H. (1975), 'The meaning of "meaning"', in Gunderson (1975)

QUINE, W. van O. (1951), 'Two dogmas of empiricism', reprinted in *From a Logical Point of View*, 2nd ed., Harvard University Press (Cambridge, Mass.), 1961

QUINE, W. van O. (1960), *Word and Object*, MIT Press (Cambridge, Mass.)

RASK, R. C. (1818), *Undersøgelse om det gamle Nordiske eller Islandske Sprogs Oprindelse*, Gyldendalske Boghandlings Forlag (Copenhagen)

RAUMER, R. (1858), 'Die sprachgeschichtliche Umwandlung und die naturgeschichtliche Bestimmung der Laute', reprinted in *Gesammelte sprachwissenschaftliche Schriften*, Heyder & Zimmer (Frankfurt a. M. and Erlangen), 1863

REICH, P. A. (1969), 'The finiteness of natural language', *Lg.*, vol. 45, pp. 831–43

REICH, P. A. (1970a), 'The English auxiliaries: a relational network description', *Canadian J. of Linguistics*, vol. 16, pp. 18–50

REICH, P. A. (1970b), *A Relational Network Model of Language Behavior* (University of Michigan Ph.D dissertation), University Microfilms (Ann Arbor, Mich.)

ROBINS, R. H. (1967), *A Short History of Linguistics*, Indiana University Press

ROBINS, R. H. (1969), Review of Langendoen (1968), *Lg.*, vol. 45, pp. 109–16

ROSS, J. R. (1972a), 'The category squish', in P. M. Peranteau *et al.* (eds.), *Papers from the Eighth Regional Meeting*, Chicago Linguistic Society (Chicago)

ROSS, J. R. (1972b), 'Doubl-ing', *LI*, vol. 3, pp. 61–86

ROSS, J. R. (1972c), 'A reanalysis of English word stress (part I)', in M. K. Brame (ed.), *Contributions to Generative Phonology*, University of Texas Press

SAMPSON, G. R. (1970), 'On the need for a phonological base', *Lg.*, vol. 46, pp. 586–626

SAMPSON, G. R. (1973), 'The irrelevance of transformational omnipotence', *JL*, vol. 9, pp. 299–302

SAMPSON, G. R. (1974a), 'Is there a universal phonetic alphabet?' *Lg.*, 50, pp. 236–59

SAMPSON, G. R. (1974b), Review of Lockwood (1972), *Lingua*, vol. 34, pp. 235–51

SAMPSON, G. R. (1975a), *The Form of Language*, Weidenfeld & Nicolson

SAMPSON, G. R. (1975b), 'One fact needs one explanation', *Lingua*, vol. 36, pp. 231–9

SAMPSON, G. R. (1976), 'The simplicity of linguistic theories', *Linguistics*, vol. 167, pp. 51–66

SAMPSON, G. R. (1978), 'Linguistic universals as evidence for empiricism', *JL*, vol. 14, pp. 183–206

SAMPSON, G. R. (1979a), *Liberty and Language*, Oxford University Press (Oxford)

SAMPSON, G. R. (1979b), 'What was transformational grammar?' *Lingua*, vol. 48, pp. 355–78

SAMPSON, G. R. (1980), *Making Sense*, Oxford University Press (Oxford)

SAPIR, E. (1921), *Language*, Rupert Hart-Davis, 1963

SAPIR, E. (1929), 'The status of linguistics as a science', *Lg.*, vol. 5, pp. 207–14

SAPIR, E. (1931), 'Conceptual categories in primitive languages', *Science*, vol. 74, p. 578

de SAUSSURE, F. (1916), *Course in General Linguistics*, ed. C. Bally and A. Sechehaye, revised English ed., Collins, 1974

Bibliography 271

SCHACHTER, P. (1977), 'Constraints on coördination', *Lg.*, vol. 53, pp. 86–103

SCHERER, W. (1868), *Zur Geschichte der deutschen Sprache*, Duncker (Berlin)

SCHLEGEL, A. W. (1818), *Observations sur la langue et la littérature provençales*, Librairie grecque-latine-allemande (Paris)

SCHLEGEL, F. (1808), *Ueber die Sprache und Weisheit der Indier*, Mohr & Zimmer (Heidelberg)

SCHLEICHER, A. (1848), *Zur vergleichenden Sprachengeschichte (Sprachvergleichende Untersuchungen*, I), H. B. König (Bonn)

SCHLEICHER, A. (1850), *Die Sprachen Europas in systematischer Uebersicht (Linguistische Untersuchungen*, II), H. B. König (Bonn)

SCHLEICHER, A. (1861), *Compendium der vergleichenden Grammatik der indogermanischen Sprachen*, vol. 1, Hermann Böhlau (Weimar)

SCHLEICHER, A. (1863), *Die Darwin'sche Theorie und die Sprachwissenschaft*, 2nd ed., Hermann Böhlau (Weimar), 1873

SCHLEICHER, A. (1865), *Ueber die Bedeutung der Sprache für die Naturgeschichte des Menschen*, Hermann Böhlau (Weimar)

SCHMIDT, J. (1872), *Die Verwantschaftsverhältnisse der Indogermanischen Sprachen*, Hermann Böhlau (Weimar)

SCHREIBER, P. A. (1974), Review of M. Tsiapera, *A Descriptive Analysis of Cypriot Maronite Arabic*, *Lg.*, vol. 50, pp. 748–55

SEBEOK, T. A., ed. (1966), *Portraits of Linguists*, vol. 2, Indiana University Press

SIEVERS, E. (1876), *Grundzüge der Lautphysiologie (Bibliothek indogermanischer Grammatiken*, 1) Breitkopf & Härtel (Leipzig)

SIMON, H. A. (1962), 'The architecture of complexity', *Proceedings of the American Philosophical Society*, vol. 106, pp. 467–82

SMITH, N. V. (1973), *The Acquisition of Phonology*, Cambridge University Press

SNOW, C., and MEIJER, G. (1977), 'On the secondary nature of syntactic intuitions', in S. Greenbaum (ed.), *Acceptability in Language*, Mouton (The Hague)

SOMMERFELT, A. (1938), *La langue et la société: caractères sociaux d'une langue de type archaïque* (Instituttet for Sammenlignende Kulturforskning, Serie A: Forelesninger, 18), H. Aschehoug & Co. (Oslo)

STAMPE, D. (1969), 'The acquisition of phonetic representation', in R. I. Binnick *et al.* (eds.), *Papers from the Fifth Regional Meeting*, Chicago Linguistic Society (Chicago)

von den STEINEN, K. (1894), *Unter den Naturvölkern Zentral-Brasiliens*, Dietrich Reimer (Berlin)

STURTEVANT, E. H. (1947), *An Introduction to Linguistic Science*, Yale University Press

TARDE, G. (1894), 'Sociology, social psychology, and sociologism', English version in Tarde (1969)

TARDE, G. (1969), *On Communication and Social Influence*, ed. T. N. Clark, University of Chicago Press

TOGEBY, K. (1951), *Structure immanente de la langue française*, 2nd ed., Larousse (Paris), 1965

TRUBETZKOY, N. S. (1939), *Principles of Phonology*, English ed., University of California Press (Berkeley and Los Angeles), 1969

TRUDGILL, P. (1974), *The Social Differentiation of English in Norwich* (*Cambridge Studies in Linguistics*, 13), Cambridge University Press

TRUITNER, K. L., and DUNNIGAN, T. (1975), 'Palatalization in Ojibwa', *LI*, vol. 6, pp. 301–16

ULDALL, H. J. (1957), *Outline of Glossematics, Pt. 1: General Theory* (*Travaux du Cercle Linguistique de Copenhague*, X_1), 2nd ed., Nordisk Sprog- og Kulturforlag (Copenhagen), 1967

ULLMANN, S. (1962), *Semantics, an Introduction to the Science of Meaning*, Blackwell (Oxford)

VACHEK, J., ed. (1964), *A Prague School Reader in Linguistics*, Indiana University Press

VACHEK, J. (1966), *The Linguistic School of Prague*, Indiana University Press

VENNEMANN, T. (1974), 'Words and syllables in natural generative grammar', in Bruck *et al.* (1974)

WALL, R. E. (1971), 'Mathematical linguistics', in Dingwall (1971)

WALLACE, A. R. (1870), 'The limits of natural selection as applied to Man', in *Contributions to the Theory of Natural Selection*, Macmillan

WALLIS, E. E., and BENNETT, M. A. (1959), *Two Thousand Tongues To Go*, Hodder & Stoughton, 1960

WANG, W. S.-Y. (1967a), 'The measurement of functional load', *Phonetica*, vol. 16, pp. 36–54

WANG, W. S.-Y. (1967b), 'Phonological features of tone', *IJAL*, vol. 33, pp. 93–105

WANG, W. S.-Y. (1969), 'Competing changes as a cause of residue', *Lg.*, vol. 45, pp. 9–25

WECHSSLER, E. (1900), 'Giebt es Lautgesetze?' in *Festgabe für Hermann Suchier*, Max Niemeyer (Halle a. S.)

WEINREICH, U., LABOV, W., and HERZOG, M. I. (1968), 'Empirical foundations for a theory of language change', in W. P. Lehmann and Y. Malkiel (eds.), *Directions for Historical Linguistics*, University of Texas Press

WEISS, A. P. (1925), 'Linguistics and psychology', *Lg.*, vol. 1, pp. 52–7

WELLS, R. S. (1947), 'De Saussure's system of linguistics', *Word*, vol. 3, pp. 1–37

WHORF, B. L. (1940), 'Science and linguistics', reprinted in Whorf (1956)

WHORF, B. L. (1941a), 'The relation of habitual thought and behavior to language', reprinted in Whorf (1956)

WHORF, B. L. (1941b), 'Languages and logic', reprinted in Whorf (1956)

WHORF, B. L. (1945), 'Grammatical categories', reprinted in Whorf (1956)

WHORF, B. L. (1956), *Language, Thought, and Reality: Selected Writings of Benjamin Lee Whorf*, ed. J. B. Carroll, MIT Press (Cambridge, Mass.)

WINCH, P. (1958), *The Idea of a Social Science and its Relation to Philosophy*, Routledge & Kegan Paul

WITTGENSTEIN, L. (1953), *Philosophical Investigations*, Basil Blackwell & Mott (Oxford)

ZWICKY, A. M. (1970), 'Greek-letter variables and the Sanskrit *ruki* class', *LI*, vol. 1, pp. 549–55

Index

Frequently used technical terms, e.g. 'morpheme', 'Received Pronunciation', are indexed only for passages defining them.

Weinreich, U., 116, 129, 245
  n. 17
Weiss, A. P., 64
Wellesley, R. C., 256 n. 3
Wells, R. S., 247 n. 11
Welsh, 18, 26, 29, 94, 242
West African languages, 254 n. 4
Western Pacific languages, 80
Whitney, W. D., 48
Whorf, B. L., 81–90, 94–7, 102,
  249 n. 5

Whorf hypothesis, *see*
  Sapir–Whorf hypothesis
Wilkins, J., 212
Winch, P., 234
Wittgenstein, L., 88, 156, 224
Word (journal), 131
word-and-paradigm (WP), 75
Wycliffe Bible Translators, 80

Zwicky, A. M., 254 n. 3